SOLITARY COMRADE

SOLITARY COMRADE

JACK LONDON AND

HIS WORK

JOAN D. HEDRICK

The University of North Carolina Press

Chapel Hill

© 1982 The University of
North Carolina Press

Manufactured in the United States of America

Library of Congress Cataloging
in Publication Data

Hedrick, Joan D., 1944–
Solitary comrade, Jack London and his work.

Bibliography: p.
Includes index.
1. London, Jack, 1876–1916.   2. Authors, American—
20th century—Biography.   I. Title.
PS3523.046Z637   818'.5209 [B]   81-2969
ISBN 0-8078-1488-1   AACR2

Jack London early in his career
(Reproduced by permission of
The Huntington Library, San Marino, California)

FOR

Jane and Paul Doran

CONTENTS

Acknowledgments
xiii

Introduction
xv

Abbreviations
xix

ONE
Initiation into Manhood,
Part One: The Lower Class
3

TWO
Initiation into Manhood,
Part Two: The Middle Class
32

THREE
Journeying Across the Ghostly Wastes
of a Dead World
48

FOUR
Descent into the Abyss
56

FIVE
The Long Sickness
72

SIX
The Call of the Wild
94

SEVEN
The Sea-Wolf, or,
"The Triumph of the Spirit"
112

EIGHT
Domesticity:
The Future of an Illusion
134

NINE
The Literary Marketplace
151

TEN
London's Socialist Fiction
169

ELEVEN
Sexual Politics in *The Iron Heel*
188

TWELVE
Martin Eden, or, Paradise Lost
200

THIRTEEN
Fading Beyond
221

Contents

Notes
239

Bibliography
251

Index
255

ILLUSTRATIONS

Jack London early in his career
frontispiece

Jack London, member of the working class
11

Charmian on horseback, Jack looking on,
at the Beauty Ranch
141

Jack and Charmian aboard the *Snark*,
just before sailing, 1907
201

Jack and Charmian in Vera Cruz, 1914
228

Jack London overlooking the Sonoma valley
231

ACKNOWLEDGMENTS

Carol Ohmann, Joseph W. Reed, Jr., and Richard Slotkin offered invaluable support and encouragement when this book was in embryo. Richard Ohmann read later drafts and gave helpful criticisms of the chapter on *The Iron Heel*. I have also benefited from close readings of all or parts of the manuscript by Phyllis Rose and Coppélia Kahn. Of the many other colleagues at Wesleyan University whose support has been essential, I would like to thank in particular Oliver W. Holmes and Donald Meyer. I would also like to thank the president and the trustees of the university for allocating funds in support of scholarship.

I am grateful to I. Milo Shepard, trustee of the Trust of Irving Shepard, for permission to quote from Jack London's published and unpublished writings. I was greatly assisted in my research by the staff of The Huntington Library, especially by David Mike Hamilton, who willingly shared his extensive knowledge of Jack London and of the archive. The late Mars and Warren Stilson made my trips to California an added pleasure. Dorothy Hay typed an earlier draft of the manuscript, and Alice Pomper provided excellent editorial assistance and typed the final draft. Sandra Eisdorfer of The University of North Carolina Press was as careful and engaged an editor as one could wish. Dianne Dumanoski will recognize her specific suggestion in the book's presentation.

I am especially grateful to Travis Hedrick, whose financial support allowed me to take a leave of absence from my teaching responsibilities and whose careful reading of the early chapters of the manuscript provoked me to clarifications of style and conceptualization. Beyond this, his appetite for books and ideas is a constant source of stimulation and companionship. I thank my daughters, Jessica and Rachel, for their interest and encouragement. Finally, I owe a debt of long standing to the people to whom this book is dedicated.

INTRODUCTION

The outward acts of Jack London's life received enormous publicity while he was living, and they continue to exercise a fascination that often eclipses his work. Like his hero, Burning Daylight, he "had the fatal facility for self-advertisement." This book is an attempt to understand the man who hid beneath the celebrated public persona. It is a study of his inner life, primarily as it is revealed in his art.

As Clarice Stasz has argued, the fictions that biographers have constructed about London's life are as obfuscating as the personae that London himself adopted.[1] The most enduring of these was formulated in Irving Stone's *Sailor on Horseback*, which reduces London's inner life to an obsession with his illegitimate birth. According to Stone, London brooded about the circumstances of his birth during the recurrent depressions that plagued him all his life, and yet his illegitimacy also "provided him with an important part of his driving power. . . . [A]lways his vigorous and full-blooded Rex complex made him feel he must be a king among men (the last shall be first, the bastard shall be king)."[2] London's alleged preoccupation with his illegitimacy has yet to be documented, but Stone's interpretation is echoed, with varying degrees of emphasis, by Richard O'Connor ("underneath the picaroon was a man tormented by the act of his illegitimate birth"), Kenneth Lynn ("not all the money or all the whiskey in the world could gainsay the shameful fact of his illegitimacy"; "to prove that a bastard could be an aristocrat meant living on 'canvasback and terrapin, with champagne'"), and in milder form, by Thomas Gossett and Kevin Starr, who argue that London's "blatant, schizoid Anglo-Saxonism compensated for the meanness of his own origins."[3]

London was in fact the illegitimate son of Flora Wellman, a young emigré to California from Massillon, Ohio. His father was, in all likelihood, Professor William Chaney, an itinerant astrologer. In his life it is easy to discern what Stone called a "Rex complex"; his desire for mastery led him to challenge the wilderness as well as the literary establishment. By the same token, his feeling that, like Martin Eden and Wolf Larsen, he had no roots, that he was the seed cast on rocky ground, led him to write, in disguised ways, of his desire for belonging. He imagined himself an exiled prince, but the kingdom he had lost was not simply the legitimate heritage of his biological parents. I take London's troubled relationship to his lower-class beginnings—his failure to achieve a sense of belonging in that subculture—to be central to an understanding of his life and art. London's failure to take root in his native subculture made him more susceptible to the dominant culture's images of reality, which in turn shaped his psychic, social, and literary development. The dominant culture to which London responded was capitalist and patriarchal. It divided humanity into hierarchies of class and gender, and the divisions of that society divided London's consciousness. His seeming preoccupation with "illegitimacy" is symptomatic of his difficulty in making contact with his authentic self, and, consequently, with comrades, kin, class, nature, God. To dwell on the literal fact of London's illegitimacy is to obscure the relationship between his yearnings and those within our culture and ourselves, and to miss, in London's own life, the wider significance of his search for belonging.

Andrew Sinclair, London's most recent biographer, does not organize his book around Stone's thesis, and he is the first writer since Stone to have access to the London papers in the Huntington Library. Although he brings important new documents to light, his book is not entirely satisfactory. Insofar as he has a new interpretation, it has to do with London's health and the medication that he believes he was taking at the end of his life. He documents London's interest in a drug for syphilis, which produced side effects similar to several of the symptoms London suffered in his final years. But it is misleading to attribute his artistic decline and the moods of depression and elation that London suffered most of his life to the effects of Salvarsan 606. At one point Sinclair seems ready to apply his medical interpretation to the psychic lives of all radicals and artists of the pre–World War I generation. Although it may be convenient to attribute "the wilder aberrations and extravagances of the period" to venereal disease, it is just possible that the disease from which these artists and radicals were suffering was a social disease of another sort.[4]

Neither Stone's myth of illegitimacy nor Sinclair's medical interpretation get us very close to London's inner life. Both have the effect of turning London into an aberration, an oddity. But the mythic appeal of his life belies his uniqueness. We may have a deep need to distance ourselves from London's "case," even as we are fascinated by his example. He was one of the last great self-made men of the nineteenth century, and his story is about the failure of success. The dialectic between public success and self-destruction that he portrays in *Martin Eden* was a parable of his own life. He lived in painful awareness of the contradictions of our society, but much of what he wrote was a veil of illusion. To understand him is to understand our society and ourselves.

The most successful interpretations of Jack London have placed the man in the historical and political context in which he lived. His daughter Joan's biography, *Jack London and His Times*, and Philip Foner's biographical essay in *Jack London: American Rebel*, are the best accounts of his political activity. Kenneth Lynn and Kevin Starr have written perceptive essays placing London in the social history of his time and the ideology of the American dream.[5] All of these works help place London within a cultural context and suggest the ways in which he was shaped by the society in which he lived. But none of them focuses primarily on London's psychic life; so far as Starr and Lynn attempt this, they simply restate Stone's hypothesis. London's inner life is best explored in his writings, but there is no book-length treatment of his major works. Earle Labor's *Jack London*, a survey of his career and the fifty-one books he wrote, comes closest to filling this need, and it is a valuable contribution. I have benefited from his work and from that of other scholars who have attempted to bring London into the humanistic literary tradition. I am particularly indebted to James McClintock's *White Logic*. This detailed analysis of London's short stories demonstrates how much can be learned by taking his art seriously and subjecting it to the close reading that is a commonplace of literary analysis, but which no one before McClintock had thought to apply to Jack London's work.

This book builds on McClintock's example, but it makes more direct use of London's autobiographical writings to understand the patterns of his fiction. Chapters 1 and 2 focus on London's early life and his initiation first into the man's world of the working class and then into the woman's world of the middle class. This double initiation defined alternate social realities against which London's psychic development was to take place, and it embodied the contradictions that, like Ahab's scar, rent his psyche and his art from crown to sole. London's first initiation revealed to him the realities of capitalist society; his second initiation was an attempt to escape from what he saw. His life and his art exhibit his ongoing struggle between reality and illusion, between truth-seeing and truth-denying. Once, in *The Call of the Wild*, London transcended this culturally determined dialectic and wrote of a dream that restored him to a kingdom he had not known he had lost.

London's vast corpus makes the task of the literary biographer one of selection. For the most part, I have expended my critical energies on what I take to be his best stories and those most revealing of dominant patterns in his life. I give scant attention to the later works, those written between 1910 and 1916. It may be objected that I thereby slight fully a third of London's active career, but I see his life and art in essentially a two-part scheme, with his working-class experiences on one side and his middle-class experiences on the other, and the "long sickness" as the watershed between them. According to this scheme, the nostalgia of *The Valley of the Moon* (1913) and the repressed sexuality of *The Little Lady of the Big House* (1915) are only decadent extensions of patterns already established in London's life and art. I have let *Burning Daylight* stand for the host of bad books London wrote in his final years. Kevin Starr's detailed treatment of the Sonoma valley novels is added reason for not dwelling on them further.

ABBREVIATIONS

BD
Burning Daylight

CW
The Call of the Wild

HL
Huntington Library

IH
The Iron Heel

JB
John Barleycorn

ME
Martin Eden

PA
The People of the Abyss

SR
Star Rover

SW
The Sea-Wolf

Road
The Road

WF
White Fang

SOLITARY COMRADE

ONE

INITIATION
INTO MANHOOD,
PART ONE:
THE LOWER CLASS

The story of Jack London's rise to middle-class success is also the story of his failure to achieve a sense of belonging within lower-class culture, and this failure shapes the opening chapter of his biography. Growing up in Oakland, California, in the 1880s and 1890s, London theoretically had the same choices available to him that any lower-class youth had. He could, through hard work, steady habits, and deferred gratification, achieve a meager respectability and a precarious stability; or he could challenge the values of work, thrift, and deferred gratification—and the whole system of legitimate means to society's rewards—by becoming a criminal; finally, he could eschew both the legitimate and illegitimate roads to success and take up the life of a tramp. Each of these choices involved the prior choice of a subculture within lower-class culture. London tried all three before he threw over this culture entirely and made his way into the middle class.

The values of the first subculture are close to the middle-class ideal of success through hard work and self-denial. In this sense it is a markedly higher-status choice than the other two. It is perhaps less obvious that the second option—becoming a criminal—has a higher status than that of becoming a tramp. In his study of crime and poverty in Columbus, Ohio, Eric Monkkonen argues that "criminal action is more aggressive and less alienated than an appeal for aid. . . . Poverty when defined as pauperism is a lower level of social oppres-

3

sion than is criminality; for those who were downwardly mobile, crime was the stop before pauperism; but for those already on the bottom, crime was a step up and not so frequently taken."[1] Others have argued that the lower-class youth's choice of the subculture to which he will belong depends on the opportunities he has to learn the ways of life they entail. Thus his choice is dependent not merely on his own motivation but on the availability of human models for his behavior through whom he has access to the values, knowledge, language, and techniques of that subculture. In other words, these subcultures, like all cultural systems, do not descend from the sky but are handed on through people and institutions. Thus it is possible to speak of the relative opportunities a lower-class youth may have to become a criminal, just as we commonly speak of the differentials in opportunity that characterize the legitimate means to success.[2] Becoming a thief is not automatically an option for a lower-class youth but is dependent upon his knowing other thieves and being initiated into the world of petty crime.

Herbert Asbury, in *The Gangs of New York*, implicitly recognizes this in his description of the career of Big Jack Zelig:

> Big Jack Zelig's name was William Alberts. He was born in Norfolk street in 1882 of respectable Jewish parents, and began his criminal career at the age of fourteen, when he ran away from home and became one of Crazy Butch's fleet of juvenile pickpockets. He was an apt pupil with a real gift for thievery, and made such rapid progress that within a year he had deserted the Fagin and was operating with great success on his own account, rolling lushes and deftly lifting pocket-books and jewelry from the crowds which thronged the Bowery and Chatham Square. [p. 328]

The language that Asbury applies to Big Jack Zelig's career in the underworld could as well be applied to an apprenticeship in the legitimate world: "apt pupil" . . . "real gift" . . . "rapid progress" . . . "great success." Because of his aptitude, Zelig later became "a prominent figure throughout the underworld" (p. 329). In *The Autobiography of Malcolm X*, the author gives a wonderful description of the different specializations that are included in the general occupation, burglar. He writes that it is "important to select an area of burglary and stick to that," in order to succeed:

There are specific specialties among burglars. Some work apartments only, others houses only, others stores only, or warehouses; still others will go after only safes or strongboxes.

Within the residence burglary category, there are further specialty distinctions. There are the day burglars, the dinner and theater-time burglars, the night burglars. I think that any city's police will tell you that very rarely do they find one type who will work at another time. For instance, Jumpsteady, in Harlem, was a nighttime apartment specialist. It would have been hard to persuade Jumpsteady to work in the daytime if a millionaire had gone out for lunch and left his front door wide open. [p. 142]

The underworld is not the realm of chaos and disorganization that it may appear to middle-class eyes. It has its own code of rules, professional techniques, and standards of success.

In other words, it is possible to be a failure in the underworld, just as one can fail in legitimate business. When the criminal fails, he falls into yet a lower social level within lower-class society: without a hustle, he becomes a panhandler and a vagabond, with no stake, legitimate or illegitimate, in society's system of rewards. In order to understand the shaping of Jack London's consciousness, it is important to see that in his lower-class career he slid closer and closer to the bottom of what he called the "Social Pit." In these depths dwelled "the people of the abyss"—those whom the social reformers called the "submerged tenth," and Karl Marx, the "lumpenproletariat." Here, by any name, humanity was at its lowest ebb. Here the struggle for survival reduced men to beasts.

London began where his family began, with the lower-middle-class belief in success through hard work. London's willingness to pursue this route was both fostered and undermined by his family's example. More than a year after she was deserted by William Chaney, and nine months after the birth of John Griffith London on January 12, 1876, Flora Wellman married John London. He was in his fifties and had five children from a previous marriage, two of whom lived with him. During his marriage to London's mother, he held many different respectable jobs: he was proprietor of a grocery store; when that failed, he took up farming; when the bank called in the mortgage on the farm, he went back to the vegetable trade. He ended his career with not what the nineteenth century called a "competence"—a modest but secure life for himself and his family—but the low wages of a night watchman and the unpredictable earnings of a constable. As London writes in *The Road*, "At one time my father was a constable and hunted tramps for a living. The community paid him so much per head for all the tramps he could catch, and also, I believe, he got mileage fees. Ways and means was always a pressing problem in our household, and the amount of meat on the table, the new pair of shoes, the day's outing, or the text-book for school, were dependent upon my father's luck in the chase" (p. 196).

By his example, John London fostered in Jack a similar belief in hard work. When he was ten years old he got up at three in the morning to deliver papers before he went to school, and he delivered an evening paper after he returned home. Saturdays he worked on an ice wagon, and Sundays he set up pins at a bowling alley.[3] This regimen characterized London's life from age ten to fifteen—his Horatio Alger period, during which he not only read Alger's books but acted out their values. Alger's hero is typified by Ragged Dick, a fourteen-year-old bootblack who escapes the streets by dint of his shrewdness (born of contact with the street) and his honesty (an innate quality that appears in Alger's homeless boys as if by genetic transmission). During his adolescence, London was devoted to Alger's belief that honesty and enterprise would be rewarded in a society that was as virtuous as the idealized hero. The Alger myth is quintessentially a child's story, for what it does not—indeed, cannot—look at are the adult relationships involved in the two initiating institutions of work and marriage. The Alger story focuses on the process through which the hero is removed from the streets. What happens after he has secured a respectable job, what kinds of demands are made upon him in his subordinate position as junior partner, what loss of independence he may experience, what courtship rituals he may expect—these are barely hinted at. The expectation is that he lives happily ever after, his salary increasing apace. The happy ending is, in the tradition of fairy tale and popular literature, supplied by the fantasies of the reading audience. (One of the earliest books London read was Ouida's *Signa*, in which the hero escapes the narrow life of a farm and experiences a social rise; in the copy that London read, the last forty pages were missing, which left even more of the ending to his imagination.)

In the Alger stories, the enterprising young hero usually has a sidekick who aids him and shares his successful struggle to respectability. In *Ragged Dick*, this is Fosdick, a bookish lad who will never get as far as Dick (for he loves learning too much for its own sake), but who proves an excellent tutor for Dick. In exchange for teaching him the rudiments of spelling and arithmetic, Dick shares his room with Fosdick, and they both get on with Franklinesque economy and self-improvement. Jack London had such a companion during his adolescence, a boy named Frank Atherton. Drawn together by their common interest in collecting cigarette papers, they shared many quiet afternoons and boyish adventures.

In his reminiscences, Atherton consciously or half-consciously casts Johnny, as London was then called, in the role of the Alger hero, and himself in the role of Fosdick, the loyal supporter who is clearly a notch below the hero in whatever magical quality it is that makes for success.[4] Atherton's family was poorer than London's, and he looked up to Johnny London as a boy of superior enterprise and accomplishment. Having had to drop out of school to support his family, Frank respected Johnny's devotion to intellectual pursuits. Between his paper route and his books, Johnny was often too busy to spend time with his friend. Atherton views London's inaccessibility as a mark of his great enterprise and determination to improve himself. In *Ragged Dick*, by contrast, self-improvement goes hand-in-hand with companionship. The satisfaction Dick and Fosdick take in their supportive companionship is at least as important as their rise to respectability, and Dick's ability to go faster and further than Fosdick does not affect the quality of their relationship. In Atherton's narrative, the difference in status between Johnny and Frank has a perceptible effect. Atherton remembers the time he was invited by Johnny London to go to a performance of a play by Shakespeare. Unfamiliar with Shakespeare's language, Atherton was unable to understand the jokes. But rather than sit by silently while others around him laughed, he determined to have a good time. Unfortunately, his zealous laughter was too often the only sound raised in appreciation, and after the play London freely ridiculed his friend's ill-timed outbursts.[5] This incident, in which London inflates his own self-worth at the expense of his friend's, portrays more realistically than Alger's stories the effects of stratification within lower-class culture. Significantly, both the class differences and the emotional

distance are heightened by the intrusion of literature into the relationship. Books were instrumental in London's rise, and later, as
he says of Martin Eden, "they were all the comrades left to him"
(*ME*, 240).

Atherton recounts two other anecdotes that reveal London's distance from another lower-class social type—the ethnic gang leader.
The first incident took place in the schoolyard of Cole School in
1886. Mike Panella, leader of a gang, tried to get London to put
down his book, which he always read at recess, and join in their play.
When Mike knocked the book out of London's hands, according to
Atherton's account, London called him a "dago" and lit into him.
London got the better of the fight, but both boys were called into the
principal's office. When the principal questioned Mike he said, "I
was only foolin' sir. I wanted him t' come an' play wid us guys."
When the principal gave the boys the choice of making up with one
another or enduring physical punishment, London preferred to take
the punishment—which won him the principal's respect and Mike
Panella's hatred. Clearly admiring London's fortitude and integrity,
Atherton understands his choice within the middle-class value of
status mobility. But looked at in lower-class terms, London has rejected a peer relationship for a relationship with books; he has lost a
potential comrade and gained the approval of a superior.[6]

London's distaste for the likes of Mike Panella was fostered at
home. Between his mother's distrust of Italians and his father's con-
stabulary job, which pitted him against the "Fish Gang" and other
youth gangs who terrorized the waterfront, London learned that
Mike Panella was the enemy. This lesson was dramatized by the
unprovoked attacks London suffered just because he was the constable's son. In the second anecdote of interest here, Atherton describes the rough district London had to pass through on his paper
route. "In the district west of Broadway, between Seventh Street and
the waterfront, one would see a class of ignorant, lawless people,
many of whom were aliens, many unable to read or write." One day
"Red Kelly," getting back at John London through his son, harassed
the young London as he was delivering his papers. Atherton's account of this set-to closely resembles Alger's account of an encounter
between Ragged Dick and the Irish gang leader, Micky Maguire. In
both stories, the frank, industrious, native American hero triumphs,

putting to rout the alien forces of a street culture mysterious and threatening.[7]

Just as subtle differences in social class distanced Johnny London from Frank Atherton, obvious differences in ethnic background distanced London from Mike Panella and Red Kelly. But the ethnic differences were only the most obvious, not the most operative factors. Mike Panella and Red Kelly, like Micky Maguire in *Ragged Dick*, have different social aspirations from our hero. They are each a leader of a gang. They are not less enterprising and industrious than London, they have simply chosen to rise *within* lower-class society rather than to step outside of it. This is clear in Alger's description of Micky Maguire:

> Now Micky was proud of his strength, and of the position of leader which it had secured him. Moreover he was democratic in his tastes, and had a jealous hatred of those who wore good clothes and kept their faces clean. He called it putting on airs, and resented the implied superiority. If he had been fifteen years older, and had a trifle more education, he would have interested himself in politics, and been prominent at ward meetings, and a terror to respectable voters on election day. As it was, he contented himself with being the leader of a gang of young ruffians, over whom he wielded a despotic power.
> {pp. 122–23}

Here we have a good example of the sort of boy the social reformers feared; for him they established the Newsboys' Lodging House, and to him Alger preached in his books, with the purpose of winning him over to more respectable and less political expressions of his energies.

London remembers his Horatio Alger years as a time of Struggle and Family and Duty. He worked long hours and turned all but a meager allowance over to his parents. Had his stepfather been younger and stronger, Johnny London might have stuck with this respectable road to lower-class manhood. But he could see, in the figure of his ill and aging stepfather, what lay ahead for him in this life of hard work and scrimping: a round of endless toil with no rest or security but the grave. His stepfather died when London was twenty-one. Although London gives little evidence of having reflected on the meaning of his stepfather's life, all the evidence on that score was in by the time London reached his majority.

When London was fifteen, he gave away his cigarette-paper collection, exchanged "Johnny" for "Jack," joined a gang, and set about becoming a man, which in some dimly understood way meant putting behind him the values of the Alger hero. With borrowed money he bought a skiff—the *Razzle Dazzle*—and began robbing the oyster beds of the legitimate fishermen of San Francisco Bay, netting $25 in one night's haul. In order to support his mother and stepfather, London was at this time in 1891 working long hours in Hickmott's cannery in Oakland for ten cents an hour. This exhausting labor left him no time or strength for the outdoor adventures that were an important part of his childhood. His rebound into crime was most immediately an escape from an insupportable amount and kind of work.

It should also be said that London, as a fifteen-year-old, urban, lower-class youth, ran a high risk of falling in with a criminal gang. The gang as a social phenomenon was especially noticeable in the post-Civil War decades, as the social fruits of industrialization appeared in the guise of a swelling population of "street people." This floating population was largely composed of young people, who often banded together for criminal purposes. Because of their numbers, their energy, and their propensity for crime, these "abandoned youth" were identified by social reformers as members of the "dangerous classes." "It should be remembered that there are no dangers to the value of property, or to the permanency of our institutions, so great as those from the existence of such a class of vagabond, ignorant, ungoverned children," warned an 1854 report of a reform society in New York:

> This "dangerous class" has not begun to show itself, as it will
> in eight or ten years, when these boys and girls are matured.
> Those who were too negligent, or too selfish to notice them as
> children, will be fully aware of them as men. They will vote—
> they will have the same rights as we ourselves, though they have
> grown up ignorant of moral principle, as any savage or Indian.
> They will poison society. They will perhaps be embittered at
> the wealth and the luxuries they never share. Then let society
> beware, when the outcast, vicious reckless multitude of New

Jack London, member of the working class
(Reproduced by permission of The Huntington Library, San Marino, California)

York boys, swarming now in every foul alley and low street,
come to know their power and *use it!*[8]

Charles Loring Brace attributed the growth of this dangerous class to
the increasing separation of youth from the apprenticeships that led
to skilled trades. This he blamed on labor unions, which allowed
fewer and fewer into the trades, and on the "increasing aversion of
American children, whether poor or rich, to learn anything thoroughly; the boys of the street, like those of our merchants, preferring
to make fortunes by lucky and sudden 'turns,' rather than by patient
and steady industry."[9] Behind the attitudes that Brace perceived
were changes in both the nature of work and in the composition of
the labor force. As wage-saving machinery eliminated many skilled
jobs, the labor unions reacted defensively to protect the jobs of
those who were already in the trade, making entry more difficult for
youth. The jobs open to youth were increasingly unskilled jobs that
led nowhere and were, like London's job in the cannery, so low-
paying and monotonous that many did choose "to make fortunes by
lucky and sudden 'turns,' rather than by patient and steady industry."

When the fifteen-year-old London turned to oyster piracy, he was
responding in a way characteristic of urban lower-class youth. Judge
Ben Lindsey wrote in 1908 that "over half the inmates of reforma-
tories, jails and prisons in this country are under twenty-five years of
age" and that "an English prison commission not long ago reported
to Parliament that the age of sixteen to twenty was the essentially
criminal age."[10] What is unusual about London's entrance into the
criminal subculture is not the nature of his choice, but the peculiar
way in which he made this entrance. He did not simply fall in with
"bad companions" who educated him in the ways of the street—or,
in his case, the waterfront. Had this happened, his niche within that
subculture would have been much more secure. Instead, he bought
his way in through an entrepreneurial scheme that was financially
dependent on his ties with the semiprosperous, respectable world.
Without the $300 he borrowed from Virginia Prentiss ("Mammy
Jenny," his wet-nurse) to buy the *Razzle Dazzle*, London would not
have had access to the world of French Frank, former owner of the
skiff. The method of London's entry is significant, for what it lacks
is the texture of cultural initiation into the signs, symbols, craft,
and fellowship of piracy. He lacked the appropriate apprenticeship.

London obtained his membership simply by a contractual exchange. That his criminal career was short-lived and may be judged a failure— in spite of his heroic accounts of his adventures—may be attributed to his abrupt and unmediated entry into this world.

Under other circumstances, London might have learned some of the secrets of piracy from French Frank, a man in his fifties; but it happened that French Frank's mistress was attracted to the young London and transferred her affections with the transfer of the *Razzle Dazzle*. French Frank subsequently tried to run London down on the bay, and only the boy's expertise at sailing saved him. London's one experienced ally was an English sailor named Shorty, who, according to London's account, distinguished himself by burning the foresail of the *Razzle Dazzle*. While it was thus crippled, it was further ravaged by vandals; biographers have speculated that the culprits were a rival gang, or perhaps London's own associates who had turned against him.[11]

London's abortive entry into this lower-class subculture may be compared to Malcolm Little's initiation into the "hip" world of Roxbury. In his autobiography, Malcolm X makes much of his ungainly appearance and his difference from the world he was about to enter: his clothes, his unconked hair, his ignorance of city ways and city speech, marked him as a country boy. But he was taken in hand by a fellow named Shorty, who was from Malcolm's home town of East Lansing, Michigan. Shorty was the ideal person to initiate Malcolm, for he belonged to both the world Malcolm was coming from and the world he hoped to enter. He could laugh at Malcolm's countrified ways without offense, for he was laughing at his former self. Malcolm could freely admit what he did not know and allow himself to be taught by the experienced Shorty. There was no embarrassment involved, for Shorty knew the boy from East Lansing for what he was and was only doing him the favor of introducing him to city ways. "Shorty's jokes about how country I had been made us all laugh. I was still country, I know now, but it all felt so great because I was accepted."[12] Malcolm X gives a detailed account of Shorty's tutelage, from how to get a hustle to how to conk his hair. Because he was Shorty's "homeboy," Malcolm was accepted by the sophisticated crowd of Roxbury, and thanks to his apprenticeship with Shorty, Malcolm Little from East Lansing was soon transformed into a smooth-talking cat in a zoot suit. When Malcolm X became a

powerful revolutionary leader, he denounced the "degrading" practice of conking hair, but surely his rise to leadership had much to do
with his early, successful integration into the black urban subculture.

London's failure to make contact with lower-class culture conditioned his later attempts at belonging; always he attempted to buy his
way, and always he missed the experience of a fellowship that was
organic and spontaneous. Without an accomplice to ease his entry,
he resorted to stratagems that had enormous implications for his
emotional life: he pretended to be what he was not—an already
initiated member-in-good-standing—and tried as best he could to
imitate the expected behavior of the gang. Always he felt the discrepancy between the public identity he was simulating and the real
identity he was experiencing.

But there was a lower-class institution that, according to London's
reconstruction of his past, effected his integration into this subculture: this was the saloon. London writes that "the things I did on
the water only partly counted. What completed everything and won
for me the title 'Prince of the Oyster Beds,' was that I was a good
fellow ashore with my money, buying drinks like a man" (*JB*, 92–93).
London calls this buying of drinks a "manhood rite" (*JB*, 96), and in
his memoirs drinking is clearly a rite of passage between boyhood
and manhood. This ritual and London's relation to it deserve careful
scrutiny, for it reveals much about what it meant to him to achieve
manhood in America.

A rite of passage in a traditional society marks the entrance of a
boy into the privileges of adulthood, as defined by the adult society
of which he has been a junior member since birth. A rite of passage
in a bourgeois society has a very different significance: typically it
marks not the full participation of a man in the society of his birth
but his departure from that given society and his entrance into a new
society (often of a higher social class), with new values and criteria of
worth. The American experience, as first defined by Crèvecoeur,
was characterized by leaving behind the whole feudal European past
and standing alone, a new man on a fresh and unexplored continent.
Thus the American typically experiences the manhood rite not as a
revelation of the familiar and a confirmation of his status within the
community but as a confrontation with an alien culture with which
he is nevertheless expected to be familiar.

The drinking London did in the Last Chance Saloon marked his departure from the values of his family (thrift, respectability, industry) and his entrance into a new subculture that valued open-handed spending, strong drink, and reckless displays of physical courage. "As a youth," London writes in *John Barleycorn*, "by way of the saloon I had escaped from the narrowness of women's influence into the wide world of men." London drank and caroused with "the spirit of revolt, of adventure, of romance, of the things done defiantly and grandly" (*JB*, 7). It is significant that London characterizes the world he is leaving as a narrow, woman's world and the world he is entering as a "wide world of men." London was always to associate the bourgeois virtues with a narrow, effeminate way of seeing and manhood with the lower-class values of Oakland street culture. This linkage of gender identity and class identity was to create predictable confusion when London later pursued his social rise.

Although London's departure from the Horatio Alger virtues marked a break from his family, in another way his drinking may be viewed as his attempt to become a man in the model of his stepfather, John London. London's biographers have pictured John London as a quiet and colorless man, not a personality to stand up to the tantrums and restlessness of Flora Wellman. That he was the less dominant force in the household surely had a bearing on young London's attempts to define his male identity. But the portrait drawn of John London by biographers may not accurately suggest the man's effect on young boys. Frank Atherton remembers his telling vivid stories of Indian warfare. To Atherton, John London was clearly a hero who moved in an aura of frontier adventure and romance. On the waterfront, he was fearless against the gangs of young toughs.

It was also important that he frequented Johnny Heinhold's Last Chance Saloon, and Atherton remembers with pleasure the time that he invited Frank and Johnny to accompany him within those portals. He recalls that John London had a running bill in Heinhold's large ledger book.[13] As a youth, London tells us in *John Barleycorn*, it became his desire to run up a similar line of credit in that book. "Almost it seemed the final badge of manhood" (*JB*, 85). London dramatizes this turn of events by describing an incident in which he was forced to choose between his industrious and thrifty habits and his newly aroused desire for acceptance into a group of men. He had to decide whether it was more important to add to his bank account like a proper Alger hero, or to add to his stock of acceptance with his peers by standing for a round of drinks. "Which was it to be? I was aware that I was making a grave decision. I was deciding between money and men, between niggardliness and romance. Either I must throw overboard all my old values of money and look upon it as something to be flung about wastefully, or I must throw overboard my comradeship with those men whose peculiar quirks made them care for strong drink" (*JB*, 83–84).

In choosing the camaraderie and romance of the saloon over the penny-pinching scruples of his newsboy's conscience, London was choosing to become a man in the model of his stepfather. In this scenario, London's mother is put in charge of the narrow, scrimping values that are now clearly viewed as limiting and limited. These represent the narrow woman's world from which he escapes into the "wide world of men." It is true that Flora Wellman was bent on getting ahead and determinedly saved money for first one investment and then another. But she also relied on magical forces outside the realm of hard work and thrift: her initial attraction to William Chaney, the atrologer, was in part her attraction to the world of séances and spiritual forces, which sometimes told her to drop what she was doing and take up a new scheme to get rich. And money that might have gone into savings often went into lottery tickets. Just as in the Alger stories, the rational forces that put the hero in control— hard work and thrift—are buttressed by implicit acknowledgment of the irrational forces—luck and magical coincidences. Flora's séances were her equivalent of John London's drinking: both were attempts to get in touch with the romance and mystery of life, and, by the same token, attempts to escape from the reality of life in the urban proletariat. They were also tacit admissions of the likely failure of the rational schemes that both of London's parents pursued with such doggedness.

Thus Flora Wellman and John London acted out a contradiction in lower-class culture between dreams of success and proletarian reality. For a child, this contradiction was hard to recognize because it was not explicitly acknowledged. London's response was to simplify the situation in a predictably child-like way. The contradiction that both of his parents had internalized and that they acted out in self-contradictory behavior was, in London's private mythology, externalized in a more clear-cut drama in which his father was the hero and his mother the villain. Together with his father in the saloon,

London escaped from women's influence and all the narrow futility of lower-class life. In this process, London did not accurately see his mother—who was just as given to escape—nor did he come close to understanding the discrepancy between dream and reality in lower-class life. In constructing this private mythology, London drew a veil between his consciousness and the social reality, and behind this veil was his mother. If she was held responsible, in some half-conscious way, for all that was wrong with lower-class life, the same pattern was to repeat itself when London made his way into the middle class and discovered the poverty of the American dream: he turned on Success as he had turned on lower-class life, and Success was a woman—a Bitch Goddess.[14]

In London's account of his initiation into the man's world of the saloon, one is struck by the disjunction between his intense desire to be accepted by the gang and his severe discomfort at undergoing the *process* of initiation. In the first place, he hated the taste of beer; he has at this point in his recollections told of several instances in which as a child he had been made violently ill by it. It is suggestive that London associates the act of fellowship with taking something poisonous and distasteful into his system. He remembers a visit to a ranch where their Italian hosts plied them with red wine. London was only seven years old, and having once got drunk on his father's beer, he did not plan to repeat the unpleasant experience. But when one of the young Italian boys pushed a tumbler of wine across the table to him, he writes, "terror descended upon me." This terror was connected with his mother's theory that "all the tribe of dark-eyed humans were deceitful." Blond herself, "she was convinced that the dark-eyed Latin races were profoundly sensitive, profoundly treacherous, and profoundly murderous. Again and again, drinking in the strangeness and the fearsomeness of the world from her lips, I had heard her state that if one offended an Italian, no matter how slightly and unintentionally, he was certain to retaliate by stabbing one in the back. That was her particular phrase—'stab you in the back'" (*JB*, 26). This Italian boy "had those terrible black eyes I had heard my mother talk about." Moved by fear of offending this dark-eyed devil and also having "some glimmering inkling of the sacredness of hospitality," London accepted the drink. Many more tumblers of wine were pushed across the table to him, and his good Italian hosts began to marvel at the child prodigy. London writes, "I was frozen,

I was paralyzed with fear." He was later violently ill from the drink, and he blamed his mother's theories for his condition (*JB*, 27–35).

London's mother, from whose lips he "[drank] in the strangeness and the fearsomeness of the world," was always in some sense removed from the small world of which she was a part. Flora Wellman had run away from her family in Massillon, Ohio, but she remembered that there they had been a solid and respected middle-class presence. By comparison, her life in California was small and sordid, as she and John London struggled to hang on to the lower-middle-class respectability that bad luck always threatened to swallow up in the commonplaces of the urban proletariat. She impressed her son with their differences from their neighbors (most of whom, in rural California, were Italian), and she insisted that the steaks be eaten on newspapers so as not to soil the tablecloths. The words that London puts in the mouth of the young boy in *The Valley of the Moon*, "Oakland's just a place to start from, I guess" (p. 267), grew out of that vision, fostered by his mother, of other, better worlds beyond the horizon. He approached that world—and the people in it—with an unstable mixture of curiosity and fear. Warned against contact with his immediate world and yet lured on by tales of the magical unknown, London was never to know rest.

In his encounter with the dark-eyed Italian, London's fear led him to subordinate himself to the wishes of the dreaded host. This mixture of outward pliability and inward paralysis was to characterize his meetings with strangers. In the next significant encounter that he relates in *John Barleycorn*, London tells of his initiation into the "manhood rite" of drinking through the agency of the waterfront pirate he so admired, "Young Scratch" Nelson. One day the twenty-year-old Nelson, passing London in front of the Last Chance Saloon, asked the inexperienced boy to have a drink with him. London remembers the intense pride he felt in being noticed by this man and included in his company. They stood at the bar and drank and talked, and after the first beer was gone, London found it strange that they "lingered at the bar. . . . We had had our beer. But who was I to lead the way outside when great Nelson chose to lean against the bar? After a few minutes, to my surprise, he asked me to have another drink, which I did." London had no taste for the beer, but, he explains, that seemed "no reason I should forego the honor of his company. It was his whim to drink beer, and to have me drink beer

with him. Very well, I would put up with the passing discomfort."
Nelson continued to order beers and the enamored London stayed
and drank with him until they had each had six rounds, at which
point London took his leave (*JB*, 78–79).

Later, when London had time to reflect, the pride he experienced
in hobnobbing with Nelson was tempered by the uncomfortable
feeling that he may not have acted properly. He "recollected that
several times other men, in couples, had entered the Last Chance,
and first one, then the other, had treated to drinks." London is overcome with shame when he realizes that he has let Nelson treat six
times without once offering to treat in return. His memory of this
realization is vivid: "I could feel myself blushing with shame. I sat
down on the stinger-piece of the wharf and buried my face in my
hands. And the heat of my shame burned up my neck and into my
cheeks and forehead. I have blushed many times in my life, but never
have I experienced so terrible a blush as that one" (*JB*, 80). As he reflects on his experience with Nelson, he suspects that Nelson drank
with him not out of friendship, but out of curiosity: "He wanted to
find out just what kind of a gink I was. He wanted to see how many
times I'd let him treat without offering to treat in return" (*JB*, 78–79).
London felt similar emotions as he recalled the transaction with
French Frank, in which, over drinks, London bought his skiff from
him. Then, as with Nelson, London did not understand why everyone lingered at the bar. "I have often thought since of how they must
have regarded me, the newcomer being welcomed into their company, standing at the bar with them, and not standing for a single
round of drinks." London is thirty-six years old as he writes this, but
still, he says, "my ears burn now as I try to surmise the things they
must have said about me" (*JB*, 71).

For London, becoming a man was inextricably bound up with
feelings of intense humiliation—the humiliation of feeling himself
the only outsider in a company of initiates. Even Nelson, cast in the
role of initiator into this new world, is suspected of treachery. The
way to overcome this humiliation, London's memoir suggests, is by
aggressive overcompensation. Did he neglect to treat Nelson? Very
well, he will return and treat him now. Not content with that, London
begins applying his new "concept," as he calls it, indiscriminately,
urging all and sundry to drink with him. One night he spends $180,
buying drinks for all who will have them. He must be in a powerful

position to avoid the paralysis that humiliated him with Nelson. "And so," London writes, "I won my manhood spurs" (*JB*, 91). The emotional pain of this initiation is balanced by a certain intellectual pleasure that London calls "pride"; he has the satisfaction of achieving what he wants: "comradeship" with men whom he admires. He attains the outward semblance of belonging in a world of men.

London's choice of the comradeship of the oyster pirates over the respectable virtues of his family may be compared to Huck Finn's choice of Tom Sawyer's gang of robbers over the Widow Douglas's respectable world of clean beds, starched clothes, and stiff moral spines. But Huck is disgusted with Tom Sawyer when he sees that he only intends to play at being robbers; the contrast between Tom Sawyer's romantic, bookish ideas of highwaymen and the stark realities of Huck Finn's life with Pap exposes the sentimental lies of the genteel culture to which Twain (and Huck) are nevertheless drawn. If in his flight from his mother London is cast in the role of Huck Finn, in his quest for adventure there is much of Tom Sawyer in him. He sought the world of the oyster pirates in order to live out the adventures he had read about in books, which he explored at an early age, reading "principally history and adventure, and all the old travels and voyages" (*JB*, 41). Books allowed him to escape from the ordinary world into a realm of adventure and great deeds. The saloon offered a similar escape from the "common every-day where nothing happened," and London repeatedly associates the romance of the saloon with the romance of books:

> In the saloons life was different. Men talked with great voices, laughed great laughs, and there was an atmosphere of greatness. Here was something more than common everyday where nothing happened. Here life was always very live, and sometimes, even lurid, when blows were struck, and blood was shed, and big policemen came shouldering in. Great moments, these, for me, my head filled with all the wild and valiant fighting of the gallant adventures on sea and land. [*JB*, 42]

His first-hand acquaintance with saloons, which were always warm and bright and welcoming, dispelled whatever notion he might have had that they were terrible places. "Terrible they might be, but then that only meant they were terribly wonderful." They were terrible "in the same way pirates, and shipwrecks, and battles were terrible"

(*JB*, 43). As he reflects on the exploits that fell to him at such a young age and that won for him the title, "Prince of the Oyster Pirates," London writes, "I had read of such things in books, and regarded them as personal probabilities of a distant maturity." He is not surprised that, in becoming prince of the oyster pirates, he has become a storybook character. He is only surprised that it happened so soon. Writing to Charmian Kittredge London years later, he explains why he took the "Queen" for his mistress. "I was making a career for myself, after a picture I had created out of the books I always kept on exchanging at the old library" (*JB*, 73).[15] Books were to London what spiritualism was to his mother and drink to his father: a momentary escape from the pain and struggle of lower-class life, a ritual space in which other possibilities might be entertained. But each of these strategies that made lower-class life more bearable also deadened consciousness; they were merely anodynes.

Just as the rite of passage in a bourgeois society signifies not full participation in one's indigenous culture but entry into an unfamiliar one, so maturity may mean not to come into one's own but to become a character in a book. London's assumption of a bookish alter ego represented the growth of a false consciousness, an identity created from without. All social mobility involves the assumption of new identities, but whether the new identity is organically assimilated depends on the presence of a trustworthy guide to the unfamiliar terrain. Lacking such a human guide, London relied on two institutions, the saloon and books, to effect his integration into the new subculture. Both conveyed to him second-hand, insubstantial personae that he attempted to integrate into his consciousness. The characters in the books were idealized, romantic figures who bore no relationship to the facts of real life as experienced from a lower-class perspective; to adopt the bookish character as an alter ego was to deny the reality of one's own experience. Similarly, alcohol suppressed London's consciousness of his real emotions—which, as we have seen, were often the uncomfortable ones of shame and humiliation. "And it was through John Barleycorn," London writes, "that I came to join this glorious company of free souls, unashamed and unafraid." He is very explicit about the effect of alcohol on his consciousness: "as John Barleycorn heated his way into my brain, thawing my reticence, melting my modesty, talking through me and with me and as me, my adopted twin brother and *alter ego*, I, too, raised my voice to show myself a man and an adventurer" (*JB*, 51). Like alcohol, the books created for London a "twin brother and *alter ego*," but instead of integrating him into his subculture this other self divided him against himself.

For several years, London drifted. He formed a partnership-in-crime with "Young Scratch" Nelson; after they were apprehended, they turned colors and worked for the Fish Patrol. London picked up odd jobs along the waterfront and, on one of them, fell in with a group of hoboes with whom he spent several weeks. When he returned to Oakland after making his way to Nevada and back, he ran for awhile with the West Oakland street gangs. Then, just after his seventeenth birthday, he signed aboard the *Sophie Sutherland* for a seven-month sealing voyage.[16]

The consciousness that London brought to the middle-class world was shaped by a lower-class career in which, unable to find a firm foothold, he slipped further and further into the Social Pit. In this process, he developed two survival tactics that became automatic responses. The first of these was his plasticity—his ability to make himself over according to the expectations of his audience. The second was his impulse to flee when the odds were against him. Both of these responses were intensified the further he slipped into the Pit and received their finishing touches when London sank into the lowest level of social oppression—the world of the tramp.

The success of the tramp depended upon his ability to tell a story that would convince his "mark." The kind of face that opened the door dictated the kind of story he would tell. Much as Huck Finn always listened carefully for cues as to who he was and became a runaway apprentice or a Tom Sawyer according to the assumptions and prejudices of his audience, the beggar had to "size up" his victim and "tell a story that will appeal to the peculiar personality and temperament of that particular victim." In his memoirs of his tramping experiences, London describes this process as a kind of apprenticeship for his writing career:

> The successful hobo must be an artist. He must create spontaneously and instantaneously—and not upon a theme selected from the plenitude of his own imagination, but upon the theme he reads in the face of the person who opens the door, be it man, woman, or child, sweet or crabbed, generous or miserly,

good-natured or cantankerous, Jew or Gentile, black or white, race-prejudiced or brotherly, provincial or universal, or whatever else it may be. I have often thought that to this training of my tramp days is due much of my success as a story-writer. [*Road*, 9]

The hobo-artist does not involve his authentic self in this transaction. He is simply a reflection of what others are (or, more accurately, of what he imagines others to be). He barters his soul for bread and creates pictures of the dominant culture. These pictures do not reflect his experiences nor are they accurate representations of those of his audience. They are only images in a hall of mirrors.

The tramp's success depended upon his ability to size up his victim before his victim had a chance to size him up. London learned that law officers could size up a tramp on the instant; the thing to do when "the bulls" were "horstile" was to make "a swift get-away." London writes, "It took me some time to learn this; but the finishing touch was put upon me by a bull in New York City." London happened to be passing by when a policeman broke up a crowd of gamins who were playing the prohibited game of pee-wee. Because he was not part of the crowd, London did not scatter with them. To his surprise, the policeman dove into him:

At the same moment, verbally, he cast the bar sinister on my genealogy.

All my free American blood boiled. All my liberty-loving ancestors clamored in me. "What do you mean?" I demanded. You see, I wanted an explanation. And I got it. Bang! His club came down on top of my head, and I was reeling backward like a drunken man, the curious faces of the onlookers billowing up and down like the waves of the sea, my precious book falling from under my arm into the dirt, the bull advancing with the club ready for another blow. And in that dizzy moment I had a vision. I saw that club descending many times upon my head; I saw myself, bloody and battered and hard-looking, in a police-court; I heard a charge of disorderly conduct, profane language, resisting an officer, and a few other things, read by a clerk; and I saw myself across in Blackwell's Island. Oh, I knew the game. I lost all interest in explanations. . . . I turned and ran. [*Road*, 208]

"Ever since that time," London writes, "it has been an automatic process with me to make a run for it when I see a bull reaching for me. This automatic process has become a mainspring of conduct in me, wound up and ready for instant release. I shall never get over it" (*Road*, 205). This "automatic process" of flight had its counterpart in London's decision to break entirely with lower-class culture and was to be intimately connected with his artistic life. In his life and his art, London's impulse to look truth starkly in the face was over and over again subverted by his "automatic" impulse to flee that truth when he felt the odds were against him. With a consciousness shaped by the experience of social oppression, he attempted to overcome that oppression and he never fully understood that he was part of the problem he was trying to eliminate.

If London lacked self-knowledge, he was gifted with an unusual clarity of vision about the society in which he lived. Indeed, it could be said that the contrast between the glaring white light of his political vision and the dark, unplumbed depths of his own psyche made life for him insupportable. In his memoirs, London associates the development of his political vision with experiences that, unlike the saloon, introduced him to the reality of working-class life. These were his experiences in the industrial shop and in prison, and they may be thought of as deeper stages of his initiation into lower-class manhood.

In the winter of 1893, London decided to quit drifting from job to job and to acquire a trade. Reasoning that the field of electricity was bound to expand indefinitely, he applied to be an electrician's apprentice. In his account of that experience he savagely satirizes his naive belief, fostered by his reading of Alger's biography of Garfield, that a canal boy could become president. London presented his eager self to the equally eager superintendent of the Oakland power plant, which supplied electricity for the street cars, and so began his initiation into the world of industrial relationships.

London stood up straight and told the superintendent of his strong body and his desire to work hard. "The superintendent beamed as he listened. He told me that I was the right stuff for success, and that he believed in encouraging American youth that wanted to rise. Why, employers were always on the lookout for young fellows like me, and alas, they found them all too rarely. My ambition was fine and worthy, and he would see to it that I got my chance. (And as I listened with swelling heart, I wondered if it was his daughter I was to marry)" (*JB*, 188–89). The superintendent explains that before the boy can learn "the more complicated and higher details of the profession, he must begin at the bottom," as a helper to the car house electricians. His duties will be sweeping up and keeping things clean; but before he can shoulder that awesome responsibility he "must pass through the engine room as an oiler"; and before he can enter the engine room ("there must be preparation for that") he must pass through the fire room. The superintendent sets the eager boy to work shoveling coal as the first step toward mastery of his profession. Being a clever manager, he assigns to the strong boy the work of two men, whom he lets go, and pays the boy $30 a month, which is $10 less than he paid *each* of the men. The boy, determined to prove himself man enough for the job, labors until his wrists are swollen and sprained. Undaunted, for he was "a husky young fellow determined to rise," he bound his wrists with straps and continued to work. He would have continued in this fashion had not an older and wiser worker told him of the manner in which he and his fellow workers were being used—and even after he learned he was doing the work of the day-shift worker and the night-shift worker, London stayed on the job long enough to prove that he could do it (*JB*, 189–201).

London's account of this experience sparkles with incisive irony. Alongside the Alger myth that characterized his young consciousness, London places a suggestive description of the organization of industrial work, an organization that rendered that consciousness obsolete. London was clearly aware, at least by 1912, if not at the time of his "electrical apprenticeship," that the techniques of scientific management made getting ahead in the traditional ways impossible. London's story may be compared with Frederick Winslow Taylor's story of "Schmidt," an immigrant and a hard-working pig-iron handler. Taylor, a manager at Bethlehem Steel Company, gets Schmidt to agree to increase his productivity from twelve and a half long tons a day to forty-seven. For this 400 percent increase in productivity, Schmidt enjoys a 60 percent increase in pay. This gain in productivity is accomplished through the more efficient use of labor power. Schmidt works exactly as Taylor directs, wasting no time on superfluous movements or needless rests. "Efficiency" is defined by the need of the industry to show a profit. That Schmidt is less efficient outside of the work place because he is so tired, that his life may be shortened by the arduousness of his work, are considerations that do not enter into Taylor's notions of efficiency.[17] London gives to the superintendent of the electrical plant notions of efficiency like Taylor's. Here the superintendent explains the importance of shoveling coal:

> ". . . you will see that even the mere handling of coal is a
> scientific matter and not to be sneezed at. Do you know that we
> weigh every pound of coal we burn? Thus, we learn the value
> of the coal we buy; we know to a tee the last penny of cost of
> every item of production, and we learn which firemen are the
> most wasteful, which firemen, out of stupidity or carelessness,
> get the least out of the coal they fire." The superintendent
> beamed again. "You see how very important this little matter of
> coal is, and by as much as you learn of this little matter you will
> become that much better a workman—more valuable to us,
> more valuable to yourself." [JB, 190–91]

There is clearly a divergence between what the young worker needs to know for the sake of his own development and what the company needs him to know. For the company, it was efficient for the young and strong to shovel coal, whatever their imaginative capacities might be. The separation of the design of the job from its execution prevented the worker from participating in the whole of the labor process, thus depriving him of the craft skill and craft knowledge that, in an earlier period, had enabled the apprentice to surpass his master, as Ben Franklin turned the tables on Keimer in Philadelphia. In short, Taylorism increased the stratification of the labor force and made it more difficult to rise. Rising through the ranks was not an option if one rank did not presuppose the knowledge learned in a previous rank; if craft knowledge resided not in the workers but in the managers, the only way to rise was from one class to another—to become a manager.

London, as we know, did not take this route, but chose to be a professional of another sort. Before he did this, he needed a clearer vision of the class structure than was afforded through his electrical apprenticeship. This vision came to him when he experienced himself, for perhaps the first time, as a member of a class. Following his "orgy of work" in the power plant, London took to the road. Marching with a contingent of Coxey's army of the unemployed, London realized what a vast number of men were out of jobs. Whatever the uniqueness of his own personality, in his economic troubles he was not alone. The experiences encountered on his march across the country were doubtless productive of a campfire fellowship, but London in his diary of those days does not dwell on any new-found feelings of solidarity. Indeed, as Andrew Sinclair remarks, his tramp diary is "almost bare of social comment, the mere record of some wandering weeks."[18] His real awakening came in the Erie County Penitentiary, where, locked up on a vagrancy charge, his class position was "hammered in" in unforgettable and "unprintable" ways.[19]

London's experience in prison may be thought of as the third in a series of initiations into "a man's world." In the first, with Nelson, London learned he could be as powerful and "manly" as the freest of swashbucklers. In the second, with the superintendent, he learned that the harder and more energetically he worked, that is, the more powerful he showed himself to be, the more complete was his exploitation. In the Erie County Penitentiary London had this lesson underscored: here, in unmistakable ways, manhood was punished; the cunning thing, the survival tactic, was to pretend to be weak and submissive. London learned this by watching what happened to "a handsome young mulatto of about twenty who got the insane idea into his head that he should stand for his rights." He observes,

> And he did have the right of it, too; but that didn't help him any. He lived on the topmost gallery. Eight hall-men took the conceit out of him in just about a minute and a half—for that was the length of time required to travel along his gallery to the end and down five flights of steel stairs. He traveled the whole distance on every portion of his anatomy except his feet, and the eight hall-men were not idle. The mulatto struck the pavement where I was standing watching it all. He regained his feet and stood upright for a moment. In that moment he threw his arms wide apart and emitted an awful scream of terror and pain and heart-break. At the same instant, as in a transformation scene, the shreds of his stout prison clothes fell from him, leaving him wholly naked and streaming blood from every portion of the surface of his body. Then he collapsed in a heap, unconscious. He had learned his lesson, and every convict

within those walls who heard him scream had learned a lesson. So had I learned mine. It is not a nice thing to see a man's heart broken in a minute and a half. [*Road*, 108–9]

This "transformation scene" represents an important and complicated event in the consciousness of Jack London. In his reminiscences he places himself in the position of an observer. He is "standing watching it all." Yet earlier in his account of his prison experiences he has explained that he managed to become a hall-man. He has further explained that it was a "rule" that whenever a prisoner was being punished, "every hall-man in sight would come on the run to join in the chastisement" (*Road*, 107). The mulatto landed on the pavement, presumably near where London was standing. It was his duty to join in the pummeling that the other hall-men had administered as the prisoner ran the gauntlet of the five flights of stairs. In that moment after the prisoner regained his feet, when "he threw his arms wide apart and emitted an awful scream of terror and pain and heartbreak," he may have been anticipating a final blow from the husky young hall-man who stood "watching it all." Whether or not it was administered before he sank into unconsciousness, who is to say? Certainly London had to administer punishments many times during his thirty days in prison or else see his job go to a more efficient hall-man.

However ambiguous London's involvement in this scene, he writes about it with humanistic engagement. This man, "wholly naked and streaming blood from every portion of the surface of his body," is not simply an object lesson to London—though he is that. The lesson that London and "every convict within those walls who heard him scream" learned depended on their recognition of the mulatto's humanity, his essential likeness to themselves. Only because of the commonality of their condition could he be a lesson to them. Yet the lesson they were expected to draw set them apart from the mulatto: as he had revolted, they were to submit. London's consciousness is divided between sympathy for the manhood that inspired this revolt and fear of the consequences it provoked. For the first time in his life, London understood that he was up against a system that was bigger than he was. As his initiation into the Erie County Penitentiary proceeded, his indignation at his arrest "ebbed away" and "into my being rushed the tides of fear," he writes. "I saw at last, clear-

eyed, what I was up against. I grew meek and lowly. Each day I resolved more emphatically to make no rumpus when I got out. All I
asked, when I got out, was a chance to fade away from the landscape. And that was just what I did do when I was released. I kept my
tongue between my teeth, walked softly, and sneaked for Pennsyl-
vania, a wiser and a humbler man" (*Road*, 97).

The lesson London failed to learn in the power plant he now
understood. In the prison there was an artificial allotment of strength
and weakness. The prisoners were dealt a position of weakness. The
hall-men held stronger cards. The guards were strongest of all. A
man's power or weakness derived not from his physical or intellectual strength but simply from the position he held. Experience with
the prison system clarified London's understanding of the nature of
his exploitation in the industrial setting. Explaining the petty extor-
tions practiced by the powerful hall-men, London asks, "[W]hat
would you do? We had to live. And certainly there should be some
reward for initiative and enterprise. Besides, we but patterned ourselves after our betters outside the walls, who, on a larger scale, and
under the respectable disguise of merchants, bankers, and captains of
industry, did precisely what we were doing" (*Road*, 101).

London is clear about what prison life did for him. By hammering
in an awareness of his class, it brought his political thought great
strides forward. He is equally clear about the effect of this experience on his emotional life: "into my being rushed the tides of fear. . . .
I grew meek and lowly." His intellectual mastery was accompanied
by the emotional experience of absolute dependency. On the one
hand, intellectual growth; on the other, emotional regression. London failed to reckon the stress that this discrepancy would cause.
This discrepancy may be articulated through Marx's distinction between "class in itself" and "class for itself." London's perception of
the class structure of the society in which he lived was his recognition of "class in itself." Although he understood that this objective
reality had implications for himself as a member of that society, he
did not experience the reality of "class for itself"; he lacked a subjective awareness of himself as a collective being. Indeed, his perception
of "class in itself" came inextricably intertwined with the desire to
escape from all that it implied. He walled himself off from the subjective awareness of class, out of an emotion he calls "terror."

Years later London wrote a prison novel, *The Star Rover*. A glance

at it will suggest one of the directions in which London's consciousness was to move. In the guise of the novel's hero, Darrell Standing,
London takes upon himself the self-assertion and the consequent
punishment that befell the mulatto in the Erie pen. London also
fleetingly and rather mysteriously makes the connection between life
within the prison and the industrial organization without.

Convicted of murder, Darrell Standing was, before his prison life,
a professor of agronomy. He presents himself as a master of scientific
farm management:

> I know the waste of superfluous motion without studying a
> moving picture record of it, whether it be farm or farm-hand,
> the layout of buildings or the layout of the farm-hands' labor.
> There is my handbook and tables on the subject. Beyond
> the shadow of any doubt, at this present moment, a hundred
> thousand farmers are knotting their brows over its spread
> pages ere they tap out their final pipe and go to bed. And yet,
> so far was I beyond my tables, that all I needed was a mere look
> at a man to know his predispositions, his co-ordination, and
> the index fraction of his motion-wastage. [SR, 6]

Standing spends most of his time in prison in the straightjacket, for
he is implicated in an escape plan of which he knows nothing; the
guards torture him to extract information he does not have. But
Standing is initially punished for an infraction of the industrial order
within the prison. Put to work in the jute mill, he soon discovers that
the prison is "an affront and a scandal of waste motion." When he
rebels against the waste and tries to show the guards "a score or so of
more efficient ways" he is put in the dungeon. When he gets out he
again tries "to work in the chaos of inefficiency of the loom-rooms,"
and again he rebels. He is "given the dungeon plus the straightjacket" (SR, 8). The hero's crime here is that he knows more about
management than those who have more power in the hierarchy.
Standing's insubordination is a protest against the new organization
of work that outlawed the exercise of knowledge by a lowly worker.
But London does not pursue this line of social criticism in *The Star
Rover*. He is more interested in punishing Darrell Standing for his
managerial consciousness than in criticizing the sociology of the
workplace.

Like the mulatto, Standing stood up for his rights; he demonstrated his knowledge and his power. But in this novel there is none of the humanistic consciousness that illuminates London's description of the breaking of a brave man's spirit. Instead, *The Star Rover* glows with the lurid light of a masochistic fantasy. Standing repeatedly provokes the guards to punish him, taunting them to harsher and harsher measures. He spends longer and longer periods in the straightjacket. This becomes enjoyable for him, as he has developed a technique, passed on to him by a fellow prisoner, for numbing his physical self so that he feels no pain. He wills his body to die, member by member. This deadening of his physical self allows his mind to leave his body and travel backward in time. The guards marvel at Standing's endurance and tighten the laces on the jacket; but Standing is fighting the Indians in the Westward migration; or enjoying the life of an Egyptian ascetic; or witnessing the events that led up to the death of Jesus, the rebel. Through Darrell Standing, London imagines a way to endure prison punishment without having the spirit broken in a minute and a half. It involves a radical disjunction between the body that is presented to the world and the self that feels. If this allows the hero to maintain the illusion of control over his situation, it also extends his punishment. What takes a minute and a half in the Erie County Penitentiary takes years in this novel of San Quentin; in the end, the only way to break Standing is to kill him.

The Star Rover was written in 1914, twenty years after London's experience in prison, and seven years after his description of those experiences in *The Road*. As a comparison of the two pieces suggests, London's consciousness moves from humanistic sympathy and outrage for the treatment of the prisoners to narcissistic identification with their suffering. In London's consciousness it was sometimes easier to take on himself the punishment of manhood than to stand "watching it all." In his writings London returned to similar scenes in which manhood was punished, and he struggled to see clearly what it meant to be a man in capitalist society. In the three initiation experiences we have explored, London was introduced to three phases of working-class life: the saloon, the industrial shop, and the prison. Each of these took him deeper into the world of men. In his next series of initiations he is introduced to middle-class culture, a culture that was, by contrast, a woman's world.

TWO

INITIATION
INTO MANHOOD,
PART TWO:
THE MIDDLE CLASS

Jack London's power as an artist came from visions that arose unbidden: ideas, emotions, and social institutions were embodied in seemingly tangible shapes. The vision that was to shape his life and his art most profoundly came to him on the road. "The woman of the streets and the man of the gutter drew very close to me. I saw the pictures of the Social Pit as vividly as though it were a concrete thing, and at the bottom of the Pit I saw them, myself above them, not far, and hanging on to the slippery wall by main strength and sweat. And I confess a terror seized me."[1] Beginning at age ten, London had worked hard with his muscles. At age eighteen, he realized that he was "beneath the point at which [he] had started." Terrified by the tenuousness of his hold on the "slippery wall" of the Social Pit, he resolved to climb out. He reasoned that muscle workers were "helpless cattle." Men who sold their muscle sold a cheap commodity; worse, it was used up in the process of exchange and could not be renewed. When the muscle-worker was old and tired, he had nothing left with which to obtain the necessities of life. The brain-worker, on the other hand, sold a commodity that was not so readily exhausted; "a brain seller was only at his prime when he was fifty or sixty years old, and his wares were fetching higher prices than ever." London determined "to become a vendor of brains."[2]

This resolve took London away from the working-class world into a middle-class world of books, lectures, music, art, and gentlemen callers—a world that Ann Douglas has characterized as a feminized culture.³ Here London was a "traveler from another world." He had to learn new speech, new manners, new behaviors. His old initiation into a man's world was no good here. All that rough and rowdy manliness had to be unlearned. Thoroughly frightened by what he had seen of raw power in the man's world, London was only too glad to become a boyish acolyte at the holy shrine of this "civilized" woman's world. If London's initiation into the man's world of the lower class had been effected by the saloon, the shop, and the prison, his initiation into the world of bourgeois respectability was effected primarily through the woman-dominated institutions of school and marriage. Along with these can be included the institutions that facilitated the courtship rituals of polite society—the Henry Clay Debating Society and the Oakland Socialist Labor party, through which London met a higher class of society.

This second initiation was in every respect an undoing of the first. Thus London's accounts of his struggles to rise in this new world of books and ideas fall right back into the pattern of the "old myths" he had seemingly discarded after his experience as an electrician's apprentice. His self-improvement through the lending library and through the discipline of regular literary exercise form an exemplary tale of a self-made man. Adopting middle-class values meant embracing the illusions of the novels and repressing the reality of his working-class experience. Horatio Alger "forgot" what happened to him in the power plant and prison. The books, which before were a slice of illusion, now became London's whole cake. The most dramatic reversals caused by this second initiation affected London's social behavior and his emotional responses.

Part of his social education in this new world involved learning a new way of courting girls, one that relied heavily on verbal and intellectual skills. In *John Barleycorn*, London incidentally contrasts the dating rituals of the working class with those of society up above. London learned the ways of the working class from a blacksmith's apprentice, Louis Shattuck. The first step in the ritual was, of course, to get a girl. In polite society there were dancing-schools and public dances through which to meet girls. But it cost money to go to dances, and, lacking entré into girls' homes, London and his chum resorted to the time-honored method of strolling the streets. "In quite primitive fashion," London writes, "I was to select [a girl] and make myself acquainted with her" (*JB*, 175). This was accomplished, as he learned under Louis's tutelage, by "a certain, eloquent glance of eye, a smile, a daring, lifted hat, a spoken word, hesitancies, giggles, coy nervousness" (*JB*, 176). Once acquainted, the courtship rituals were again shaped by the straitened financial circumstances of the boys. They pooled their meager resources and managed the carfare out to Blair's Park, or bought ice-cream or tamales. When London met a girl named Haydee at a Salvation Army meeting, he courted her by sending her a note and arranging a meeting. They never went anywhere, "not even to a matinée," but stole half-hours together in which, with shy eagerness, they touched hands and exchanged kisses (*JB*, 181).

The difference between these informal "street" methods of getting to know girls and those employed in more polite society is briefly suggested when London tells of his social rise:

> Boy and girl love was left behind, and along with it, Haydee and Louis Shattuck, and the early evening strolls. I hadn't the time. I joined the Henry Clay Debating Society. I was received into the homes of some of the members, where I met nice girls whose skirts reached the ground. I dallied with little home clubs wherein we discussed poetry and art and the nuances of grammar. I joined the socialist local, where we studied and orated political economy, philosophy, and politics. I kept half-a-dozen membership cards working in the free library and did an immense amount of collateral reading. [*JB*, 205]

Still lacking money, London found that ideas and books provided an intellectual dance floor on which boys might pursue girls with much assurance of success. The rules of the game were formalized here and less "primitive" than the methods London and his chum used in street meetings. Significant glances were replaced by significant statements, and physical ardor was sublimated in intellectual questions of intense mutual concern.

Relationships in polite society were much less overtly sexual than in the working class, and yet even the working-class rituals of courtship into which London was initiated by Louis Shattuck represented to him a level of sophistication and formality with which he was not only unfamiliar but in some sense beyond. For the innocent boy and girl adventures that he pursued with Louis Shattuck came after his

waterfront adventures with Nelson and his experience in the Erie
County Penitentiary. At age sixteen he had enjoyed the favors of
French Frank's mistress; now, at age eighteen, he had somehow to
forget those experiences in a man's world and play the game of being
a young boy—to pretend, in short, that he was sexually inexperienced, and, together with genuinely inexperienced young girls, to
grope his way to polite adulthood. This involved quite a juggling act:
as the girls were struggling, with various degrees of awareness, to
develop and *express* their sexuality, London was struggling manfully
to *repress* his. In order to play the game with them and to draw them
out with either coy glances or clever statements, he had to act the
part of one who was also a novice in the ways of love. And, paradoxically, he *was* a novice, as far as the courtship rituals were concerned. He had known sexual experience on a much more direct and
unmediated plane, and he was bashful and backward in the presence
of young girls. One possible psycho-sexual effect of this initiation
into more formal courtship rituals is described by London in *Martin
Eden*; as the proper heroine is sexually awakened under the restrained
courtship of Martin Eden, Eden himself loses sexual desire. It is
possible that the strain of "forgetting" earlier sexual experiences for
the sake of the innocent middle-class girl can result in an irreversible
repression of sexuality. The proper girl is sexually awakened at the
expense of the working-class man: for Martin Eden, to become a
little boy again after he was in reality grown up, was to become not a
sexual initiate, but a eunuch.[4]

This psychological difficulty typifies the contradictions involved in
London's second initiation into "manhood": whatever social advance
his entry into the middle class marked, psychologically it involved a
regression. The nineteen-year-old London, who had been a sailor
before the mast and self-sufficient for many years, went back to high
school and said "Yes, ma'am," and "No, ma'am" to a teacher who,
he hoped, would provide him with the proper way of talking and
the tools with which he could open the world of books and ideas.
This was the period in which secondary education was so dominated
by unmarried women that a strenuous hue and cry was raised by
G. Stanley Hall and Theodore Roosevelt to the effect that education
was becoming "feminized."[5] The gates of the intellectual mecca to
which London aspired were guarded by those who understood how
to speak properly, and these grammarians were, in London's mind,

women. Mabel Applegarth, the first proper woman to whom he was attracted, used to correct his punctuation in the letters that he wrote her.[6] Mabel was the original of Ruth Morse, the prim and proper heroine of *Martin Eden* who presides over the hero's initiation into the middle class, and something of the emotional regression brought on by this initiation is suggested through their relationship. Ruth studies literature in college, converses fluently on Swinburne, and delivers pithy lectures to Martin on the double negative and the agreement of parts. Here is a specimen:

> "There is no such word as 'ain't,' " she said, prettily emphatic.
> Martin flushed again.
> "And you say 'ben' for 'been,' " she continued; " 'I come' for
> 'I came'; and the way you chop your endings is something
> dreadful."
> "How do you mean?" He leaned forward, feeling that he
> ought to get down on his knees before so marvellous a mind.
> "How do I chop?"
> "You don't complete the endings. 'A-n-d' spells 'and.' You
> pronounce it 'an.' 'I-n-g' spells 'ing.' Sometimes you pronounce
> it 'ing' and sometimes you leave off the 'g.' And then you slur
> by dropping initial letters and diphthongs." [*ME*, 58–59]

London presents Eden as a rough naif, a man who becomes as a little child in order to enter the middle-class kingdom of heaven. Ruth is "a spirit, a divinity, a goddess" (*ME*, 4), and she brings to Martin "the message of immortality." Martin's ambition urges him "to grasp at eternal life." He is willing to enter this world on his knees, and, though he blushes and perspires when Ruth corrects his grammar, he is humbly grateful to her for giving him the keys to the pearly gates. "His mood," London writes, "was essentially religious. He was humble and meek, filled with self-disparagement and abasement" (*ME*, 24). Ruth is touched by his humble desire for knowledge. "He seemed such a boy, as he stood blushing and stammering his thanks, that a wave of pity, maternal in its prompting, welled up in her" (*ME*, 22).

London escaped from the open and direct oppression evident in the prison to an indirect and manipulative world in which women lacking in real power wielded the cultural symbols of power. As he portrays Ruth Morse, she is unconscious of the desire for mastery that leads her to mold Martin in the ways of her class. London's own initiation into this woman's world was capped by his precipitous marriage to Bessie Maddern in 1900. London found this gentle yoke more galling than the outright exercises of power he had known before he retreated into domesticity. Soon after his marriage London wrote to Anna Strunsky:

> I remember now, when I was free. Where there was no restraint, and I did what the heart willed. Yes, one restraint, the Law; but when one willed, one could fight the law, and break or be broken. But now, one's hands are tied, and one may not fight, but only yield and bow the neck. After all, the sailor on the sea and the worker in the shop are not so burdened. To break or to be broken, there they stand. But to be broken while not daring to break, there's the rub.[7]

The bind that London describes here is characteristic of the conflicting emotions a child feels toward a mother: he is unable to express the deep resentment at the power wielded over him because it is entangled with feelings of love and guilt. London's difficulty in coming to terms with power relationships, his fearful retreats into postures of submission, surely has roots in his early experiences, in the politics of his own family relationships. But the politics of the family mirror the political relationships in the larger society. If London had a penchant for self-defeating mechanisms, the class structure of his society gave him ample stage on which to indulge them. If London was emotionally still a little boy, the sociology of the workplace, the prison, and the feminine literary establishment fostered a society of little boys who won approval through submission to the proper forms.

Jack's way of rebelling against the ties of domesticity was not original: he pursued his growing interest in another woman. He had met Anna Strunsky, a woman of considerable intelligence and emotional depth, through their common interest in socialism. His letters to her are full of deep emotion, honest disagreement, the joy of discovering a soul-mate. These letters suggest she came closer than anyone else in his life to being a true comrade. When he addressed her as "Comrade Mine," his salutation conveyed more than their engagement in a common social cause, as the following passage in a letter makes clear: "Comrades! And surely it seems so. For all the petty surface turmoil which marked our coming to know each other, really, deep down, there was no confusion at all. Did you not notice it? To me, while I said 'You do not understand,' I none the less felt the happiness of satisfaction—how shall I say?—felt, rather, that there was no inner conflict; that we were attuned, somehow; that a real unity underlaid everything."[8] The bonds of this comradeship were strong, yet loose enough to allow the surface disagreements about which they argued at length in *The Kempton-Wace Letters* (the book on which they collaborated) and in their private letters. When Anna urged Jack not to attend an execution in San Quentin (for she thought his presence would be an implicit statement of his approval of capital punishment), he wrote a long and impassioned letter in response, explaining that his life had been different from hers and had shaped him differently and that to be true to his own sense of himself and his relationship to the realities of his society, he must attend the execution. He articulates a conception of their relationship that allows both of them space to be themselves, allows both to be strong and equal, allows them to disagree: "We are so different, that to live we must live differently. Is it necessary that we should be like to be friends? Is it not well that we should reach out hands to each other, like captains of great hosts, in alliance?—neither of us compromising, neither of us giving over or diminishing? Surely such things can be, and are. Is it meet that friends lose themselves in each other? Away with such friendships."[9] The most obvious stumbling block to the consummation and sustenance of Jack and Anna's relationship was of course Jack's marriage to Bessie Maddern, a marriage contracted rather on the spur of the moment, when Jack's relationship with Anna was quickening and deepening. Just months after his marriage, he is writing Anna "brokenly and stumblingly," ready to declare his love for her but restrained by "this false thing, which the world would call my conscience."[10] By 1902 this restraint had broken down to the extent that London was writing her avowed love letters. But, as we shall see, he sacrificed their intimacy to his greater need for security.

In 1896 London joined the Oakland Socialist Labor party. This was a period of heady intellectual stimulation for him, in which he derived more from socialist gatherings and sociology books than from his classes that year at the University of California. This was also a period in which he became increasingly aware of leaving be-

hind an old self and acquiring a new one. London the sailor and the
hoodlum was giving way to London the intellectual and the writer.
His socialist activities, while remaining an intellectual link with his
former self, represented a social break from his working-class identity, for there were few of the Oakland proletariat in the Socialist
Labor party.[11] As Kenneth Lynn has pointed out, for London the
Socialist Labor party functioned primarily as a vehicle of social and
intellectual advancement. The party enabled him to associate with a
group for whom ideas were common playthings. London admits that
these socialist meetings seemed to him a mere foretaste of the ideal
(bourgeois) world on whose doorstep he stood.[12]

The emotional dependence that characterized the coming of age
of his political thought, in the Erie County Penitentiary, led London
to idolize both socialism and the middle-class world of culture—
almost in the same breath. They represented salvation, the way out,
a heaven that would save him from the lower-class hell. In the socialists London found "warm faith in the human, glowing idealism,
sweetnesses of unselfishness, renunciation, martyrdom." In London's exalted language are the seeds of his inevitable disillusionment: "All about me were nobleness of purpose and heroism of
effort, and my days and nights were sunshine and starshine, all fire
and dew, with before my eyes, ever burning and blazing, The Holy
Grail, Christ's own Grail, the warm, human, long-suffering and
maltreated, but to be rescued and saved at the last."[13] This intoxi-
cating intellectual atmosphere combined in London's mind with his
notions of the middle-class heroines he read about in the "Seaside
Library" novels to form an idealized portrait of the class he was
entering through his "socialism." London's subsequent shock and
outrage at his discovery that the middle classes were composed of
human beings with human flaws and that beneath their hypocritical
veneer of civilization they were guilty of egregious exercises of
capitalistic power is registered both in his essay "What Life Means
to Me" and in *Martin Eden*. He knows, by the time of his 1906
essay, that his faith was misplaced. No more will he believe in the
middle class: "I went back to the working-class, in which I had
been born and where I belonged. I care no longer to climb."[14] This
essay was written during a period in which London's gentlemanly
Ruskin Club socialism was giving way to a firebrand advocacy of
the "PEOPLE." But this change in style did not signal a change in

stance. London did not abandon his search for idols. He merely replaced the clay god of middle-class socialism with the earthen god of the "PEOPLE." Nowhere in the many accounts of his successive disillusionments does London ever suggest that the problem lay in his need to find an idol before which he could abase himself, a cause in which he could lose himself. It was just that the idols were not good enough. After each successive disillusionment London is re-invigorated with a conviction of his superiority to the fallen idol.

Imagining a great gulf between himself and the middle-class world, he was surprised and disappointed to discover how ordinary were its inhabitants. From believing in his own unworthiness to touch the hem of the garment of the middle-class woman, he swung to an exaggerated sense of his own worth when he discovered that "the Colonel's Lady and Judy O'Grady are sisters under the skin." It is apparent that London condemned himself to this syndrome of self-abasement and self-exaltation as long as he persisted in positing superior worth outside himself. It is also apparent that the class structure, with its distinctions of speech, behavior, dress, education, and occupation reinforced the tendency to make distinctions of worth, to impute superiority to those higher up in the class structure. London reasoned that he had two alternatives: to be a master or to be a slave. These were culturally determined options, and London's acceptance of them in one sense testifies to his maturity and social adjustment. By the same token, it could be argued that his acceptance of them made him neurotic in socially acceptable ways, that is, he patterned his life on a neurotic pattern in his culture. In adopting the choices determined by his society, London repressed what his society repressed: the need for intimacy. Intimacy is essentially a relationship between equals. The political term for this relationship is fraternity, or brotherhood, or comradeship.

If London left behind the man's world into which he had been brutally initiated, he also left behind his companions from those days. London's new friends included Fred Jacobs, who worked at the Oakland library and was preparing himself for the University of California; Bessie Maddern, who tutored high school students; Edward Applegarth, who taught him chess; and his sister, Mabel Applegarth, who knew music and moved in an aura of Swinburne and Browning.[15] In *John Barleycorn* London admits that he never "regretted those months of mad deviltry" with Nelson, but he is also clear about the

shabbiness and futility of the life of petty crime. Nelson was dead—
"shot to death while drunk and resisting the officers." Other companions from those days were either dead or in prison (*JB*, 168–69).
Clearly, in choosing to get an education, London was choosing a
better life.

But there is evidence that suggests that London weaned himself
slowly from those early experiences of adolescent camaraderie. In
1899 he wrote to Cloudesley Johns (a new writing friend) of a revealing experience. London was out on a date with Bessie Maddern,
soon to become his wife. They were on the ferry from Sausalito to
San Francisco when a gang of lively young rowdies "took the deck
and raised hell generally." London was "attacked by all kinds of
feelings" as he witnessed the scene:

> Why, my longing was intense to jump in and join them after
> the fashion of my wild young days, and go on after we arrived
> at 'Frisco and make the night of it which I knew they were
> going to make. Alluring? I guess yes.
>
> And then again, I could feel how I had grown away from
> that—lost touch. I knew if I should happen to join them, how
> strangely out of place it would seem to me—duck-out-of-
> water sort of feeling. This made me sad; for while I cultivate
> new classes, I hate to be out of grip with the old. But say, it
> wouldn't take me long to get my hand in again. Just a case
> of lost practice.[16]

In *John Barleycorn* London recalled an experience in which he did
answer the call of the wild life he had left behind. After taking his
college entrance exams, for which he had crammed for four months,
London rebounded and went "on the adventure-path." He borrowed
a boat and sailed out of the Oakland estuary to Benicia, the haunt of
his oyster-pirate days. As he tells the story in *John Barleycorn*, he had
not planned to stop at Benicia, and he did so only because, for the
first time in his life, he was conscious of a desire to get drunk. He
castigates both himself (for the desire) and society (for making alcohol so available). But he does not seem to be conscious of another
desire that is conveyed in the texture of his language: his desire for
the companionship of his old friends. As he makes his way on shore,
he is surrounded: "Charley Le Grant fell on my neck. His wife,
Lizzie, folded me to her capacious breast. Billy Murphy, and Joe

Lloyd, and all the survivors of the old guard, got around me and their arms around me" (*JB*, 214). Beer and whiskey are called for. The arrival of the man who was Nelson's partner before London arouses memories of the man who "had stretched out his great shoulders for the last long sleep in this very town of Benicia; and we wept over the memory of him, and remembered only the good things of him, and sent out the flask to be filled and drank again" (*JB*, 215). London eventually takes himself away from this group, returns to his boat, and continues his cruise in an intoxicated state, singing songs from his oyster-pirate days like "Shenandoah" and "Ranzo, Boys, Ranzo." In this reminiscence London again tells of meeting friends, this time at Antioch, "where, somewhat sobered and magnificently hungry," he anchored next to "a big potato sloop that had a familiar rig." He ends with the following lyrical passage:

> Here were old friends aboard, who fried my black bass in olive oil. Then, too, there was a meaty fisherman's stew, delicious with garlic, and crusty Italian bread without butter, and all washed down with pint mugs of thick and heady claret.
>
> My salmon boat was a-soak, but in the snug cabin of the sloop dry blankets and a dry bunk were mine; and we lay and smoked and yarned of old days, while overhead the wind screamed through the rigging and taut halyards drummed against the mast. [*JB*, 217–18]

London does not tell us who these friends are, but that does not diminish the feeling of warmth, animal contentment, and easy comradeship. Indeed, that London does not name or describe his companions intensifies the experience; he is *one* of them. The loss of self-consciousness and the easy communion with the rest of physical nature suggested in this passage is reminiscent of Huck Finn's lyrical descriptions of nights and days on the raft with Jim. Although London has made explicit in *John Barleycorn* his organic linkage of fellowship and alcohol, he seems unaware of the extent to which he associated fellowship with the lower-class man's world he had left behind in his efforts to rise.

London's emotional ties to his past were repressed by his conviction that he was choosing a better life and by his fear of the dreary ends that were prophesied for those in the old life. When he viewed those old days from his new vantage point within the parlors of polite society, they appeared brutal and savage. London often uses the language of social Darwinism to describe his rise or that of his lower-class heroes. The movement from the Social Pit to the middle class was a movement from savagery to civilization, from the wild to the domestic, from the brute to the scholar. As the above passages show, the "wild" also implied spontaneity, warmth, and friendship, but London does not invoke these associations when he speaks of his rise. Thus in a letter to Mabel Applegarth, defending his decision to hold out for the uncertain rewards of a writing career rather than accept the security of an unskilled job, he writes:

> If I had followed [the call of duty, which said "get a job"] what
> would I have been to-day? I would be a laborer, and by that
> I mean I would be fitted for nothing else than labor. . . . If I had
> followed that, would I have known you? If I had followed that,
> who would I now know whose companionship I would esteem?
> If I had followed that from childhood, whose companionship
> would I now be fitted to enjoy?—Tennyson's? or a bunch of
> brute hoodlums on a street corner?[17]

London puts a very limited choice to himself: he may enjoy either the rough companionship of a street gang or a bookish companionship with a sentimental Victorian poet. It is a choice between the man's world of raw power and the woman's world of poetry and "culture," a choice between Wolf Larsen and Maud Brewster. Over and over again London was to choose the sentimentalities of middle-class culture over the "old sad savagery" that he had known. But in his longing for a "Man-Comrade," in the lyrical intensity of *The Call of the Wild*, London harbored a largely unconscious vision of a fellowship that was beyond both the sloppy sentimentality of drinking buddies and the prescribed sentimentality of Victorian love-making.

Why could London not bring this vision into his consciousness and pursue it openly? The answer lies partly in his terror of the kind of relationship and the kind of aloneness that true comradeship implied. The terror was, on the one hand, a fear of being known for himself, that is, a fear of letting the invulnerable public mask slip aside to expose the vulnerable inner self, the "real" self. In an extraordinary letter to Charmian Kittredge, his second wife, he speaks of his great desire to be frank and yet his shrinking from "the pain of intimacies which bring the greater frankness forth. Superficial frankness is comparatively easy, but one must pay for stripping off the dry husks of clothing, the self-conventions which masque the soul, and for standing out naked in the eyes of one who sees. I have paid, and like a child who has been burned by fire, I shrink from paying too often." Struggling to explain to Charmian why he cannot speak from his heart to her, why the voice of the inner self is "automatically, instinctively" stilled by the memory of "old pains, incoherent hurts, a welter of remembrances," he writes:

> I wonder if I make you understand. You see, in the objective facts of my life I have always been frankness personified. That I tramped or begged or festered in jail or slum meant nothing by the telling. But over the lips of my inner self I had long since put a seal—a seal indeed rarely broken, in moments when one caught fleeting glimpses of the hermit who lived inside. How can I begin to explain? . . . My child life was uncongenial. There was little responsive around me. I learned reticence, an inner reticence. I went into the world early, and I adventured among different classes. A newcomer in any class, I naturally was reticent concerning my real self, which such a class could not understand, while I was superficially loquacious in order to make my entry into such a class popular and successful. And so it went, from class to class, from clique to clique. No intimacies, a continuous hardening, a superficial loquacity so clever, and an inner reticence so secret, that the one was taken for the real, and the other never dreamed of.[18]

London wrote in a similar vein to Anna Strunsky, who had accused him of smiling at her enthusiasm. London replied that if he smiled, it was "almost an envious smile," that he had lived "twenty-five years of repression" in which he had "learned not to be enthusiastic." Of his attempt to forget that "hard lesson," he writes almost incoherently: "I begin to forget, but it is so little. At the best, before I die, I cannot hope to forget all or most. I can exult, now that I am learning, in little things, in other things; but of my things, and secret things doubly mine, I cannot, I cannot. Do I make myself intelligible? Do you hear my voice. I fear not. There are poseurs. I am the most successful of them all."[19] In *Martin Eden* London was to create a character who leads a double life, an outward life in the world and a secret life in his thoughts. London's secret self was both his strength and his weakness: from it he drew his energy as a writer and with it he experienced the pain of self-inflicted solitude.

London chose this solitude, paradoxically, out of a terror of being alone. Although his terror of comradeship was, on the one hand, a fear of being known for himself, it was, on the other hand, a fear of the separateness that an egalitarian relationship implies in the very act of communion. London's longings for comradeship are often expressed as a desire to merge with the other, to lose his identity in the other. London writes to Charmian, "Surely we are very ONE, you and I!" He goes on to confess to her "a dream of [his] boyhood and manhood." Through all his loves he has felt, he writes, "that there was a something greater I yearned after, a something that beat upon my imagination with a great flowing light and made those woman-loves wan things and pale, oh so pitiably wan and pale!" This "something greater" is his dream of "the great Man-Comrade":

> I, who have been comrades with many men, and a good comrade I believe, have never had a comrade at all, and in the deeper significance of it have never been able to be the comrade I was capable of being. Always it was here this one failed, and there that one failed until all failed. And then, one day, like Omar, "clear-eyed I looked, and laughed, and sought no more." It was plain that it was not possible. I could never hope to find that comradeship, that closeness, that sympathy and understanding whereby *the man and I might merge and become one in understanding and sympathy for love and life.*
>
> How can I say what I mean? *This man should be so much one with me that we could never misunderstand.*[20]

The relationship London dreams of has no misunderstandings, no risk, no pain. It is indeed like communing with himself: all his thoughts and desires meet identical sympathies in the Man-Comrade. Such a relationship does not celebrate and confirm one's identity but rather knells a narcissistic death.

Erich Fromm has analyzed the desire for total identity with the other, which he calls "symbiosis" and which characterizes both sadism and masochism. "Symbiosis, in this psychological sense, means the union of one individual self with another self (or any other power outside of the own self) in such a way as to make each lose the integrity of its own self and to make them completely dependent on each other."[21] The object of both sadistic and masochistic strivings is loss of the individual self. People who characteristically view their options as between mastery and submission, argues Fromm, are afraid of the freedom that an egalitarian relationship entails. In his analysis of the masochistic strivings Fromm suggests the many ways in which this fear may be served:

> As long as I struggle between my desire to be independent and strong and my feeling of insignificance or powerlessness I am caught in a tormenting conflict. If I succeed in reducing my individual self to nothing, if I can overcome the awareness of my separateness as an individual, I may save myself from this conflict. To feel utterly small and helpless is one way toward this aim; to be overwhelmed by pain and agony another; to be overcome by the effects of intoxication still another. The phantasy of suicide is the last hope if all other means have not succeeded in bringing relief from the burden of aloneness.[22]

Especially toward the end of his life, London courted pain, intoxication, and fantasies of suicide to escape the intolerable burden of self. But his most productive way of losing himself was through his art, which allowed him to break the fetters of his prison and to experience a collective awareness of what it means to be human.

The two-stage initiation that London experienced was to become a significant pattern to both his life and his art. His first initiation revealed to him the realities of the lower-class world; his second initiated him into the middle-class world of culture and books. Because the second initiation annulled the first by rendering it insufficient and inapplicable, it was fundamentally contradictory in character: insofar as it was an initiation, it partook of the growing-up process, but insofar as it annulled the first initiation, it was more akin to regression than to growing up. The first initiation, as we have seen, was rent by a similar contradiction. To grow up in the lower class meant to become aware of the power relationships that set capital over labor, bosses over workers, captains over seamen, guards over hallmen, hall-men over prisoners. It meant seeing a vision of one's dependency and powerlessness. Manhood, under these circumstances, was a contradiction. By going from the man's world of the lower class to the woman's world of the middle class, London only exchanged the illusion of power for the illusion of weakness.

Twice London attempted to become a man, and twice he was reduced to childish dependence in the process. It is not surprising that his frustrated attempts gave rise to an obsession with manhood and with proving himself in strenuous physical feats, nor that his normal, human drive to become an adult should have sometimes been transformed into a swollen and unhealthy desire for mastery. What remains mysterious and awe-inspiring is the tenacity with which he struggled—in the face of the contradictions of his society— to become truly a man. Through art, London imagined choices that his society did not allow. By becoming an artist, London embarked on a continually renewed quest to realize himself fully, to do what neither the lower-class nor the middle-class world had allowed him to do—to become human. Through his art he would struggle to see and articulate a humanistic vision, to put together what his society had rent asunder. Often he failed, and the human would degenerate into the bestial, or would be counterfeited in megalomaniacal fantasies of power. But when he succeeded, he opened up old worlds of forgotten emotions. To follow the development of his fiction from the early Alaskan tales to the consummatory myth of *The Call of the Wild* and the terrible illusions of *The Sea-Wolf*, to understand the double consciousness that informs *The People of the Abyss*, "South of the Slot," and *Martin Eden*, is to understand a man who struggled to be human in a society that divided feeling from thought, muscle from brain, masculine from feminine, worker from artist.

THREE

JOURNEYING ACROSS
THE GHOSTLY WASTES
OF A DEAD WORLD

His purse exhausted after a year at the University of California, in
1897 London joined the second wave of fortune-hunters in the Klondike. He returned with little more than a case of scurvy to show for
his efforts, but the stories he wrote from his Alaskan experience
established his literary career. In them we can see the lineaments of a
hero who would never appear in London's "civilized" fictions. He
represents the most fully mature and human character London was
to imagine. The aloneness of this Alaskan hero is different from the
aloneness of London's romantic heroes. Martin Eden's aloneness
grows out of a syndrome of self-abasement and self-exaltation like
that which was operating in London's consciousness as he entered
the middle class. The Alaskan hero's aloneness is based on a more
realistic assessment of his strengths and weaknesses. He understands
that there is something stronger than he—Death. Death is the ultimate equalizer, and in this awareness London wrote a handful of
stories that imply the need for human solidarity.

In *Jack London and the Klondike*, Franklin Walker provides a carefully researched account of London's day-by-day adventures, against
which he parallels his use of similar experiences in his fictions. Walker
contributes significantly to our knowledge of London's sources and
artistic techniques, but he does not analyze the more subtle movements that occurred in London's inner life, as he internalized the
white landscapes of Alaska. For this, one must turn to James Mc-
Clintock's *White Logic*. McClintock traces the movement of London's consciousness from the affirmation, in the early Malemute

Kid stories, of the individual's ability to master the universe, to an awareness of "a more complex view of reality" in which "limited protagonists . . . [reach] an accommodation with a hostile, chaotic cosmos by living by an imposed code," to a loss of faith in the ability of the code to order the universe. Then the cycle begins over again, as London "turns to race identification" to provide the illusion of mastery that the individual hero could not sustain.[1] McClintock's ground-breaking analysis of London's Northland stories is the starting point for this chapter, and his work makes it unnecessary to dwell in detail on London's Alaskan fictions. It is sufficient to point out the pattern that emerges from a comparison of three stories: "The White Silence," "In a Far Country," and "To Build a Fire."

The first story is about three people (plus one unborn) traveling in mutual comradeship; the second is about two men who are together but who are not bound by comradely ties; in the third story "the man," as he is designated, insists on defying sourdough wisdom and traveling alone. Death enters each story. "In a Far Country" and "To Build a Fire" deal with unnecessary death—death that could have been avoided had the protagonists the imagination to perceive their finitude and their need to rely on others for mutual support and protection. The relationship between Cuthfert and Weatherbee in "In a Far Country" hinges on mutual fear and suspicion. Together in a cabin for the duration of the Alaskan winter, their distrust of each other encourages waste of food and fuel rather than the economy that is necessary for mutual survival. In the end they kill each other over a cache of sugar. The man in "To Build a Fire" believes that "a man who is a man" travels alone. He reads no message in the vast Alaskan landscape, nor does he understand, in human, mortal terms, the significance of sixty-five degrees below zero. When he breaks through the ice and wets himself to his knees, his limbs begin to freeze before he can get a fire started to dry himself out. Only when death is upon him does he realize his own mortality.

These deaths were avoidable, and the way to avoid them is clearly through human solidarity. But if solidarity can prevent some unnecessary deaths, it cannot, of course, undo the inevitability of death. That is the reality London faces in "The White Silence." The Malemute Kid is traveling with Mason, his close companion of five years, and Mason's Indian wife, Ruth. London establishes the odds early in the story. They have two hundred miles to travel and only enough

food for six days. The reader may expect a tale of struggle and sacrifice in which—perhaps—the trio united can cope with nature's odds
against them. But this is not, London hints in the following passage,
simply a tale of heroic struggle. It is a tale of human finitude:

> The afternoon wore on, and with the awe, born of the White
> Silence, the voiceless travellers bent to their work. Nature
> has many tricks wherewith she convinces man of his finity,—
> the ceaseless flow of the tides, the fury of the storm, the shock
> of the earthquake, the long roll of heaven's artillery,—but the
> most tremendous, the most stupefying of all, is the passive
> phase of the White Silence. All movement ceases, the sky
> clears, the heavens are as brass; the slightest whisper seems
> sacrilege, and man becomes timid, affrighted at the sound of his
> own voice. Sole speck of life journeying across the ghostly
> wastes of a dead world, he trembles at his audacity, realizes that
> his is a maggot's life, nothing more. Strange thoughts arise
> unsummoned, and the mystery of all things strives for utterance.
> And the fear of death, of God, of the universe, comes over
> him,—the hope of the Resurrection and the Life, the yearning
> for immortality, the vain striving of the imprisoned essence,—
> it is then, if ever, man walks alone with God.[2]

Death comes unexpectedly, from an unexpected quarter. There is
still food, and in the three travelers, warmth and energy. But an old
pine, "burdened with its weight of years and of snow," falls and
crushes Mason. He is half-paralyzed but not dead. He urges the
Malemute Kid to go on with his wife and the unborn child she carries
—urges him to save his family and leave him to his inevitable death.
He only asks that he not have to face death alone. "'Just a shot,
one pull on the trigger,'" he asks of the Kid before they leave. The
Kid is reluctant to part with his traveling companion of five years
with whom, "shoulder to shoulder, on the rivers and trails, in the
camps and mines, facing death by field and flood and famine," he had
"knitted the bonds of . . . comradeship."[3] He asks that they wait
with Mason for three days, hoping for a change of luck. Mason
agrees to a one-day wait. The Kid's request for a delay turns out to
be costly. He is unable to kill a moose, and, when he returns to
camp, he finds the dogs have broken into their food cache. They now
have "perhaps five pounds of flour to tide them over two hundred

miles of wilderness." But fear of death is not, in this story, as great as the fear of aloneness.

The Kid sends Ruth on ahead, and then sits by Mason's side, hoping that he will die so that he will not be obliged to shoot him. Mason is in pain and knows he is dying, but his torment is not as acute as the Kid's. Mason places his hopes in the continuation of life through his wife and the child ("flesh of my flesh") she will bear. During his last day his mind wanders euphorically back to scenes of his early manhood in Tennessee. Although Mason bears some resemblance to London's description of his ideal Man-Comrade, who, he wrote, should be both "delicate and tender, brave and game," and "who, knowing the frailties and weaknesses of life, could look with frank and fearless eyes upon them," he also has traces of the "smallness or meanness" that was explicitly not a part of London's conception.[4] For, earlier in the story, Mason—over the Kid's gentle protest—brutally whipped a dog who was unfortunate enough to fall in the traces. The weakened dog is subsequently devoured by her teammates. Mason is very much an ordinary man, loving his wife, loving life, having no grand philosophy but only a realistic practicality that says life must go on. He does not appear an idealized Man-Comrade but only a garrulous traveling companion, full of stories and gab. Indeed, the extent to which his rambling monologues fill up the story makes all the more awesome his death—marked by a sharp report, followed by silence.

In this story London portrays death as an event with a human character that quickly yields to a nonhuman force—the White Silence, which "seem[s] to sneer" in the moment before the Kid performs his last act of comradeship. Death is clearly harder for the survivor than for the dying. It is easier for Mason to die than for the Kid to live with the knowledge of death. He has been forced to participate in a ritual confirmation of death's power and man's finitude. Worse, he has had, in the name of comradeship, to break the bond that makes death human, that made death bearable for Mason. He is now alone. In terror, he lashes the dogs across the waste of land.

Unlike the man in "To Build a Fire," the Malemute Kid has the imagination to perceive in the vast silences of the Northland the message of his finitude. He knows the value of comradeship. But neither his imagination nor his sensitivity can protect him from the pain of loss, the pain of experiencing death before death through the death of another to whom he is bound. Written within months after London learned of John London's death (he died while Jack was in Alaska), this story probably draws on the emotions of that loss. In one stroke London lost a father, a comrade, and a model of male working-class identity. In "The White Silence" the Kid is almost in the role of a redeemer: he takes the suffering of Mason on himself; by acquiescing in Mason's request that he not be left to die alone, the Kid takes that aloneness on himself. He redeems Mason's death and renders it human. But the unspoken question hanging in the silence, the question that fills the Kid with fear, is this: Who will redeem his own death?

As McClintock writes, this story ends in an ambiguous balance between human significance and human futility.[5] The Kid has shown himself to be a true comrade. It remains to be seen whether or not someone will yet be a true comrade to him. This future, which is beyond the scope of the story, depends on whether or not the Kid can be open and trusting of others, whether or not he can be passively receptive to the significance that others might invest in his life; whether or not, in religious terms, he can leave his salvation up to others. If he cannot, then it is hard to escape the conclusion that, by severing the bond between himself and Mason, he has condemned himself to a living death.

"In a Far Country," written probably a few months after "The White Silence," suggests that death may also come in nonredemptive ways. Cuthfert and Weatherbee are bound together by their situations, but, not being bound emotionally, they engage in a ghastly inversion of comradely rituals. They are united not in life-giving rituals like washing and eating, but in their mutual disregard for cleanliness, order, and economy. London suggests that the reasons for their mutual suspicion are their class differences. Weatherbee is a lower-class clerk, Cuthfert a Master of Arts who writes and paints. Both think of themselves as gentlemen but, London pointedly remarks, "a man can be a gentleman without possessing the first instinct of true comradeship." Master of Arts Cuthfert "deemed the clerk a filthy, uncultured brute, whose place was in the muck with the swine, and told him so." The sensuous, adventure-loving clerk calls the Master of Arts "a milk-and-water sissy and a cad."[6] They perceive each other through class stereotypes, and the mechanical nature of their togetherness is like the articulation of classes and occupations in a capitalist society in which a physical interdependence of parts is accompanied by emotional anomie. Having killed each other, they die in each other's arms. Like the "devil dog" and his cruel master, LeClerc, in London's story "Bâtard," like Hawthorne's Dimmesdale and Chillingworth, they are bound not by love but by a dark necessity.

The stories in which London writes of such false comradeship tend to dwell on a materialistic, positivistic view of man.[7] The inevitable degeneration of the characters in these stories is rendered in laboratory detail as if all that were at stake were a piece of flesh. Thus in "Love of Life," which looks at the struggle of a man who has been abandoned by his traveling mate, although the protagonist survives, he is described as an "it," a squirming mass of cells.[8] This is the positivistic view of man that Wolf Larsen propounds to Van Weyden in *The Sea-Wolf*. The loss of human significance in these stories of comradeship betrayed make survival a sorry boon.

In "To Build a Fire," written after that period of disillusionment he called the "long sickness," London takes the next logical step. If comradeship inevitably will be betrayed, one might as well travel alone. When the man in this story finally realizes that he is going to die, he "entertained in his mind the conception of meeting death with dignity." But what sort of dignity is available to him? It was possible for Mason in "The White Silence" to meet death with dignity without cutting his emotional ties to life—because of his comradeship with the Kid and his biological link through Ruth to the next generation. But when one travels alone, death holds all the cards. The only way to meet it with dignity is to surrender oneself totally to it. The man in "To Build a Fire" gives himself drowsily to these thoughts. "Well, he was bound to freeze anyway, and he might as well take it decently. With this new-found peace of mind came the first glimmerings of drowsiness. A good idea, he thought, to sleep off to death. It was like taking an anaesthetic. Freezing was not so bad as people thought. There were lots worse ways to die."[9] Several years later London described Martin Eden's attempt to drown himself: "He breathed in the water deeply, deliberately, after the manner of a man taking an anaesthetic" (*ME*, 380). Unable to take charge of the life-forces, the characters who travel alone maintain a modicum of dignity by giving themselves willingly to their deaths.

"To Build a Fire" and "In a Far Country" plot a retreat from the comradeship of "The White Silence." The solace of comradeship is supplanted in "To Build a Fire" by the whispers of a dreamless sleep. The fire has gone out, and along with it, all hope of campfire fellowship. If we are to judge from "The White Silence," London's reason for retreating from the bonds of comradeship is not simply that his comrade failed him. Mason may have differed with the Kid, but as he lay dying he apologized for his mistreatment of the dog. The only way in which Mason betrayed his comradeship was in the very act of death itself, when of mortal necessity he left the Kid behind. Perhaps this "betrayal" was more than the Kid could bear. It brought him up against the irrefragable aloneness of each human being. He was afraid. The delicate ecological balance London achieves in "The White Silence" between the forces of life and the forces of death is perhaps all that human beings should hope for in their living and dying. For London, it was not enough.

Like so many American writers, Jack London early in his career realized a vision that he could not sustain. The decline of artistry in his later fictions paralleled his retreat from the knowledge apprehended in "The White Silence." It was a retreat from death, from limitation, from aloneness. In his search for a way out of the human condition, London did, in a measure, deny himself humanity. By retreating from all that life has to offer in the way of human solidarity, London exiled himself. Like Hawthorne's Wakefield, he was an "outcast of the universe." Just as Wakefield, by leaving his marriage partner, lost his "place" in human society, so London, by leaving the lower class, found himself with no niche, no place to rest himself. The decline of London's writing career in many ways parallels that of Nathaniel Hawthorne's. Both men began their careers with short stories of superior quality, followed by a novel that became a classic. For London this was not his first novel, *A Daughter of the Snows*, but his second, *The Call of the Wild*. London followed with novels of mixed quality, like *The Sea-Wolf*, just as Hawthorne followed *The Scarlet Letter* with the less forceful *The House of the Seven Gables*, and then succumbed to the repressed sexuality of *The Blithedale Romance* and the tortured symbolism of *The Marble Faun*. But the real similarities are in their choices of theme and in their modes of retreat from the primary truth of their earlier work. Both write about characters who suffer from their aloneness. Hawthorne was able to distinguish between an aloneness that is human and necessary, indeed, inescapable, and an aloneness that is inflicted on oneself out of over-weening pride, that is to say, between the aloneness of the modern hero, Hester Prynne, and that of the romantic hero, Arthur Dimmes-dale. Both London and Hawthorne attempted to retreat from alone-ness through the sentimental Victorian strategy of love and marriage. What neither of them fully understood was that, in using a platitudi-nous domesticity to shield them from the terror of aloneness, what they were seeking was not a comrade, a mate, a wife, but something altogether different: a mother.

The fire of the Victorian hearth did not burn as brightly as the Alaskan campfire. It replaced intimacy with sentiment and comrade-ship with courtship. For a relationship between equals, struggling against mutual dangers, it substituted a relationship between a boy-man and a girl-woman who played at being grown-ups. This ploy enabled London to come out of the long sickness and to resume life, but it vitiated his art and provided only a stay of execution for his life.

FOUR

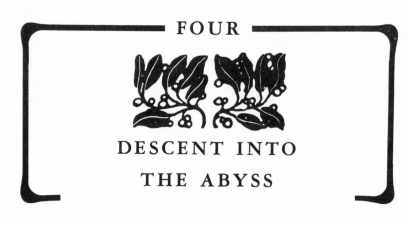

DESCENT INTO
THE ABYSS

The comradeship that London wrote about in his Alaskan tales was not part-and-parcel of the daily life of the professional writer. That work had to be done alone. The solitariness that is the writer's lot insofar as he is practicing his art was for London intensified by his awareness that, viewed from the working-class expectations of his family and friends, he was doing something odd by choosing to be a writer. In 1898, unpublished and unsupported, he complained to Mabel Applegarth that no one had ever understood his aspirations. "The whole thing has been by itself. . . . So be it. The end is not yet. If I die I shall die hard, fighting to the last, and hell shall receive no fitter inmate than myself. But for good or ill, it shall be as it has been—alone."[1] London threw all of his energies into this battle, and by 1902 he had won it. He had published three volumes of short stories, a children's adventure tale, and his first novel. He had fought and survived. Now he began to look hard at who and what had survived.

His letters of the first week of the new year, 1902, suggest the mood of reflection and reevaluation that characterized that year in his life. On January 5 he wrote to Anna Strunsky:

> You look back on a tumultuous and bankrupt year; and so I. And for me the New Year begins full of worries, harassments, and disappointments. So you? I wonder?
>
> I look back and remember, at one in the morning, the faces I saw go wan and wistful—do you remember? or did you notice?—and I wonder what all the ferment is about.
>
> I dined yesterday, on canvasback and terrapin, with cham-

pagne sparkling and all manner of wonderful drinks I had never
before tasted warming my heart and brain, and I remembered
the sordid orgies and carouses of my youth. We were ill-clad,
ill-mannered beasts, and the drink was cheap and poor and
nauseating. And then I dreamed dreams, and pulled myself up
out of the slime to canvasback and terrapin and champagne,
and learned that it was solely a difference of degree which art
introduced into the fermenting. And I thought of you, and I
wondered.[2]

If his backward look is not nostalgic, his view of his new social position is tinged with disillusionment. He now sees that the middle-
class world that he had so desired differed only in degree from the
sordidness of his lower-class youth. It was all sordid, all a mere
ferment of biological necessities. London had clearly thought to resolve fundamental questions of value by pursuing his "dreams," but
having won to canvasback and terrapin, he still finds himself wondering "what all the ferment is about," that is to say, what makes life
humanly significant and worth living. London poses this philosophic
question directly in his letter of the following day to Cloudesley
Johns. "But after all, what squirming, anywhere, damned or otherwise, means anything? That's the question I am always prone to put:
What's this chemical ferment called life all about? Small wonder that
small men down the ages have conjured gods in answer. A little god
is a snug little possession and explains it all. But how about you
and me, who have no god?"[3] London goes on to articulate his own
beliefs, which, he says, he has recently formulated. "I have at last
discovered what I am. I am a materialistic monist, and there's damn
little satisfaction in it."

It is significant that this crystalization of his materialist philosophy
comes during the period in which he wrote tales that, as we have
seen, charted a retreat from the value-giving experience of comradeship. Now, as he tries to articulate his philosophy, London sees the
ferment of life but no underlying or transcendent pattern to it all. It
is just a "squirming." He tries to face this honestly, without inventing
a god he has not experienced. Several times in the following months
London alludes to his attempts to find himself, to work out a philosophy. London writes to George Brett, his publisher, "there are
big books in me and . . . when I find myself they will come out. At

present I am just trying to find myself and am busy gripping hold of life."[4] London believed that it was essential for a writer to have a philosophy of life if he would have his writing strong and true.[5] But he was pulled into a vortex of pessimism as he tried to work out the details of his "materialistic monism." This was not a philosophy that gave coherence and meaning to life; rather, it gave an orderly description of a world without human values. By July, he had made little progress on his philosophy. He writes to Johns:

> I am moving along slowly, about $3000 in debt, working out a philosophy of life, or rather, the details of a philosophy of life, and slowly getting a focus on things. Some day I shall begin to do things, until then I merely scratch a living.
>
> Between you and me, I wish I had never opened the books. That's where I was the fool.[6]

In *John Barleycorn* London writes obliquely of a period in his life when he "read too much positive science" and "made the ancient mistake of pursuing Truth too relentlessly" (*JB*, 253–54). That was the beginning of his "long sickness." As London remembered that experience in 1913, he did not question whether or not the terrible vision of the Truth, seen with the eyes of positive science, was an accurate description of life. He only knew, then as at the time of that vision, that no one could live with such a philosophy, and that, having seen such a picture of the squirming ferment called life, the sanest thing one could do was to cover it with illusions. Neither in *John Barleycorn* nor in his 1902 letters does London connect his materialism and his pessimism with the idea of comradeship, nor does he explore the relationship between the ideas he is shaping and the feelings he is experiencing as he cuts himself off from his roots and embraces middle-class life. The closest he comes to an awareness of the source of his philosophic malaise is his statement to Johns: "I wish I had never opened the books. That's where I was the fool." Five years later, in *Martin Eden*, London was able to articulate more clearly the loneliness of the literary aspirant who has removed himself from the class into which he was born.

It was in this mood of pessimism and disillusionment that London sailed for England in July. What followed was for London a mock return to his roots. In order to write a journalistic exposé of the conditions in the East End of London, a sprawling ghetto of poverty,

London put on old clothes and played the part of a down-at-the-heels American sailor. This experience, which was to put the last nail in the coffin of his working-class identity, was conceived of by London as he rode the train across country to New York. According to his daughter Joan's account, the contrast between the "plush and polished elegance of a Pullman" and his memories of riding the rails in his hobo days conjured up the project: he would go to England and report the coronation of Edward VII from the point of view of the English working class.[7] He was at that time on assignment for the American Press Association, en route to Africa to report on the aftermath of the Boer War, but when that assignment was cancelled, his publisher encouraged him to pursue his own idea. At a time when London was groping for connections, a time when he saw his terrapin and champagne diet to be less glamorous than it had appeared from the vantage point of a hungry newsboy, London saw his old self in the English sailors and carters and dockers. He saw, and he recoiled from the images of what he had been. But this reaction, which was cumulative and which received cathartic expression only after the experience was over, was also mixed with the understanding and sympathy he brought to his materials in *The People of the Abyss*, which he later said was, of all his books, closest to his heart.

London entitled the first chapter of his book "The Descent." Deliberately and self-consciously, with a significant measure of control over his fate, London lowered himself into the Social Pit whose slippery walls had so terrified him in 1894. Then he had perceived the Pit for the first time and had seen himself slipping willy-nilly into it. Now he was safely on the outside: he had become a brain worker and was visiting the abyss to write a comparative study. What could be clearer and safer than that? But for London, intimacy with the people of the abyss was fraught with psychic peril.

In some ways London's second experience in the Social Pit was worse than his experience in America had been. For one thing, conditions in the East End of London were objectively worse than the rural poverty of California and the urban unemployment of Oakland. "As a vagrant in the 'Hobo' of a California jail," London remarks, "I have been served better food and drink than the London workman receives in his coffeehouses; while as an American laborer I have eaten a breakfast for twelve-pence such as the British laborer would not dream of eating" (*PA*, 234–35). For another, London was coming from softer circumstances now. When he had taken to the road, he had done so to escape the brutalizing labor of the coal room in the Oakland power plant. Now he was leaving a middle-class wife and child and a comfortable home. Then he had fled the industrial scene; now he was (perhaps) fleeing the domestic scene. As he puts on the second-hand clothes that are to be his street disguise, London notices the roughness of the fabric against his skin, and he reflects "upon the fair years and fat, which had made my skin soft and brought the nerves close to the surface" (*PA*, 13).

London's plunge into the English slums has elements of the stock naturalistic plot, worked out in Frank Norris's *Moran of the Lady Letty* and later repeated in London's own *The Sea-Wolf*, in which an upper-class hero discards his fancy duds and is reborn into life in the raw. This plot, as Kenneth Lynn argues, has its social origins in the new affluence of the post-Civil War middle class. Frank Norris, David Graham Phillips, and London himself would write about the ennui and purposelessness of the "second-generation," the sons and daughters of Gilded Age luxury, whose comfortable upbringing distanced them from the sordid necessity of earning a living and made it difficult for them to discover their role in industrial America. Lacking the direction of a career or a consuming purpose, they suffered from ennui, neurasthenia, and the fashionable diseases that were then called women's complaints. The naturalistic tale took these soft, aesthetic sufferers, and, by placing them in primitive surroundings, reinvigorated them with purpose, direction, will to live.[8] This plot usually involved taking the protagonist away from the city (over-civilization), to the country, the high seas, or the Klondike (the frontier). Here the veneer of civilization falls away from the aesthete and he is reborn in the image of an earlier social type: the self-made man. Instead of relying on his father's income, he learns to do for himself. In becoming self-sufficient, he becomes revitalized, healed. He also, as Lynn suggests in his analysis of Frank Norris's career, recreates himself in the image of his father.[9]

This nostalgic re-creation of an earlier America was an attempt to salvage the American dream of success, a dream that may never have been realized by many, but one that lived on in the Horatio Alger books, the self-help manuals, and the entrepreneurial dreams of the Mark Twains and Jack Londons. Because the reworking of this ideology depended upon the illusion that the past could be recovered

("Can't repeat the past?" cries the hero of *The Great Gatsby*, incredulously, "Why of course you can!"),[10] it was essential for these tales to take place in a setting removed from the straitened circumstances of the urban proletariat. When this plot unfolds within an urban setting, the result is quite different. Instead of the naturalistic story of rebirth, it gives rise to its counterpart—the naturalistic story of degeneration. Frank Norris's *McTeague*, subtitled "A Story of San Francisco," works out the degeneration of the erstwhile self-made man, who demonstrates not vitality and energy, but apathy. McTeague's animal torpor is consonant with London's characterization of the English proletariat as degraded animals. This characterization of the urban worker bears a strong resemblance to the world view of London's "materialistic monism," which viewed man as only a bit of animal protoplasm, making feeble and futile efforts to survive, without benefit of a usable past or, indeed, any culture worth the name.

London's perception of the London proletariat was conditioned by his already developed view of the American proletariat, as seen from his new middle-class identity. En route to London he wrote to Anna Strunsky: "A week from today I shall be in London. I shall then have two days in which to make my arrangements and sink down out of sight in order to view the coronation from the standpoint of the London beasts. That's all they are—beasts—if they are anything like the slum people of New York—beasts, shot through with stray flashes of divinity."[11] In *The People of the Abyss* London uses language that underscores the "bestial" nature of the ghetto-dwellers. On the benches in Spitalfields Garden, London writes, "it was a welter of rats and filth, of all manner of loathesome skin diseases, open sores, bruises, grossness, indecency, leering monstrosities, and bestial faces" (*PA*, 62). The hops pickers, leaving the slums to harvest the hops in the country, seem to London "some vile spawn from underground" (*PA*, 168). He describes the "new race" of "street people" that has sprung up: "They pass their lives at work and in the streets. They have dens and lairs into which to crawl for sleeping purposes, and that is all. . . . When they have nothing else to do, they ruminate as a cow ruminates" (*PA*, 229–30).

But London's application of animal language to the poor reflects only their degraded circumstances. He has an unsentimental sympathy for them, although he is repelled by the conditions in which they live. The creation of this population of beasts he unequivocally attributes to the political structure of England: "Class supremacy can rest only on class degradation; and when the workers are segregated in the Ghetto, they cannot escape the consequent degradation. A short and stunted people is created,—a breed strikingly differentiated from their masters' breed, a pavement folk, as it were, lacking stamina and strength" (*PA*, 220). The ghetto children are born with "all the qualities which make for noble manhood and womanhood." But, he writes, "the Ghetto itself, like an infuriated tigress turning on its young, turns upon and destroys all these qualities, blots out the light and laughter, and moulds those it does not kill into sodden and forlorn creatures, uncouth, degraded and wretched below the beasts of the field" (*PA*, 275–76). The law of the jungle, which London glorifies in his next book, is flatly rejected in this urban setting. In its place London suggests the Golden Rule; he tells his readers that if they do not want their children reared in the East End, they should not want those of others reared there. "Political economy and the survival of the fittest can go hang if they say otherwise" (*PA*, 213).

London's perception of the city as an urban jungle culminates in "A Vision of the Night," in which he tells of walking down to the docks. "It is rather hard to tell a tithe of what I saw. Much of it is untellable. But in a general way I may say that I saw a nightmare. . . ." He sees "a menagerie of garmented bipeds that looked something like humans and more like beasts, and to complete the picture, brass-buttoned keepers kept order among them when they snarled too fiercely" (*PA*, 284). His fear gives a hysterical edge to his telling. (He is now in his own clothes, which make him appear a likely "mark.") He is "afraid of their hands, of their naked hands, as one may be afraid of the paws of a gorilla." He fantasizes about their "ferocious, primordial strength to clutch and gripe and tear and rend," and in his language is the perceptible fear of a violent assault: "When they spring upon their human prey they are known even to bend the victim backward and double its body till the back is broken. . . . They are a new species, a breed of city savages. The streets and houses, alleys and courts, are their hunting grounds. As valley and mountain are to the natural savage, street and building are valley and mountain to them. The slum is their jungle, and they live and prey in the jungle" (*PA*, 285).

London's full articulation of the metaphor prepares him for his next departure. If fear has overcome sympathy, this emotional withdrawal is followed by a quite self-conscious repulsion from modern civilization. "If this is the best that civilization can do for the human, then give us howling and naked savagery. Far better to be a people of the wilderness and desert, of the cave and the squatting-place, than to be a people of the machine and the Abyss" (*PA*, 288). *The Call of the Wild*, written in a white heat several months later, was a celebration of "howling and naked savagery." As Joan London remarks with characteristic perception, "despite its Klondike setting, *The Call of the Wild* stems just as certainly, though less directly, from [London's] experiences in the East End as *The People of the Abyss* itself."[12]

The People of the Abyss opens and closes on the same emotion: fear. The fear London experienced as he walked down to the docks, which he recounts near the end of the book, is similar to his initial reaction to the East End. Interestingly, London expressed his initial "fear of the crowd" in a metaphor of drowning. "It was like the fear of the sea; and the miserable multitudes, street upon street, seemed so many waves of a vast and malodorous sea, lapping about me and threatening to well up and over me" (*PA*, 8). Here, as in his "Vision of the Night," London is dressed in clothes that mark him as of another social class. After he dons his second-hand clothes he experiences a revolution in his identity and in his consciousness:

> No sooner was I out on the streets than I was impressed by the difference in status effected by my clothes. All servility vanished from the demeanor of the common people with whom I came in contact. Presto! in the twinkling of an eye, so to say, I had become one of them. My frayed and out-at-elbows jacket was the badge and advertisement of my class, which was their class. It made me of like kind, and in place of the fawning and too-respectful attention I had hitherto received, I now shared with them a comradeship. [*PA*, 13–14]

He finds himself addressed as "mate" instead of "sir" or "governor," and he delights in his ability to meet the English people "on a basis of equality": "they talked as natural men should talk, without the least idea of getting anything out of me for what they talked or the way they talked." This comradely interaction overcomes London's fears for his safety. He finds that he has become part of the crowd that he had so feared. "The vast and malodorous sea had welled up and over me, or I had slipped gently into it, and there was nothing fearsome about it. . . ." At the same time that his emotional security is strengthened, he finds he must be "more lively in avoiding vehicles," for, he reports, "my life has cheapened in direct ratio with my clothes" (*PA*, 15).

London's next act suggests the rhythm of immersion and withdrawal that structures *The People of the Abyss*. The rebirth effected by his old clothes could be undone by escaping to dry land. London plans a "port of refuge" not far from the East End, where he can bathe and change clothes. "Also in such port I could receive my mail, work up my notes, and sally forth occasionally in changed garb to civilization." This port of refuge has an emotional equivalent in the recurrent feeling London conveys of giving thanks that he is not *really* in the desperate condition of the urban beasts he beholds. He plays the game of slumming, only to retreat to the half-crowns and florins tucked away in his pockets. These escapes alternate with feelings of sympathy and outrage for the condition of the urban proletariat (*PA*, 19). London himself provides a concise description of his consciousness: he was "a gentleman leading a double life" (*PA*, 20).[13]

London's consciousness of leading a "double life" is of course produced by his dual class allegiance. Although he is meeting "the English lower classes face to face, and [knowing] them for what they [are]" (*PA*, 15), *they* are not meeting and knowing London for what he is. They think he is a furloughed American sailor. They do not suspect that his real identity is Jack London, writer-on-assignment. But the irony of the situation can be turned on its head; who *is* the real Jack London? Is it the writer-on-assignment? Or is the real Jack London his old self, sailor Jack? Precisely these questions were to close in on Martin Eden; unable to find a social space in which he could be "real," he slipped gently into the sea and it closed over him, providing a final suffocation for a life that felt itself suffocated and in need of air and space it could never find.

As London makes his way through the East End, he meets characters who remind him of his former self. First he meets an English sailor, whose working-class background, life of petty pilfering and manual labor, and philosophy of life (he lived for "booze") closely parallel the career of Jack London, oyster pirate. London sees, as does the English sailor, the downward curve of this life: "A young sot; a premature wreck; physical inability to do a stoker's work; the gutter or the workhouse; and the end." But though the sailor sees this all, "it held no terrors for him"—as it had for London. London bunks with the English sailor, and, as he watches him stripping for bed, he admires the strong and perfect body of this "young god," who is bent on wasting it in a few short years and whose disdain for home life (for he has never known a home worthy of the name) means that he will "pass hence without posterity to receive the splendid heritage it was his to bequeath" (PA, 39). Again, London articulates that which has removed him from his old self: London's choice of a wife, home, and posterity set him apart from the rootless, futile existence of the lumpenproletariat. These domestic, middle-class accoutrements, which he seems to have chosen more for their ability to create a new self than for their intrinsic appeal, were waiting for him in America.

London next meets two companions who together recall London's double consciousness as he entered the middle-class world of college and Ruskin clubs. The one is a sweated worker, the other a "burning young socialist." London's mockery of the young socialist's lust for heroic martyrdom suggests that London had by this time seen the inadequacies of the gentlemanly socialism that had been his entré into the middle class. Described as "a slender lad of nineteen," "slight and frail," the socialist regales London and the sweated worker with tales of many exciting scrapes in pro-Boer meetings: of "climbing on the platform to lead the forlorn hope, when brother speaker after brother speaker had been dragged down by the angry crowd and cruelly beaten; of a siege in a church, where he and three others had taken sanctuary, and where, amid flying missiles and the crashing of stained glass, they had fought off the mob till rescued by platoons of constables; of pitched and giddy battles on stairways, galleries, and balconies" (PA, 54–55). But when he is shown the degradation of Spitalsfield Garden, where he and London have been taken by the sweated worker, "the burning young socialist" does not have the stomach for it. "'Oh, why did you bring me here?'" he demands, his "delicate face white with sickness of soul and stomach sickness"

(*PA*, 64). London implies that he has the heart for the romantic
heroism of the cause of the Boers but will not, cannot, look at what
is happening before his eyes. He is all heart, no liver. London's sympathies are nearer to those of the sturdy sweated worker than to
those of the middle-class socialist whose company, in America, he
has more recently left.

The final meeting that has significance for its relationship to London's old life does not have an exact counterpart in one of London's
selves, but rather cuts across a number of the experiences London
had as a member of the American working class. In line for a bed in
the workhouse, London meets a man who had been in the navy. That
he is no longer in the navy is owing to the following circumstances.
One day, as he was discharging his duties, his lieutenant, who was
perhaps in a foul mood, called him a name. It was, London writes,
"not a nice sort of name. It referred to his mother. When I was a boy
it was our boys' code to fight like little demons should such an insult
be given our mothers; and many men have died in my part of the
world for calling other men this name" (*PA*, 69–70). Accordingly,
the sailor immediately struck the lieutenant over the head with the
iron lever he happened to be holding, knocked him overboard, and
jumped in after him to finish him off. He was denied this opportunity when another ship pulled alongside. The sailor was given a sea
trial in which he was stripped of his rank, dismissed from the navy,
and sentenced to fifty lashes and two years in prison. This, London
pointedly remarks, was "the punishment of a man who was guilty of
manhood" (*PA*, 70). The sailor's crime was like that of the mulatto in
the Erie County Penitentiary. It was the crime of every lower-class
person who dared presume to equal rights and equal dignity.

The other side of the coin of this assertion of manhood was the
fawning respect that the lower classes customarily paid to their social
betters. London describes the "degraded humility" that his companions in the workhouse line display for the benefit of the workhouse porter, for whom one must not ring the bell too loudly or
insistently (*PA*, 84). London himself is the object of this behavior
after he reveals his identity as investigative reporter and treats his
companions to their first full meal in days. Immediately "they shut up
like clams. I was not of their kind; my speech had changed, the tones
of my voice were different, in short, I was a superior, and they were
superbly class conscious" (*PA*, 86).

These incidents suggest the protean identity that allowed London to float in and out of several selves, several class allegiances. London recognized this trait in Martin Eden, whom he described as "a fluid organism, swiftly adjustable, capable of flowing into and filling all sorts of nooks and crannies" (*ME*, 25). In one of his autobiographical notes, London describes himself as "plastic, fluid, flowed into any environment."[14] In *The People of the Abyss*, a consummate expression of this protean identity occurs in the passage in which London describes his visit to a working-man's hotel. As the men sleep, London goes "from bed to bed [and looks] at the sleepers." He sees that "they were not bad-looking fellows. . . . They were lovable, as men are lovable. They were capable of love" (*PA*, 249). London's identity goes out to that of the poor men, soothing them and loving them, enfolding them, much as Walt Whitman's protean "I" was able to encompass "you." In the emotional texture of London's language is the implication that his sexual identity is as plastic as his class allegiance.

London's protean identity was effectively extinguished by his experiences in the East End, taken as a whole. His cumulative reaction was a fear similar to that which he had experienced when he had his first vision of the Social Pit in 1894. Then, as now, intimacy with the people of the abyss made London determined to put distance between their situation and his. This movement can best be seen in the letters London wrote from the East End. Repeatedly he registers his shock at the conditions there. He writes to Anna on August 16, "The whole thing, all the conditions of life, the immensity of it, everything is overwhelming. I never conceived such a mass of misery in the world before." Several days later he writes again, "Am rushing, for I am made sick by this human hell-hole called London Town. I find it almost impossible to believe that some of the horrible things I have seen are really so."[15] Rush he did, completing the research and writing of *The People of the Abyss* in a total of seven weeks. He finished the manuscript on September 28, and immediately began a letter to Anna Strunsky to tell her that "the book is finished." He quotes to her the last paragraph of his book, then interrupts the letter to go to a meeting of the East End socialists, of which he gives a brief account when he returns later that day. He finishes the letter the following day, in the meantime having received a letter from Anna, to which he responds. Near the end of this twice-interrupted letter London writes:

And now it is all over and done with. So be it. Henceforth
I shall dream romances for other people and transmute them
into bread and butter.

Did I tell you I had finished the book? I did yesterday
afternoon.[16]

The terse "so be it," which London often uses to indicate that he is
turning down a page in his life, here is a monument to his working-
class self. Horrified by what he has seen, he makes a resolve, just as
eight years ago he had made a resolve after looking into the depths
of the Pit. "Henceforth I shall dream romances for other people and
transmute them into bread and butter." This letter allows us to date
with precision Jack London's private burial of his working-class consciousness. Despite the rebirth of his socialism from 1903 to 1907, in
an irrevocable sense London had "closed certain volumes in [his] life
on a certain day in London."[17] He had walled off his consciousness
from a social reality that was too painful. Specifically, he had walled
off his consciousness from his proletarian roots.

The way this manifested itself in his political thought is succinctly
stated by Joan London. She notes that her father had long harbored
"a contradiction . . . between [his] belief in the destiny of the working
class and his lack of belief in its ability to achieve this through its own
efforts." The East End experience intensified this tendency: "if his
faith in the ability of the working class to throw off its yoke had
formerly been weak, it had now practically ceased to exist."[18] The
change effected in his consciousness was likewise an intensification
of contradictions that he had long harbored, which were now given a
less flexible cast. After this experience his protean social identity was
fixed more securely within the middle class; the energies he formerly
had directed toward his working-class consciousness were henceforth to be diverted into hating the middle class. Thus the energies
that might have been expended in a socially productive way, in some
form of collective action, were now turned inward in a destructive
cycle, as the determinedly bourgeois Jack London detested his bourgeois self. "In retrospect," writes Joan London, "it has seemed to
some of Jack London's older friends that by 1903 he was an entirely
different person."[19] It is significant that London later declined an
opportunity to do a similar journalistic exposé of child labor in the

cotton mills of the South. And though he made notes for "an American People of the Abyss," he was never to write it.[20] Intimacy with the proletariat was too dangerous.

Andrew Sinclair puts an entirely different construction on London's statement that "it is all over and done with." This, and London's statement several months later to the effect that he had closed certain volumes in his life on a certain day in London, Sinclair believes refers to the breaking-up of the relationship between Jack London and Anna Strunsky.[21] After he returned from the East End, something had changed in their relationship, but it was not, as Sinclair speculates, that Anna had broken with Jack. I imagine Sinclair was led into this interpretation by what London writes in response to Anna's letter (which apparently does not survive), the letter he received in the middle of writing his of September 28–29. He writes: "What rot this long-distance correspondence is! About the time you are receiving harsh letters from me, I am receiving the kindest letters from you." He goes on to tell of the knock-out, bewildering effect of his receiving "that frightful letter from you." Apparently in response to the "frightful" letter he had received, he had written a harsh letter to her, and now he apologizes for it, saying he "should have taken the knock-out clean and not put up any defense."[22] From this I conclude that they had been having a transatlantic argument (they differed on many issues) and that now it was resolved, after several crossed letters. London does begin the next paragraph, "And now it is all over and done with," but this seems clearly to refer to what follows ("Did I tell you I had finished the book"), not what has come before. The letter does not appear to be that of a rejected lover. Sinclair, led far afield by this letter, provides this obfuscating comment on London's reaction to the East End: "He confused the fury of his disappointed love for Anna with his hatred of an unjust industrial system that had ruined his youth."[23]

London's decision to pursue bread-and-butter goals certainly affected his relationship with Anna, a committed socialist, but the burden of his letters clearly has reference to what writing *The People of the Abyss* did to his consciousness. Although there is nothing in them that suggests that Anna broke with him, there is evidence that London's response to the misery of the East End was to affirm the middle-class values of wife, home, and posterity. These values, as the

following letter of December 20, 1902, suggests, were asserted in
opposition to the East End, working-class life, socialism—and Anna.
Writing apparently in response to a question she had asked about his
frame of mind, London says "No, Dear Anna, I am neither in joy
nor sorrow. I closed certain volumes in my life on a certain day in
London. These volumes will remain closed. In them I shall read no
more." He next replies that yes, he has happiness in his daughter
Joan: elaborating on his involvement with his daughter, he uses his
posterity as a shield against his intimacy with Anna. He writes:

> The mystery of man and woman is behind me. I am deep in the
> mystery of father and daughter. You do not understand this.
> You are about seventeen to-day. And between seventeen and
> twenty-seven you will linger until you die. [He has earlier said
> he feels fifty years old.] You will never get beyond the man-
> and-woman mystery. Theoretically, at least, you will remain
> always lost in it.[24]

Whether or not Anna failed to meet London's expectations in some
way, we shall probably never know. Clearly, he has backed away
from the relationship. The pattern that emerges is of a young man,
for the second time terrified by a vision of the Social Pit, who resolves that he will sacrifice all (even intimacy) to make sure that he
does not lose his middle-class port of refuge, his home. In this attempt to bind himself to stabilizing forces, London places great emphasis on his posterity. The energies he had once invested in the
cause of socialism will now be invested closer to home: "Behold, my
seed comes after me. I am joyed with it, satisfied. Still you pursue,
wrestling with angels and demons without end, when all the wrestling
is without avail. Not so, you say, and I am coward to sit down and
leave the fight. And I reply: so be it. I am so made, as you are otherwise made. I prefer least to nothing. You prefer nothing or all to
less."[25] Anna, a Jewish intellectual who was born in comfort, remained true to her socialist ideals. She regarded London's pursuit of
marketplace glory a sellout of the cause. He, threatened by the possibility of slipping into the Abyss, reacted to the objective conditions
of his society with one goal in mind: his personal survival.

Having already cut himself off from his working-class friends,
from his middle-class socialist friends, from his working-class roots,

London now walled himself off from his relationship with Anna. There remained his home and family, but, having chosen them for the wrong reasons—not for the companionship they would bring to him but for the new and stable identity they would create for him, London was within a year to turn down the page on his domestic life. It is no wonder that in 1903 he began slipping into the slough of despond he called the "long sickness."

FIVE

THE LONG SICKNESS

The depression that engulfed Jack London in 1903 was a turning point in his life. It coincided with important events in every area of his experience: with the height of his early success, with the crystallization of his middle-class identity, and with the breakup of his marriage. He was only twenty-seven, but he surveyed the struggles of his youth from the vantage point of one prematurely old and jaded. London's long sickness and his response to it are the key to the remaining thirteen years of his life. Through an enormous act of will London pulled himself out of the slough of despond, but he never recaptured his sense of wonder and his vital engagement in the world. His recovery was only apparent; at the back of his consciousness lay the sleeping dogs—quiet only because they were under heavy sedation. Remove the anodynes, the sweet illusions, and all was plunged in blackness again. His "cure" took him from the land of the suicidal to the land of the living dead.

In *John Barleycorn*, London describes his depression in this way: "Mine was no uncommon experience. I had read too much positive science and lived too much positive life. In the eagerness of youth I had made the ancient mistake of pursuing Truth too relentlessly. I had torn her veils from her, and the sight was too terrible for me to stand. In brief, I lost my fine faiths in pretty well everything except humanity, and the humanity I retained faith in was a very stark humanity indeed" (*JB*, 253–54). At this point London cuts short his description with the words "this long sickness of pessimism is too well known to most of us to be detailed here." He does, however, enumerate the "fine faiths" that went by the board.

> The things I had fought for and burned my midnight oil for, had failed me. Success—I despised it. Recognition—it was

dead ashes. Society, men and women above the ruck and the muck of the water-front and the forecastle—I was appalled by their unlovely mental mediocrity. Love of woman—it was like all the rest. Money—I could sleep in only one bed at a time, and of what worth was an income of a hundred porter-houses a day when I could eat only one? Art, culture—in the face of the iron facts of biology such things were ridiculous, the exponents of such things only the more ridiculous.
[*JB*, 254–55]

Success, recognition, society, money, art, culture—these terms have in common the bourgeois values that London had unequivocally embraced when he resolved in his letter to Anna Strunsky to "dream romances for other people and transmute them into bread and butter." The incongruous term in his list is "love of woman," which London says "was like all the rest." In this incongruity we have a significant unconscious revelation: to Jack London, love of woman carried the same emotional connotations as success, recognition, society, money, art, and culture. Objectively, it was indeed "like all the rest": it was simply another item for conspicuous consumption; subjectively, success, recognition, and so on were sought for the emotional satisfaction of love and intimacy. In *Martin Eden* the hero cannot distinguish his desire to succeed from his desire to win the love of the middle-class Ruth. Intimacy with this mother-goddess was to be the final fruit of the struggle to make it in a bourgeois world.

The peculiar language in which London describes his positivistic vision of the Truth unconsciously makes this association. Truth is a woman whom London had pursued "relentlessly." He had "torn her veils from her," but instead of consummating this rape-like union, London flees from a sight that was, he says, "too terrible for me to stand." This experience plunges him into a depression, the only cure for which is repression of the awful vision: "I pursued Truth less relentlessly, refraining from tearing her last veils aside even when I clutched them in my hand. I no longer cared to look upon Truth naked. I refused to permit myself to see a second time what I had once seen. And the memory of what I had that time seen I resolutely blotted from my mind" (*JB*, 256–57). In Jack London's psycho-sexual imagination, the woman who personified Truth was supposed to be spiritual, sexless, above the "iron facts of biology." To look upon her naked was to see a vision of the mother-goddess as a whore. The ambiguities of London's consciousness are wonderfully suggested in his repressive solution for this nightmare vision: he will continue to pursue Truth, but he will leave her partially clothed and will blot from his mind the memory of her genitals.

That this sexual imagery is not incidental and is centrally related to London's pursuit of bourgeois values is confirmed if we look at the language he uses to describe his disillusionment: "Society opened its portals to me. I entered right in on the parlor floor, and my disillusionment proceeded rapidly. I sat down to dinner with the masters of society, and with the wives and daughters of the masters of society. The women were gowned beautifully, I admit; but to my naive surprise I discovered that they were of the same clay as all the rest of the women I had known down below in the cellar. 'The colonel's lady and Judy O'Grady were sisters under their skins'— and gowns."[1] London uses this quotation from Kipling on several other occasions; each time this sexual innuendo stands for his general disappointment with the class he struggled to enter.[2]

In *Martin Eden* London puts a positive construction on this revelation about middle-class women, but in the end the result is the same. While Martin is courting Ruth, they have an exchange in which Ruth tells him she has never loved before. When Martin tells her that *he* has never known love before either, she scoffs and throws up to him the debauched sailor's life he has led. Martin accepts her characterization of him as having had "a wife in every port," but he denies that this is love. She bursts into tears at the thought of these "other women," and, to Martin's wonder, her tears can be driven away only by caresses. As he embraces her, the line from Kipling runs through Martin's mind, and "though the novels he had read had led him to believe otherwise," he realized that Kipling was right:

> His idea, for which the novels were responsible, had been that only formal proposals obtained in the upper classes. It was all right enough, down whence he had come, for youths and maidens to win each other by contact; but for the exalted personages up above on the heights to make love in similar fashion had seemed unthinkable. Yet the novels were wrong. Here was a proof of it. The same pressures and caresses, unaccompanied

by speech, that were efficacious with the girls of the working-class, were equally efficacious with the girls above the working-class. They were all of the same flesh, after all, sisters under their skins; and he might have known as much himself had he remembered his Spencer. [*ME*, 166–67]

Martin takes "great consolation" in this truth, for he feels that it brings Ruth closer to him. "There was no bar to their marriage. Class difference was the only difference, and class was extrinsic. It could be shaken off." He could rise to Ruth, and Ruth, "under her purity, and saintliness, and culture, and ethereal beauty of soul" was really "just like Lizzie Connolly and all Lizzie Connollys. All that was possible of them was possible of her." This knowledge does not condemn Ruth in Martin's eyes—quite the contrary—and yet the novel is structured around Martin's repulsion from this daughter of the bourgeoisie whom he had sought so avidly. And in this scene there is a suggestion of hypocrisy in Ruth's tears over the other women, which turn into a not-so-subtle seduction. Her hypocrisy will be underscored later in the novel when, after Martin is a successful and rich writer, the prim-and-proper Ruth offers herself to Martin, with her family's knowledge and encouragement.

London's convolution of "love" and "success" is of course not original. When William James labeled success the "bitch-goddess," he succinctly captured the contradictory expectations many men had of the middle-class woman. She was both an idealized goal and a sexual betrayer of her own imputed purity. The way women figured in the romantic imagination of the self-made man is epitomized in Scott Fitzgerald's description of his hero's love for Daisy in *The Great Gatsby*. In his inimitably suggestive prose, Fitzgerald tells of a magical autumn night:

> . . . they had been walking down the street when the leaves were falling, and they came to a place where there were no trees and the sidewalk was white with moonlight. They stopped here and turned toward each other. Now it was a cool night with that mysterious excitement in it which comes at the two changes of the year. The quiet lights in the houses were humming out into the darkness and there was a stir and bustle among the stars. Out of the corner of his eye Gatsby saw that the blocks of the sidewalks really formed a ladder and mounted to a secret

place above the trees—he could climb to it, if he climbed alone, and once there he could suck on the pap of life, gulp down the incomparable milk of wonder.

His heart beat faster and faster as Daisy's white face came up to his own. He knew that when he kissed this girl, and forever wed his unutterable visions to her perishable breath, his mind would never romp again like the mind of God.
[p. 112]

The magic of this night has less to do with Daisy than with Gatsby's perception that the "blocks of the sidewalks really formed a ladder and mounted to a secret place above the trees"—an image of Gatsby's climb to success. Yet we know that this does have to do with Daisy, for she is the inspiration for his climb. If the imagery is to be trusted, there is also a woman at the end of the quest, though she is not a seductress but a nurturant mother: there, above the trees, "he could suck on the pap of life, gulp down the incomparable milk of wonder." If the goal of the quest is to be suckled by a cosmic mother, it is clear that the flesh-and-blood Daisy will not suffice. In the last sentence of this passage, the physical consummation of love destroys Gatsby's dream and the possibility of god-like postures. He can reach "the secret place above the trees" only if he climbs alone. He must not "wed his unutterable visions to her perishable breath," for that will destroy the illusion—which promises the satisfaction not of sexual intimacy but of an idealized love more appropriate to a suckling babe and mother.

If we turn from such patterns in American fiction to the pulpy versions pedaled in success manuals, the relationship between "love" and "success" is more baldly stated. In *Think and Grow Rich*, Napoleon Hill reveals the hidden power of sex attraction: "*Man's greatest motivating force is his desire to please woman*! The hunter who excelled during prehistoric days, before the dawn of civilization, did so because of his desire to appear great in the eyes of woman. Man's nature has not changed in this respect. The 'hunter' of today brings home no skins of wild animals, but he indicates his desire for her favor by supplying fine clothes, automobiles, and wealth" (p. 195). (In *The Great Gatsby*, Daisy cries as Gatsby heaps in front of her specimens of his lavish wardrobe, obtained to please her.) Hill argues that all successful men "have been of a highly sexed nature." But the mere possession of sexual energy is not sufficient for success. "The energy must be *transmuted* from desire for physical contact, into some *other* form of desire and action before it will lift one to the status of a genius" (p. 185). Anyone who wishes to romp with the mind of God will not do anything so unseemly as to express physical love. "Far from becoming geniuses because of great sex desires, the majority of men *lower* themselves, through misunderstanding and misuse of this great force, to the status of the lower animals" (p. 185). The higher purpose to which Hill would have men direct their sexual energies is not far to seek: "Master salesmen attain the status of mastery in selling because they consciously or unconsciously *transmute* the energy of sex into sales enthusiasm" (p. 188). Hill believes he has discovered why men seldom succeed before they are forty, and "do not strike their real pace until they are well beyond the age of fifty." Until that time they have dissipated their energies "through over-indulgence in physical expression of the emotion of sex" (p. 185). In Hill's scenario the woman is a dynamo that is best kept at a far remove from the aspiring man whom she energizes. The sexual energies she arouses in him are not returned to her, as the logical receptable for them, but directed away from her, into economic activity.[3] In relationships between men and women, the human economy must be interrupted in the interest of generating more market activity; sexual energies expressed directly between people are lost as far as the market is concerned. These same energies, "when harnessed and transmuted into action, other than that of physical expression, may raise one to great accomplishment."[4]

The way that the political economy of the market structures relationships between men and women was brilliantly analyzed by Charlotte Perkins Gilman, a feminist theorist and contemporary of Jack London. The year that London broke into the *Overland Monthly* with his first Alaskan stories, Gilman published her first book, *Women and Economics* (1898). A brief look at her analysis will underscore the systemic nature of London's emotional responses to success and will also suggest the limits of his political analysis, which he never extended to the realm of personal relationships.

In the first chapter of *Women and Economics* Gilman argues that women are economically dependent on men and that this dependency leads to "excessive sex differentiation," that is, those characteristics in women that sexually attract men are unnaturally exaggerated:

> Where the two sexes obtain their food under different con-
> ditions, and where that difference consists in one of them being
> fed by the other, then the feeding sex becomes the environ-
> ment of the fed. Man, in supporting woman, has become her
> economic environment. Under natural selection, every creature
> is modified to its environment, developing perforce the qualities
> needed to obtain its livelihood under that environment. Man,
> as the feeder of woman, becomes the strongest modifying
> force in her economic condition. [p. 38]

Sex attraction thus becomes the basis of women's economy: "the
personal profit of women bears but too close a relation to their
power to win and hold the other sex. From the odalisque with the
most bracelets to the debutante with the most bouquets, the relation still holds good,—woman's economic profit comes through the
power of sex-attraction" (p. 63). Gilman aptly describes the political
economy that makes logical and necessary the "transmutation of sex
desire" described by Napoleon Hill. Gilman writes: "She gets her
living by getting a husband. He gets his wife by getting a living. It is
to her individual economic advantage to secure a mate. It is to his
individual sex-advantage to secure economic gain. The sex-functions
to her have become economic functions. Economic functions to him
have become sex-functions" (p. 110). In these terms, marriage is not
different from prostitution; both involve the same "sexuo-economic
relation," and Gilman points out our inconsistent attitudes toward
these two institutions: "When we confront this fact boldly and plainly
in the open market of vice, we are sick with horror. When we see the
same economic relation made permanent, established by law, sanctioned and sanctified by religion, covered with flowers and incense
and all accumulated sentiment, we think it innocent, lovely, and
right" (p. 63). Our repulsion from prostitution is a "true instinct," but
the same physical and psychic evils result from marriage, were we
willing to admit this. Woman's economic dependence makes the
woman and the mother "a hideous paradox," for we expect her to
"get gain through love." "No wonder," Gilman wrote, "that men turn
with loathing from the kind of women they have made" (p. 98).

Gilman locates man's repulsion from woman not in woman herself, but in the sexuo-economic relationship in which both man and

woman are enmeshed. By looking at women as a part of the economy, she is able to recognize and explain private horrors that may be difficult for individual men to admit and consciously feel. She cuts through the sentimental lies that clouded London's political vision whenever he dealt with women and the private sphere, and she provides a penetrating economic analysis of why "good" women despise "vicious" ones:

> The virtuous woman stands in close ranks with her sisters, refusing to part with herself—her only economic goods—until she is assured of legal marriage, with its lifelong guarantee of support. Under equal proportions of birth in the two sexes, every woman would be tolerably sure of obtaining her demands. But here enters the vicious woman, and offers the same goods—though of inferior quality, to be sure—for a far less price. Every one of such illegitimate competitors lowers the chances of the unmarried woman and the income of the married. No wonder those who hold themselves highly should be moved to bitterness at being undersold in this way. It is the hatred of the trade-unionist for "scab labor." [pp. 109–10]

London wrote a lucid economic analysis of "The Scab," but never does he mention women and prostitution. He followed Truth only up to the portals of the boudoir; behind those doors Truth remained veiled.

London's naiveté about women constricted his political vision. His refuge from the brutalities of capitalism was an idealized middle-class woman (or a feminized middle-class society—class and sex are hopelessly conflated here). His confusion about the nature of bourgeois society is reflected in the posture that he unconsciously adopted in his struggle to rise: that of a young boy who passionately believes in the sexlessness of his mother at the same time that he secretly desires her. His bitter disillusionment with success grew out of his naive assumption that by leaving the working class he was escaping from the oppression of class. When he entered the parlor floor of society, he discovered not only that he was still within the class structure of capitalist America, but also that this class brought with it oppressions only more discreetly camouflaged than those he had experienced as a sweated worker. For his part, he preferred the "naked simplicities" of life, as they were frankly espoused by the working class, to the sentimental selfishness of the middle class. Or so he sometimes said.

The reason it was difficult to look upon these "naked simplicities" is that they rendered human life a worthless affair. People became, in fact, commodities. He realized this when he saw himself slipping into the abyss:

> I saw the naked simplicities of the complicated civilization in which I lived. Life was a matter of food and shelter. In order to get food and shelter men sold things. The merchant sold shoes, the politician sold his manhood, and the representative of the people, with exceptions, of course, sold his trust; while nearly all sold their honor. Women, too, whether on the street or in the holy bond of wedlock, were prone to sell their flesh. All things were commodities, all people bought and sold.[5]

Even "in the holy bond of wedlock, [women] were prone to sell their flesh." Sexuality belonged to the world of commodities, and a hint of sexuality in a love relationship tainted it and turned it into a market relationship. In order to imagine a noncontractual human relationship, sexuality had to be repressed. An unconscious desire for a noncontractual relationship drew London to embrace the middle-class woman. At her feet he sought his heart's desire: the unqualified love and acceptance that (ideally) a mother gives to her child—not for what the child has done for her or given to her but for the very fact of the child's existence. But London, like Martin Eden, discovered that this woman was "like all the rest." She did not love him for himself but for what he was worth in the literary marketplace.

The psychic and social sources of London's long sickness should be clear. He had embraced the bourgeoisie in the belief that he was affirming home, motherhood, security, love, only to discover that he had been taken to bed by a shameless whore who would rob him of his manhood. There seemed only two possible defenses: to run away—and to be deprived of the promised (but illusory) emotional satisfactions of union, or, like Moll Flanders and her lover, to lie together in the mistaken belief that virtue was sufficient protection against amorous indiscretion. Unwilling to give up his dream of a noncontractual union, London chose the latter alternative. As he says at the end of "What Life Means to Me," "I retain my belief in the

nobility and excellence of the human. I believe that spiritual sweetness and unselfishness will conquer the gross gluttony of today."[6]
The contradictions of his society were mirrored in London's choice:
he prostituted himself—for love.

To dream of a better world is not the same as to have illusions
about the present social reality. London confounded dream and illusion: isolated within his bourgeois self, he could not believe in the
possibility of social change, and only in wish fulfillment were the
emotional satisfactions of solidarity available to him. Unable to see
how a better world could be brought into being, he took refuge in
illusions of "nobility and excellence," of "spiritual sweetness and
unselfishness." These were illusions not because they did not exist
but because Jack London had not experienced them, yet he continued to believe in them as abstractions. They were elements in the
ideal world that his working-class consciousness had attributed to
the middle class. Now, however, as he "went back to the working-
class," he added to his list of illusions his belief in the "PEOPLE." The
realities of working-class life were now, in his bourgeois consciousness, transformed into ideals. He believed in the "PEOPLE" with the
same abstract passion with which he had believed in the purity of the
middle-class woman. He was in fact to be pulled out of the long
sickness by *both*.

In *John Barleycorn* London reports that during his long sickness he
was not tempted by drink. "Never the remotest whisper arose in my
consciousness that John Barleycorn was the anodyne, that he could
lie me along to live" (*JB*, 255). He found other anodynes, other lies.
"What really saved me," he writes, "was the one remaining illusion—
the PEOPLE." During this period he "meditated suicide coolly," and
he was so preoccupied with the idea of ending his life that he gave
away his revolver for fear he might do away with himself in his sleep.
This self-protective gesture is of a piece with his recommitment to
the cause of the people, as is suggested by London's syntactical con-
junction of the two acts:

> I grew afraid of my revolver—afraid during the period in which
> the radiant, flashing vision of the PEOPLE was forming in my
> mind and will. So obsessed was I with the desire to die, that
> I feared I might commit the act in my sleep, and I was com-
> pelled to give my revolver away to others who were to lose it

for me where my subconscious hand might not find it.

But the PEOPLE saved me. By the PEOPLE was I handcuffed to life. [*JB*, 255–56]

London had of course been active in socialism since 1896, and had
even, in 1901, run for mayor of Oakland on the Socialist Labor party
ticket; but at this time of personal crisis he "threw all precaution
to the winds, threw [himself] with fiercer zeal into the fight for
socialism" (*JB*, 256). From this period date a number of his propa-
gandistic essays and stories. "How I Became a Socialist" appeared
in 1903. "The Class Struggle" appeared in the New York *Independent*
of November 5, 1903, and "The Scab" in the *Atlantic Monthly* of
January, 1904. In "What Life Means to Me" (1904), London con-
fessed his errant ways, denounced the bourgeoisie, and claimed to
have returned "to the working class," which was, he says, where "I
had been born and where I belonged. I care no longer to climb."[7]
His rededication of himself to the Holy Grail of socialism reached a
pitch in the following two years. As Philip Foner writes: "The years
of 1905–1907 marked the period of Jack London's greatest activity
for the socialist movement. During these years he lectured frequently
to socialist organizations, toured the East for the Intercollegiate
Socialist Society, raised money for the movement and for various
labor causes, wrote numerous essays and stories in which he brought
the socialist message before the American reading public, and completed his most important contribution to the literature of socialism,
The Iron Heel."[8]

This was not the first time that London had discovered the way in
which he was, through socialism, "handcuffed to life." On December
10, 1900, London wrote this revealing passage in a letter to Elwyn
Hoffman: "You seem to be in the dumps, the blues, or something.
So am I, I get them regularly, and thereby am greatly flattered. It is a
penalty, you know, which must be paid by the higher organisms." He
goes on to provide a long quotation from Huxley that shows that the
higher the culture, the greater the stimulation, exhaustion, and consequent ennui. Then he suggests that this penalty does not always
have to be paid.

I know many bright, talented fellows, and women too, who
escape the futile regret and morbid anxiety by addressing themselves to the work of ameliorating so many factors in present-

day society which are causes of futile regret and morbid anxiety. Look at the socialists, for instance—men who immolate self upon the altar of the Cause, and so immolating self, forget self, and exchange the pains of self for the pleasures of struggle and altruism. Now don't say this is all bosh. I have been so blue as to have spent a day contemplating suicide, and gone forth in the evening to lecture before some socialist organization,— and in the battle forgot self, been uplifted out of self, and in the end returned home happy, satisfied. The thing works; it's bound to.[9]

London's language makes clear both the nature of the sickness and the nature of the cure. Socialism releases him from "the pains of self" and allows him to "forget self," to be "uplifted out of self." He strikes a suicidal note even in his cure, for he twice speaks not just of losing self-consciousness but of immolating himself on the altar of the Cause. Socialism was Jack London's holy war. It gave him the psychic release of a religion and the physical release of a fight. Yet had socialism truly functioned as a religion? If it had truly engaged London as a member of a living, believing community and so allowed him a social identity "uplifted out of self," it seems unlikely that he would have needed the "battle" in order to forget that painful self. In the context of London's other struggles against colossal odds, his commitment to socialism does not appear very different from the fights he seemed to need in order to continue living. They were all a way to forget self, to break out of the prison of consciousness. As he writes in *John Barleycorn*, "I was born a fighter. The things I had fought for had proved not worth the fight. Remained the PEOPLE" (*JB*, 255). Only through violent action could the pent-up self be momentarily released from captivity.

Since London specifically counterposes the anodyne of the PEOPLE to the anodyne of John Barleycorn, it is significant that one of his few expressions of socialist brotherhood came arm-in-arm with the saloons that, in *John Barleycorn*, provide London with the much-desired sense of comradeship. Writing Anna Strunsky from Rome in 1902 London declares: "I belong to the greatest brotherhood in the world, the greatest and finest the world has ever seen; and I meet my brothers wherever I wander. In Paris, for instance, I find the guide on the street corner a socialist. In the Latin Quarter I had a most

wonderful time with anarchists and socialists—all chance acquaintances. I shall never forget one night there, in a students' cafe, with
two Italians and a Dutchman."[10] He reminisces of yet another night,
in Spezzia, Italy, in which they went ashore and "ran upon nests of
socialists, and one of my strongest impressions of that night is a
crowd of us, speaking divers tongues, but all chanting the 'Mar-
sellaise' as we marched along the streets. Oh, it was glorious." The
feeling of brotherhood is strong, but one is struck as well by the
"foreignness" of the experience. London is temporarily expatriated,
these are all "chance acquaintances," and all are "speaking divers
tongues." It is easier, perhaps, to feel kinship with those so obviously
removed in nationality and language than it is with those whose
likeness and familiarity are threatening. It is also easier to experience
this brotherhood in the familiar haunts of his working-class days—
the café, with its clean, well-lighted promise of fellowship and jollity.

Homeopathic doses of the PEOPLE kept London alive but did not
restore his humanity. He was indeed "handcuffed to life." He was
serving a life sentence. A prisoner of his own consciousness, he was
very like the "masters of society" whom he describes as "the unburied dead."[11] In stark contrast to "the radiant, flashing vision of the
PEOPLE" are Jack London's subsequent encounters with real flesh-
and-blood people. After his long sickness, he finds he can tolerate
the company of others only if he is loaded with liquor; here begins
the cycle that will lead to his early death:

> . . . as soon as I got in the company of others I was driven to
> melancholy and spiritual tears. I could neither laugh with nor
> at the solemn utterances of men I esteemed ponderous asses;
> nor could I laugh with nor at, nor engage in my old-time
> lightsome persiflage, with the silly superficial chatterings of
> women, who, underneath all their silliness and softness, were
> as primitive, direct, and deadly in their pursuit of biological
> destiny as the monkey women were before they shed their
> furry coats and replaced them with the furs of other animals.
> [JB, 259–60]

London was not able to repress completely the vision he had seen
when Truth stood naked before him: there they were again, the
monkey women—"primitive, direct, and deadly in their pursuit
of biological destiny." London's invocation of "biological destiny"

underscores the way in which sexuality and materialism were linked in his mind with a positivistic vision in which life was a mere biological squirming in which the big ate the little, a ferment with no human significance, no ideals, no love. London expresses his removal from the land of the living in another striking metaphor, in which he likens the people around him to actors on a stage and himself to a jaded theater-goer. He could no longer enjoy the show because he had gone "behind the scenes" and was too aware of the artifice to enjoy the art:

> I had seen the same show too often, listened too often to the same songs and the same jokes. I knew too much about the box-office receipts. I knew the cogs of the machinery behind the scenes so well, that the posing on the stage, and the laughter and the song, could not drown the creaking of the wheels behind.
>
> It doesn't pay to go behind the scenes and see the angel-voiced tenor beat his wife. Well, I'd been behind, and I was paying for it. [*JB*, 260]

He concludes, "social intercourse for me was getting painful and difficult." His organic connection to human society has been snapped; the beauty and wonder of life have been replaced by "box-office receipts." The show is not real, nor are the people, nor is the viewer. All is a creaking of machinery, a farce got up for fools who could not see through it. "And now," writes London, "we begin to come to it. How to face social intercourse with the glamour gone?" He found the answer in his bottle of Scotch:

> A cocktail or two, or several, I found, cheered me up for the foolishness of foolish people. A cocktail, or several, before dinner, enabled me to laugh whole-heartedly at things which had long since ceased being laughable. The cocktail was a prod, a spur, a kick, to my jaded mind and bored spirits. It recrudesced the laughter and the song, and put a lilt into my own imagination so that I could laugh and sing and say foolish things with the liveliest of them, or platitudes with verve and intensity to the satisfaction of the pompous mediocre ones who knew no other way to talk. [*JB*, 261–62]

Alcohol, the ritual draught of his initiation into the lower class, had become essential to his continued existence as a social creature.

"When I thought of fellowship, the connotation was alcohol. Fellowship and alcohol were Siamese twins. They always occurred linked together" (*JB*, 340). Only with the aid of alcohol could London "join [his] fellows and make one with them" (*JB*, 279).

The final chapters of *John Barleycorn* are exquisitely painful. London's voice comes from beyond the grave. He cannot be touched by human hands, yet his rational, detailed exposition of his distress demands a response from the reader. At the same time, London's diseased egotism, his utter contempt for those around him, turn aside the sympathetic response that a reader might otherwise give London's humanity. The only response of the reader for which London seems to care is the box-office receipts. As London prepares to entertain his dinner guests, armed with a glass of scotch, he exclaims to the reader, "The clown's the thing! The clown! If one must be a philosopher, let him be Aristophanes" (*JB*, 331). London turned the very stuff of his existence, even his pain, into an entertaining show for the benefit of his public and the lining of his pocket.

The contrast between London's private desperation and his forced jollity recalls an incident he recounts earlier in *John Barleycorn*. On the night the politicians opened the bars, London got dangerously drunk, and neither Nelson nor his other companions were aware of his critical condition. London tried to communicate his distress through his physical acts, but his companions were only amused by his antics. "And I remember," writes London, "the fleeting bitterness that was mine as I realized that I was in a struggle with death and that these others did not know. It was as if I were drowning before a crowd of spectators who thought I was cutting up tricks for their entertainment" (*JB*, 137). His private self gesticulates dumbly, fails to communicate, and drowns. If this is poignant and painful, it is also self-pitying. How can the reader extend to London sympathy when he so readily does that himself? And in fact he does not ask for sympathy but for pity, not for understanding and sharing but for a bestowal of feeling from one whose very removal from the distress allows him to give with largesse. That is to say, in the very act of requesting pity London rears a wall of difference between the reader and himself. London's style and stance, like that of John Barleycorn, raises a wall between his public and his private selves, a wall that enables the entertainer to go on with his tricks, the spectators to laugh, the show to go on. There is something perverse in London's building the wall yet higher while complaining bitterly that no one tries to surmount it. This tactic enables London both to feel superior to his spectators and to be abused by them. He is both master and slave, abuser and abused, knower and known. He lives within the walls of a sado-masochistic prison.

London's placement of himself as an observer behind the scenes endowed him with powers both god-like and demonic. He was the stage manager, changing scenes, cranking the machine that would make the angel fly. At the same time, he had no emotional investment in what was happening on stage. London conveys his detachment from life in the mechanistic metaphors—the cogs and the wheels—which he uses to describe human intercourse. All is mechanical contrivance. Moments of intimacy are transformed into diabolical probings into the hearts of others. London's glowing memory of drinking and sharing intimacies with his sailor friend, Scotty, may be seen by the reader in a slightly more lurid light: "It was memorable. . . . Among other things, I had got into the cogs and springs of men's actions. I had seen Scotty weep about his own worthlessness and the sad case of his Edinburg mother who was a lady. . . . I had got behind men's souls" (*JB*, 60). Is this a true intimacy, or the scientific prying of a Chillingworth into the heart of a Dimmesdale? Is true intimacy possible, or is all intimacy a lurid violation?

London's mechanistic metaphors are often interchangeable with his biological metaphors. This is most clearly evident when he speaks of his body as a "flesh-machine," which "was running smoothly on" (*JB*, 309). London's uncertain status as a member of the "unburied dead" gives rise, in *John Barleycorn* and in his life, to a preoccupation with his physical health. Yet even as his doctor assures him he is in fine physical shape, the Noseless One jeers at him. Emotionally dead, he can think only that the most intolerable thing is the death of his body. At the same time, he is detached even from that body. London engages in interior dialogues with what he calls the "White Logic," which asks: "Is this flesh of yours you? Or is it an extraneous something possessed by you? Your body—what is it? A machine for converting stimuli into reactions. Stimuli and reactions are remembered" (*JB*, 327). The White Logic speaks for the dominant culture, which sees human beings not as sentient organisms but as labor power to be set in motion. The "animating principle . . . is

the view of human beings in machine terms," as Harry Braverman
explains of scientific management:

> The human being is here regarded as a mechanism articulated
> by hinges, ball-and-socket joints, etc. Thus an article in the
> *British Journal of Psychiatry* aptly entitled "Theory of the
> Human Operator in Control Systems" says: ". . . as an element
> in a control system, a man may be regarded as a chain consist-
> ing of the following items: (1) sensory devices . . . (2) a com-
> puting system which responds . . . on the basis of previous
> experience . . . (3) an amplifying system—the motor-nerve
> endings and muscles . . . (4) mechanical linkages . . . whereby
> the muscular work produces externally observable effects."[12]

Only in rare moments was London able to see human beings for
what they could be rather than for what they were reduced to through
capitalist modes of production. One such moment occurs in *John
Barleycorn* when he forgets for the moment about his own body and
writes of a dray horse. He is consciously struggling here for words
in which to express to the "untraveled reader" the "lunatic and
blasphemous . . . realm" into which John Barleycorn has led him.
Implicit in London's explanation is the assumption that he is a traveler from another land, another culture, another tribe, and that he
has even a language of his own, "the language of John Barleycorn's
tribe. It is not the language of your tribe, all of whose members
resolutely shun the roads that lead to death and tread only the roads
that lead to life. For there are roads and roads, and of truth there are
orders and orders. But have patience. At least, through what seems
no more than verbal yammerings, you may, perchance, glimpse faint
far vistas of other lands and tribes" (*JB*, 305). It is characteristic of
London's bourgeois consciousness that he views himself communicating with people who have not shared his experience. In his effort
to explain the difference between the orders of truth, London introduces the dray horse:

> Alcohol tells truth, but its truth is not normal. What is normal
> is healthful. What is healthful tends toward life. Normal truth
> is a different order, and a lesser order, of truth. Take a dray
> horse. Through all the vicissitudes of its life, from first to last . . .
> it must believe that life is good; that the drudgery in harness

is good; that death, no matter how blind-instinctively apprehended, is a dread giant; that life is beneficent and worthwhile;
that, in the end, with fading life, it will not be knocked about
and beaten and urged beyond its sprained and spavined best;
that old age, even, is decent, dignified, and valuable, though
old age means a ribby scarecrow in a hawker's cart, stumbling a
step to every blow, stumbling dizzily on through merciless
servitude and slow disintegration to the end—the end, the
apportionment of its parts (of its subtle flesh, its pink and
springy bone, its juices and ferments, and all the sensateness
that informed it), to the chicken farm, the hide-house, the
glue-rendering works, and the bone-meal fertilizer factory.
To the last stumble of its stumbling end this dray horse must
abide by the mandates of the lesser truth that is the truth of
life and that makes life possible to persist (*JB*, 305–6).

In this passage London eloquently expresses his perceptions of growing old in the traces. His description of the dray horse draws its power
from the tension between two conflicting value systems. On the one
hand is the horse's "blind-instinctively apprehended" belief that life
is good, "that old age, even, is decent, dignified, and valuable." But
this vision is interrupted—in mid-sentence—with a vision of the
social reality of growing old in America. The dray horse will be
forced to work right up to the end, to work beyond its strength, and
to suffer blows for its failing energy. The "slow disintegration" of its
body will, upon death, be replaced by a rational "apportionment of
its parts . . . to the chicken farm, the hide-house, the glue-rendering
works, and the bone-meal fertilizer factory." Still within the frame of
this one remarkable sentence London juxtaposes to this vision of
horseflesh as commodity a humanistic description "of its subtle flesh,
its pink and springy bone, its juices and ferments, and all the sensateness that informed it." The distance between London's humanistic
vision and his vision of the social reality is deeply moving. Likewise,
the distance between the terrifying implications of the dray horse
and the beautiful, precise, supple language in which it is described
arouses deep aesthetic pleasure in the reader.

In such poetic passages as this, London overcomes all the barriers
of language, class, and tribe and communicates intimate knowledge
to his readers. He does so by truly forgetting himself and his disinte-

grating body and expressing his feelings through sympathy with another living creature. Significantly, London chooses a dumb animal,
not a human being, to carry the burden of his sympathy. It was easier
for him to identify with an inarticulate beast than with the humanity
from whom he was estranged. When he wrote about people, too often
he either cast them in his own public image and made them gods, or
he created cardboard foils to his god-like self-characterization. (His
Northland stories are the important exception.) In this portrait of
the dray horse London was able to achieve the sympathy and the
distance necessary for art, just as he did through his canine hero in
The Call of the Wild. The animal world provided London with a way
out of the positivistic, mechanical, biological way of seeing. The
animal world was a repository of humanistic values in a dehumanized
society. If London could not experience his unity with other human
beings, at least he could sense, in a "blind-instinctively apprehended"
way, his place within the natural order.

If the natural order drew London in an unconscious way, he was
consciously committed to a deadly logic that assumed a hierarchy of
values. In his "order of truths," the positivistic vision emanating from
capitalist social relationships is the primary truth. The normal truth,
the humanistic vision that makes toward life, is a "lesser order of
truth." After his description of the dray horse, London comments
that "to man, alone among the animals, has been given the awful
privilege of reason. Man, with his brain, can penetrate the intoxi-
cating show of things and look upon a universe brazen with indifference toward him and his dreams" (*JB*, 307). The "privilege" of
reason raises man high above the other animals, yet all this avails
him is a vision of "a universe brazen with indifference toward him
and his dreams." What makes man distinctively human also makes
life not worth living. Better "that man should accept at face value the
cheats of sense and snares of flesh, and through the fogs of sentiency
pursue the lures and lies of passion." Yet to do this—according to
London's logic—is to back away in another way from what it means
to be human, for it is to deny that reasoning capacity that sets man
apart from the animals.

London is enmeshed in a logic that makes it impossible for him to
be human, a logic rooted in the social and functional divisions of the
class structure. London's dialogues with the White Logic are not only
contests between the primary truth revealed by John Barleycorn and

the lies that allow life to go on, they are also dialogues between Jack London's working-class past and his middle-class identity. Riding across his ranch, London notices an old Italian immigrant who is one of his workmen: "He has toiled like a beast all his days, and lived less comfortably than my horses in their deep-strawed stalls. He is labor-crippled. He shambles as he walks. One shoulder is twisted higher than the other. His hands are gnarled claws, repulsive, horrible. . . . His brain is as stupid as his body is ugly" (*JB*, 317–18). The White Logic joins in and chuckles at the illusions of this human dray horse who "is convinced that the universe was made for him." He has no idea that he is a "cosmic joke":

> "But you, who have opened the books and who share my awful confidence—you know him for what he is, brother to you and the dust, a cosmic joke, a sport of chemistry, a garmented beast that arose out of the ruck of screaming beastliness by virtue and accident of two opposable great toes. He is brother as well to the gorilla and the chimpanzee. . . .
> "Yet he dreams he is immortal," I argue feebly. "It is vastly wonderful for so stupid a clod to bestride the shoulders of time and ride the eternities."
> "Pah!" is the retort. "Would you then shut the books and exchange places with this thing that is only an appetite and a desire, a marionette of the belly and the loins?"
> "To be stupid is to be happy," I contend.
> "Then your ideal of happiness is a jelly-like organism floating in a tideless, tepid, twilight sea, eh?" [*JB*, 318–19]

Just as London once posed to himself the choice of being intimate either with street-corner thugs or with Tennyson's poetry, he again poses a limiting choice: he can either "shut the books" and be a stupid clod, or he can be intellectually aware and mortally unhappy. And even as he argues against the sneering voice of the White Logic, London entertains an opinion of the Italian workman that is just as condescending. The sympathetic identification that London felt with the dray horse is missing in this description of a human being. London cannot help sneering at the ignorance he imputes to this man. It is all right for a dray horse to be unconscious of his true condition, but it is inexcusable for a human being.

London gives us no indication that he has really plumbed the intelligence of the Italian workman; he simply cannot imagine an intellectually alive worker. It was a contradiction in terms. London internalized the logic of his society that attributed bones and muscle to the working class and reason and books to the middle class. He accepted the dominant culture's view of the workman as a subhuman creature. He is a "garmented beast"—a phrase that echoes the language London used to describe the English workingman in his vision of the urban jungle. This man's beastliness is not like the beastliness of the natural order; it is something "monstrous." Nor can London take comfort in the fact that this Italian workman is "brother to [him] and the dust," for all this means is that both are "brothers as well to the gorilla and the chimpanzee." This is not a humanistic brotherhood that affirms life, but a positivistic vision in which they are linked only in a cosmic joke: death. London cannot imagine a fellowship growing out of this common cosmic condition, for so lacking in consciousness is London's workman that he does not even know he is going to die. To London alone has been imparted this primary truth.

The White Logic was based on a hierarchical mode of thought that made certain equivalencies and assumptions. It assumed that man was higher than other animals, that the middle class was higher than the working class, that reason was higher than emotion, that primary truth was higher than the sane and normal secondary truths, that death was higher than life. The White Logic represented London's bourgeois consciousness, in which to be a human being was to be a rational member of the middle class. The forces that divided society into classes divided Jack London's consciousness against itself. Only in moments of unconsciousness was London able to feel himself at one with the universe. The White Logic removed London from this natural communion and substituted a demonic communion with himself. Consciousness of others became exclusive consciousness of self; dialogue with others became dialogue with self. Several times in *John Barleycorn* he refers to himself as an "intimate" of John Barleycorn. Sharing the "awful confidence" of the White Logic (*JB*, 318), London is engaged in a "dreadful intimacy" (*JB*, 308). "You are at any moment what you are thinking at that moment. Your I is both subject and object; it predicates things of itself and is the things predicated. The thinker is the thought, the knower is what is known, the possessor is the thing possessed" (*JB*, 328). London's bourgeois consciousness, like a beautiful Narcissus, was condemned to drown in self-contemplation.

But in other passages London speaks not with the voice of the White Logic, but with the voice of a human being struggling for words in which to communicate his subjective reality to another. He finds an image that does this, and it is an image from his Alaskan landscapes. The White Logic, he writes, is

> the argent messenger of truth beyond truth, the antithesis of life, cruel and bleak as interstellar space, pulseless and frozen as absolute zero, dazzling with the frost of irrefragable logic and unforgettable fact. John Barleycorn will not let the dreamer dream, the liver live. He destroys birth and death, and dissipates to mist the paradox of being, until his victim cries out, as in "The City of Dreadful Night": "Our life's a cheat, our death a black abyss." And the feet of the victim of such dreadful intimacy take hold of the way of death. [JB, 308]

This image of a white and frozen land that obliterates human life and human values evokes the same emotion Melville plays upon in his description of "The Whiteness of the Whale"—terror.

In his bourgeois consciousness, London felt himself to be in a class by himself. He was a member of John Barleycorn's tribe, he spoke John Barleycorn's language, and this was not understood by the "untraveled reader." Yet as we have seen, London does communicate when he allows himself to speak of the visions that well up from his unconscious. In this dream language of images, London reaches out of his isolation, touches the reader, and perhaps evokes a shock of recognition.

SIX

THE CALL OF
THE WILD

During his long sickness Jack London wrote two of his major novels, *The Call of the Wild* and *The Sea-Wolf*. Both books delve into London's past, but the first book loses itself in the "womb of time," while the second resolutely takes the story into the bright light of the present. As James McClintock has suggested, *The Sea-Wolf* affirms the illusions that London had consciously decided to live by.[1] It is a book from his "recovery." *The Call of the Wild*, by contrast, came out of that black abyss into which London had sunk after his experiences in the East End of London. If *The Sea-Wolf* is a justification of the middle-class self that London had decided was his only rational option, *The Call of the Wild* is a lyric not to what is possible or logical but to what the heart desires.

The book is, indeed, mysteriously moving. Through Buck, his dog hero, London was able to release emotions he perhaps did not know he harbored. The act of creation took London by surprise, as this letter to his publisher suggests: "The whole history of this story has been very rapid. On my return from England I sat down to write it into a 4000 word yarn, but it got away from me and I was forced to expand it to its present length."[2] Written just after his vision of the urban jungle and its city savages, this book conveys London's revulsion from modern life as it expressed itself in this escape to the "howling and naked savagery" of a wilderness jungle. At the same time that this was an escape, it was also, paradoxically, a return. Upon completion of *The People of the Abyss*, London had consciously closed the book on his working-class past. That self dwelt in a black and slippery pit to be recalled only in dreams. But in *The Call of the Wild* London was able, through his canine hero, to return to the scenes of his past, and, having got in touch with them, to imagine a different future.

Like *The Sea-Wolf* and many another naturalistic tale, it begins with the abrupt transportation of a sheltered upper-class hero "into the primitive." At Judge Miller's estate in the Santa Clara valley, Buck is the favorite dog. Referring to the judge's buildings and grounds, London writes "over this great demesne Buck ruled" (*CW*, 17). It is his privilege to accompany the judge and his sons and daughters and grandchildren wherever they go, and Buck "stalked imperiously" before the other dogs, "for he was king,—king over all creeping, crawling, flying things of Judge Miller's place, humans included" (*CW*, 18). When gold is discovered in the Klondike, a premium is put on dogs like Buck, who are strong and have warm furry coats. One night when the judge is away, Manuel, an underpaid gardener, steals Buck and sells him to cover his gambling debts. Here begins Buck's education as to his true estate. When a rope is put around his neck, he accepts it with "quiet dignity," still trusting in the wisdom of human masters. But when the end of the rope is handed to a stranger, Buck "growls menacingly," believing that "to intimate was to command" (*CW*, 20). Instead of hearkening to his royal wishes, this stranger tightens the rope around his neck. When Buck springs at the man, the rope tightens and Buck is helpless—and enraged. "Never in all his life had he been so vilely treated, and never in all his life had he been so angry" (*CW*, 21). Buck's anger waxes as, instead of being released, he is put into a cage, tormented through the bars by his keepers, and finally put on an express car. After having changed hands many times, Buck meets the man in the red sweater who is the dog-breaker. Against this man is unleashed the mighty anger that has waxed in the heart of this "kidnapped king." "Straight at the man he launched his one hundred and forty pounds of fury, surcharged with the pent passion of two days and nights." But in mid-air, Buck's hurling body is stopped by the blow of a club. "He had never been struck by a club in his life, and did not understand." Again and again he launches himself against this man, for "his madness knew no caution." But each time "the club broke the charge and smashed him down" (*CW*, 28). The man in the red sweater finishes him off with a blow directly on his nose, and a final "shrewd blow" knocks him unconscious. As an onlooker comments, this man is "no slouch at dog-breakin'." The man later brings Buck water and food, and Buck allows him to touch him and even eats from his hand.

London is clear about the effect of this experience on Buck. "He was beaten (he knew that); but he was not broken. He saw, once for all, that he stood no chance against a man with a club. He had learned the lesson, and in all his after life he never forgot it. That club was a revelation" (*CW*, 30). The lesson is reinforced as Buck watches other dogs being initiated. "Again and again, as he looked at each brutal performance, the lesson was driven home to Buck: a man with a club was a law-giver, a master to be obeyed, though not necessarily conciliated. Of this last Buck was never guilty, though he did see beaten dogs that fawned upon the man, and wagged their tails, and licked his hand. Also he saw one dog, that would neither conciliate nor obey, finally killed in the struggle for mastery" (*CW*, 31). This initiation serves Buck well in the Northland, where he must take on a new psychology—the psychology of a dependent people—if he is to survive. When the "kidnapped king" is put in harness, "his dignity was sorely hurt by thus being made a draught animal, [but] he was too wise to rebel" (*CW*, 42). He has not forgotten his kingly heritage, but he cunningly hides his desire for mastery, "bid[ing] his time with a patience that was nothing less than primitive" (*CW*, 74).

Buck's experiences to this point parallel the experiences that befell Jack London when, walking down the street early one morning in Niagara Falls, he was arrested for vagrancy, summarily tried, and sent by box car to the Erie County Penitentiary. Although London was at that time a tramp and not a pampered pet of the upper classes, like Buck, he was rudely awakened to the realities of his estate. He, along with sixteen other hoboes, was sentenced to thirty days by a judge who, without the aid of witnesses, took fifteen seconds to hear the charge, "Vagrancy, your Honor," leveled against each of the men before he handed out the sentence. London watched and could not believe that the same things would happen to him.

> They are poor dumb cattle, I thought to myself. But wait till
> my turn comes; I'll give his Honor a "spiel." . . . my American
> blood was up. Behind me were the many generations of my
> American ancestry. One of the kinds of liberty those ancestors
> of mine had fought and died for was the right of trial by jury.
> This was my heritage, stained sacred by their blood, and it

devolved upon me to stand up for it. All right, I threatened
to myself; just wait till he gets to me. [*Road*, 78, 79–80]

When his turn comes, London does begin speaking of his rights, but
the judge cuts him off with "thirty days!" When London continues
talking, the judge pauses long enough in his administration of justice
to tell him, "Shut up!" and then continues with the next name on the
list. London's outrage under this treatment grows, and he remembers
another right his fathers had fought for—*habeas corpus*:

I'd show them. But when I asked for a lawyer, I was laughed at.
Habeas corpus was all right, but of what good was it to me
when I could communicate with no one outside the jail? But
I'd show them. They couldn't keep me in jail forever. Just wait
till I got out, that was all. I'd make them sit up. I knew something about the law and my own rights, and I'd expose their
maladministration of justice. Visions of damage suits and sensa-
tional newspaper headlines were dancing before my eyes when
the jailers came in and began hustling us out into the main
office. [*Road*, 81]

As he is handcuffed, shaved, and put in convict stripes, London
counts the indignities to which he, a patriotic American citizen, is
subjected. But like Buck, his rash anger will be replaced by cunning.
He hears stories from the other prisoners, "of personal experiences
with the police of great cities that were awful. And more awful were
the hearsay tales they told me concerning men who had died at the
hands of the police and who therefore could not testify for themselves" (*Road*, 96). London scoffs at these tales—until he sees with
his "own eyes, there in that prison, things unbelievable and monstrous" (*Road*, 97). London gives no hint of the initiatory rites that he
himself suffered. Perhaps he was too cunning an observer of what
happened to others to challenge the law of the club, or perhaps some
experiences are best unrecorded and unremembered. Certainly he
learned an unforgettable lesson from the mulatto, just as Buck did
from the experience of the dog "that would neither conciliate nor
obey," who was "finally killed in the struggle for mastery."

The "revelation" effected on London and his dog hero by the rule
of the club revolutionizes their moral universe. Neither the prisoners

nor the dogs are fed enough to maintain their strength. When Buck steals a chunk of bacon London writes, "This first theft marked Buck as fit to survive in the hostile Northland environment" (*CW*, 53). London subtly satirizes the false consciousness Buck's civilized life had developed: "Civilized, he could have died for a moral considera-tion, say the defence of Judge Miller's riding-whip; but the complete-ness of his decivilization was now evidenced by his ability to flee from the defence of a moral consideration and so save his hide" (*CW*, 54). In the Erie County Penitentiary, London discovered that the long-timers got more food than the short-timers, and while he was a trusty he used to "steal from their grub while serving them" (*Road*, 99). This was only one of the many petty grafts that were practiced there, where the strong preyed upon the weak. London's initiation "into the primitive" tore the scales from his eyes and en-abled him to see clearly the society in which he lived. Adapting to the new, hostile environment meant discarding the myths that hid one's true condition, just as it meant looking sharp and imitating the old-timers, whether that meant, for Buck, learning to burrow into the snow to sleep, or, for London, learning from his "pal" ways to sneak personal possessions past the wardens and guards.

The careers of author and dog, closely parallel at this point, are on divergent trajectories, for while Buck was moving from civilization to savagery, Jack London was moving from savagery to civilization. This difference affects the way the respective heroes handle their latent "desire for mastery." London is frank in his treatment of Buck's kingly pretensions and his determination that some day he will be king again. It was his blood right, and Buck has the imagination and strength to assert his prerogatives. He competes with Spitz for his position and wins leadership of the sled dogs. In the end, he will compete with the wolves and win the right to run at the head of the pack. On the surface this appears to parallel London's determination to make it in the middle-class world. He competed in the market-place and won literary renown and rich royalties. But, in succeeding, London found himself a ruler with no kingdom or subjects, whereas Buck is the recognized leader of a tribal community. A master with no subjects is master of himself alone, making him both master and subject at once. The internalization of the desire for mastery pro-duced, on the one hand, a psyche divided against itself, and on the other, an ideology of racial supremacy. London's embarrassing, half-baked notion of the Aryan masters, the "zone-conquerors" and pioneer race-wanderers, was the product of his search for a respectably bourgeois equivalent of the "call of the wild." This call, to which Buck responds, is the "song of a younger world," a precapitalist world in which the rhythms of life are rooted in the traditions of a folk culture.

The Call of the Wild is the story of an animal who, having been domesticated, was artificially removed from his rightful culture and traditions, and who is, in the story, restored to that heritage. The first step in that process is the initiation, which reveals to him his true state. Then gradually Buck is restored to the older tradition from which he had been cut off. Although Buck hears the call of the wild insistently and responds dramatically at the end of the tale, he begins to hear the notes of this call in the second chapter, after his introduction into the Northland. As he finds himself a member of a group of dogs (some of whom, like himself, have been kidnapped, but others of whom are Alaskan dogs), Buck finds himself awakening to forgotten racial memories:

> In vague ways he remembered back to the youth of the breed, to the time the wild dogs ranged in packs through the primeval forest and killed their meat as they ran it down. It was no task for him to learn to fight with cut and slash and the quick wolf snap. In this manner had fought forgotten ancestors. They quickened the old life within him, and the old tricks which they had stamped into the heredity of the breed were his tricks. They came to him without effort or discovery, as though they had been his always. And when, on the still cold nights, he pointed his nose at a star and howled long and wolflike, it was his ancestors, dead and dust, pointing nose at star and howling down through the centuries and through him. And his cadences were their cadences, the cadences which voiced their woe and what to them was the meaning of the stillness, and the cold, and dark. [*CW*, 56]

As this "ancient song surged through him," Buck "came into his own again" (*CW*, 57). Were London writing about people returning to their roots, as he does in *The Valley of the Moon*, he would romanticize this old life of the "primitive ancestors" and emphasize racial homogeneity as a bonding agent. But his description of Buck's return to his cultural roots does not romanticize that lost world; rather, London underscores the primitive emotions—woe, pain, fear of the dark—which bind this community together and produce the collective expressions of its culture.

> Every night regularly, at nine, at twelve, at three, [the dogs] lifted a nocturnal song, a weird and eerie chant, in which it was Buck's delight to join.
>
> With the aurora borealis flaming coldly overhead, or the stars leaping in the frost dance, and the land numb and frozen under its pall of snow, this song of the huskies might have been the defiance of life, only it was pitched in minor key, with long-drawn wailings and half-sobs, and was more the pleading of life, the articulate travail of existence. It was an old song, old as the breed itself—one of the first songs of the younger world in a day when songs were sad. It was invested with the woe of unnumbered generations, this plaint by which Buck was so strangely stirred. When he moaned and sobbed, it was with the pain of living that was of old the pain of his wild fathers, and the fear and mystery of the cold and dark that was to them fear and mystery. [*CW*, 78–79]

This younger world to which Buck hearkens recognizes the "fear and mystery" of life; the explicit acknowledgment of the irrational, of powers that lurk in the dark, forms the basis of the community. By contrast, the bourgeois consciousness was for London associated with the assertion of reason and the separation of man from the animal world of primitive fears. Because the irrational forces were not explicitly acknowledged, the expressions of that culture lacked the basis of a collective experience, and instead it formulated ideologies that promised a collective identity but in fact could not deliver the ecstasy that carried Buck out of himself and "into his own again."

In *A Daughter of the Snows*, London's first novel and a resounding failure, he attempted the same plot as *The Call of the Wild*: the decivilization of the hero in the Northland. But because his protagonist is Frona Welse, a woman and not a dog, the "call" she hears is a confused babble of Norse mythology and racist, imperialist ideology. The following exchange occurs between Frona and her suitor, Vance

Corliss, as they witness the funeral cortège of one of the Northland pioneers:

> "A zone-conquerer," Frona broke voice.
> Corliss found his thought following hers and answered,
> "These battlers of frost and fighters of hunger! I can understand
> how the dominant races have come down out of the north to
> empire. Strong to venture, strong to endure, with infinite faith
> and infinite patience, is it to be wondered at?" [pp. 146–47]

At this point Frona is too choked with emotion to respond, but instead of acting like a human being she begins to chant a saga and to sway "like a furred Valkyrie" above what she imagines to be the final carnage of men and gods. That her extraordinary response is out of proportion to the stimulus provided by the plot is not the most ludicrous element of this scene. We are asked to believe that Frona is responding to the call of the race life, and yet, unlike Buck, who moans and sobs with the cadence of his ancestors, whose cadences are his cadences, Frona does not even know the language she is speaking. She is in an ecstasy of sorts, but she is speaking in tongues rather than hearing the songs of her ancestors. (She is Welsh and Irish; the saga she chants is about Yggdrasil and Jötien Luck, Surt, Hrym, and the ship Najhfar.) Cut off from her traditions, her past, her culture, she cannot find that organic link that sends the song coursing through Buck. Buck is part of a collective life and ongoing tradition: "He linked the past with the present, and the eternity behind him throbbed through him in a mighty rhythm to which he swayed as the tides and seasons swayed" (*CW*, 154). Frona Welse is not a member of a tribe and thus has no culture worth the name. She hears only a babel of tongues.

The heritage on which London prides himself and which is outraged in the Erie County Penitentiary is not a transcendent racial mythology like Frona Welse's. It is simply the indigenous experience of his "American ancestors." He speaks repeatedly of his "American blood" and his "patriotic American citizenship" (*Road*, 80, 77), of the rights his ancestors fought and died for. He is invoking the indigenous American tradition of "equal rights," which was, according to Allan Dawley, a live tradition among the shoemakers of Lynn, Massachusetts, until shortly before the time Jack London writes about.[3]

The shoemakers' consciousness of a noble heritage gave them a collective energy and common words in which to oppose the indignities that industrial capitalism was visiting upon their craft and their lives. London has a glimmer of this consciousness, but it seems to burn itself out as his anger is replaced by fear. Unlike Buck, who never licks the hand of his master—except Thornton, whom he loves—and who never forgets his mutinous intentions and his real identity, Jack London was confused and removed from his American heritage; he conciliated masters in a half-aware way, and, not knowing whom he could trust, trusted no one. Fear, the cement of the primitive community to which Buck is recalled, keeps London from finding that community.

Buck's restoration to his rightful kingdom proceeds in four stages, which are characterized by the contrasting masters under whom he works. Perrault and François, the government couriers under whom Buck first works, are just and efficient masters. The taciturn Perrault, chosen for his job because "nothing daunted him," labors grimly from dawn to dark, his consciousness focused only on the job of delivering the despatches as speedily as possible. His garrulous companion, François, is endowed with a bit more imagination and humor than Perrault, but he is just as concentrated on the job at hand. Both are expert managers of their dogs, upon whose energy and cooperation depends the task of delivering the mail. François's impartial administration of justice keeps peace among the huskies and wins Buck's respect. Although Buck accepts the rule of François and Perrault, he challenges the authority of Spitz, whose role as lead dog is analogous to that of a foreman on a line. Spitz keeps discipline among the dogs. The order and efficiency of the team is disrupted by Buck's challenge to his authority, which sends a mutinous ripple throughout the ranks. François understands that the competition between the dogs will eventually end in a fight to the death, but he does not see all the petty insubordinations with which Buck cunningly lays down his challenge to Spitz. Buck, the onetime pet of the upper class, is now like a blond beast, riding high within a system in which the strong eat the weak. After Buck has fought Spitz to the death, the other dogs, who have been hungrily waiting, close in to feast on the victim. "Buck stood and looked on, the successful champion, the dominant primordial beast who had made his kill and found it good" (CW, 89).

Buck's desire for mastery is now spent upon his fellow dogs. In a later stage of his restoration he will question the authority of his human masters, but even in this first stage Buck's consciousness is more developed than that of most of his teammates. This may be seen in the contrast between Buck and two of the most experienced and knowledgeable dogs, Dave and Sol-leks. The joy of work is strong in all of the sled dogs, but in Dave and Sol-leks, it is a passionate pride. Apathetic under most circumstances, they are reborn when put in the traces. When the team hits the trail for Dyea, Buck's attitude is contrasted with theirs:

> Buck was glad to be gone, and though the work was hard he found he did not particularly despise it. He was surprised at the eagerness which animated the whole team and which was communicated to him; but still more surprising was the change wrought in Dave and Sol-leks. They were new dogs, utterly transformed by the harness. All passiveness and unconcern had dropped from them. They were alert and active, anxious that the work should go well, and fiercely irritable with whatever, by delay or confusion, retarded that work. The toil of the traces seemed the supreme expression of their being, and all that they lived for and the only thing in which they took delight. [*CW*, 49]

The petty fights that break out among the other dogs do not interest Dave and Sol-leks. Nor do they seek advancement through the ranks. After Buck has killed Spitz, François harnesses Sol-leks, whom he judges to be "the best lead-dog left," in the coveted position. When Buck asserts his prerogatives and springs upon Sol-leks, the old dog is only too eager to give over the position to Buck, of whom he is afraid (*CW*, 94). Although the endurance and pride of dogs like Dave and Sol-leks are admirable, they do not have the imagination of Buck, who is able to see beyond the toil of the traces to a larger game. Dave and Sol-leks are, for all their pride, destined to be work-beasts.

The importance of Buck's larger vision becomes evident in the next interlude; François and Perrault depart, and a "Scotch halfbreed" takes charge of the team, which becomes part of a large mail train en route to Dawson. The drivers are considerate of their dogs and do what they can for them, but conditions are against men and dogs. The dogs are exhausted from their earlier runs and should have

had a week's rest before starting out again. The mail is heavy, and
daily snowfalls increase the friction on the runners. The dogs' pride
in their work remains, but competing for attention in London's descriptions are details that suggest the industrial routine in which they
labor: "Buck did not like it, but he bore up well to the work, taking
pride in it after the manner of Dave and Sol-leks, and seeing that his
mates, whether they prided in it or not, did their fair share. It was a
monotonous life, operating with machine-like regularity. One day
was very like another" (*CW*, 100–101). Buck challenges three other
dogs and wins leadership of the team, but this fact goes almost un-
noticed, so lacking in drama is it after the elaborately prepared-for
battle with Spitz. The glamour of being a "blond beast" is subtly
undermined by a vision of the limits of this route to mastery. The
chapter ends, significantly, with the death of Dave. He dies as he has
lived, in the traces, and in his passing there is an ambiguous message.
Under the increasing hardship of the trail Dave develops an internal
illness that makes pulling in the traces extremely painful for him.
Nevertheless, he refuses to be replaced:

> He pleaded with his eyes to remain there. The driver was
> perplexed. His comrades talked of how a dog could break its
> heart through being denied the work that killed it, and recalled
> instances they had known, where dogs, too old for the toil,
> or injured, had died because they were cut out of the traces.
> Also, they held it a mercy, since Dave was to die anyway, that he
> should die in the traces, heart-easy and content. So he was
> harnessed in again, and proudly he pulled as of old, though
> more than once he cried out involuntarily from the bite of
> his inward hurt. [*CW*, 108–9]

This passage may be compared to London's description of the dray
horse in *John Barleycorn*. Both the dray horse and Dave die on the
job, but the dray horse is pushed beyond his energy (even though he
is not aware of this) while Dave insists, out of pride, on working up
to the end. Dave's death is also dignified by the understanding of the
men, who permit him to die "heart-easy and content." And neither
are his remains sent off to the chicken farm and fertilizer plant. The
consciousness that informs this passage is unequivocally humanistic,
and yet the reader understands that the cause of Dave's death is the

exhausting pace he and the other dogs have been forced into. As in "The White Silence," there is a tenuous balance here between the humanistic forces that make for life and a competing set of forces that look with "brazen indifference" on life's best efforts. The final scene of the chapter is quite close in setting and mood to that of "The White Silence." When morning comes, Dave is too weak to drag himself into the traces. The men and dogs leave without him and "hear him mournfully howling till they passed out of sight behind a belt of river timber." At this point the train halts. "The Scotch half-breed slowly retraced his steps to the camp they had left. The men ceased talking. A revolver-shot rang out. The man came back hurriedly. The whips snapped, the bells tinkled merrily, the sleds churned along the trail; but Buck knew, and every dog knew, what had taken place behind the belt of river trees" (*CW*, 110). Here ends the chapter, with no further reflection from either dog or author. If Dave's death is viewed in a humanistic rather than positivistic light, it is also true that the emphasis is more on mortality than immortality, and what Buck achieves in his apotheosis is immortality.

Buck's third set of masters may be dispensed with quickly. The dogs are not allowed to recover their now seriously flagging energies before they are sold to three incompetents from the States, who are, interestingly, "a nice family party"—a husband and wife and the wife's younger brother—rather than a work team. They quarrel, they overload the sled, they get late starts every morning, and worse, they miscalculate the amount of food they must carry for the dogs. The dogs begin to die, one by one, and the remaining team and drivers are finally swallowed up when the men insist on crossing the ice during the spring thaw. Buck is saved from this end by his refusal to obey the command to cross the ice. He does not trust these masters, and, oppressed by a sense of impending calamity, he lies down in the traces and refuses to budge, even though he is whipped repeatedly. He was prepared to die in this mutiny, but a man watching the beating forcefully intervenes. This man is John Thornton, destined to become Buck's last and most beloved master.

Up to this point, Buck's situation has worsened with each change of masters. The limits that are placed on dogs by their dependency on human masters have been starkly dramatized in the last episode, in which the masters are not competent enough to look out for even their own best interests. It is at this point, when Buck might most logically have made a run for freedom and independence, that London introduces him to a master who is qualitatively different. The bonds that tied Perrault and François to Buck were bonds of duty and work and were lightly snapped. The bonds that tie Buck and John Thornton are bonds of love and can be broken, if at all, only by death. The chapter entitled "For the Love of a Man" treads a fine line between sentimentality and deep emotion; the balance comes down on the side of deep emotion, and one doubts that London could have achieved this were he writing about a father and his child rather than a man and his dog. "This man had saved his life, which was something; but, further, he was the ideal master. Other men saw to the welfare of their dogs from a sense of duty and business expediency; he saw to the welfare of his *as if they were his own children, because he could not help it*" (*CW*, 149; my emphasis). As Thornton saved Buck's life, Buck will later have the opportunity to save Thornton's life. The covenant thus forged between man and dog cannot be measured in ordinary terms, nor is Buck's trust of Thornton a calculated thing. When Thornton, in a moment of thoughtless whim, commands Buck to jump over a cliff, Buck responds instantly and unthinkingly, for he had already demonstrated that he would give his life for Thornton if he requested it. (Only Thornton's last-minute scramble to grab Buck at the edge of the cliff prevents his jumping.) Besides these heroic demonstrations of their bonding, Thornton and Buck have a language in which they communicate their affection from day to day. "Buck had a trick of love expression that was akin to hurt. He would often seize Thornton's hand in his mouth and close so fiercely that the flesh bore the impress of his teeth for some time afterward. And as Buck understood [John Thornton's] oaths to be love words, so the man understood this feigned bite for a caress" (*CW*, 150).

The emotional peak of their relationship occurs when Thornton—again rather thoughtlessly—asserts in front of others that Buck can break out a sled loaded with one thousand pounds of goods. Bets are placed. Buck is harnessed to a sled loaded with one thousand pounds of flour. Thornton does not know whether or not Buck can perform this extraordinary feat, but he grabs the dog's head and shakes it back and forth as was his affectionate habit and whispers to the dog, "As you love me, Buck. As you love me" (*CW*, 170). Buck does it for love.

Thornton fell on his knees beside Buck. Head was against head, and he was shaking him back and forth. Those who hurried up heard him cursing Buck, and he cursed him long and fervently, and softly and lovingly.

"Gad, sir! Gad, sir!" spluttered the Skookum Bench king. "I'll give you a thousand for him, sir, a thousand, sir—twelve hundred, sir."

Thornton rose to his feet. His eyes were wet. The tears were streaming frankly down his cheeks. "Sir," he said to the Skookum Bench king, "no, sir. You can go to hell, sir. It's the best I can do for you, sir."

Buck seized Thornton's hand in his teeth. Thornton shook him back and forth. As though animated by a common impulse, the onlookers drew back to a respectful distance; nor were they again indiscreet enough to interrupt. [*CW*, 172–73]

Buck has worked harder than he ever has before, and is, in his blind love of John Thornton, more dependent than he has ever been before. Yet this love dependency, this total giving up of self to another and total entrusting of his life to another is necessary before Buck can strike out on his own and be restored to the culture and traditions from which he has been separated. *The Call of the Wild* is set apart from all of London's other quest stories by the emotional satisfaction granted the hero (and the reader). This quest is different from the others, too, in that the hero seeks not a nurturant mother, who inevitably reveals her rapacious designs, but a father, who remains to the end the good father, who cares for his dogs "as if they were his own children, because he could not help it."

Having truly been a child, Buck is now prepared to grow up. More and more insistently he hears a call from the forest: "It filled him with a great unrest and strange desires. It caused him to feel a vague, sweet gladness, and he was aware of wild yearnings and stirrings for he knew not what. Sometimes he pursued the call into the forest, looking for it as though it were a tangible thing, barking softly or defiantly, as the mood might dictate" (*CW*, 183). Buck listens to "the subdued and sleepy murmurs of the forest, reading signs and sounds as man may read a book, and seeking for the mysterious something that called—called, waking or sleeping, at all times, for him to come" (*CW*, 185). One night he is awakened from his sleep by a call "distinct and definite as never before,—a long-drawn howl, like, yet unlike, any noise made by husky dog." Buck sets off in pursuit of this call, which he recognizes "in the old familiar way," and in an open place in the trees he sees, "with nose pointed to the sky, a long, lean, timber wolf." Buck approaches him cautiously, mingling threats and friendly overtures in his movements. The timber wolf flees, but Buck continues his friendly advances and the timber wolf, "finding that no harm was intended, finally sniffed noses with him" (*CW*, 187). They frolic together and then the timber wolf sets off purposefully.

> He made it clear to Buck that he was to come, and they ran side by side through the sombre twilight, straight up the creek bed, into the gorge from which it issued, and across the bleak divide where it took its rise.
>
> On the opposite slope of the watershed they came down into a level country where were great stretches of forest and many streams, and through these great stretches they ran steadily, hour after hour, the sun rising higher and the day growing warmer. Buck was wildly glad. He knew he was at last answering the call, running by the side of his wood brother toward the place from where the call surely came. [*CW*, 187–88]

Before they reach the place from where the call came, Buck remembers John Thornton and turns back to the camp, in spite of the whining entreaties of his "wood brother." When he regains the camp, he jumps wildly on John Thornton, and for two days and two nights, he "never let Thornton out of his sight" (*CW*, 189). But the call "began to sound more imperiously than ever," and Buck is "haunted by recollections of the wild brother." He begins to wander in the woods, "but the wild brother came no more." He begins to stay away from camp for longer and longer periods, "seeking vainly for fresh sign of the wild brother, killing his meat as he traveled" (*CW*, 190). Buck's hunting exploits are an important part of this interlude. "The blood-longing became stronger than ever before. He was a killer, a thing that preyed, living on the things that lived, unaided, alone, by virtue of his own strength and prowess, surviving triumphantly in a hostile environment where only the strong survived" (*CW*, 191).

Through these exploits he develops "a great pride in himself which communicated itself like a contagion to his physical being" (*CW*, 191). Just before his apotheosis, Buck is pictured in the prime of his life: "His muscles were surcharged with vitality, and snapped into play sharply, like steel springs. Life streamed through him in splendid flood, glad and rampant, until it seemed that it would burst him asunder in sheer ecstasy and pour forth generously over the world" (*CW*, 193). In his desire for larger and larger prey, Buck runs down a great moose, having patiently trailed him for four days. After feasting on the moose, he turns back toward the camp, but as he goes, he is "oppressed with a sense of calamity" (*CW*, 200). When he reaches the camp, he finds it has been raided by the Yeehat Indians, who have left their victims riddled with arrows. Buck madly avenges himself on the Yeehats, and then returns to look for John Thornton. He follows his scent "down to the edge of a deep pool," which "effectually hid what it contained, and it contained John Thornton" (*CW*, 204). Buck broods by the side of the pool, feeling "a void which ached and ached, and which food could not fill." He also feels pride when he remembers that in avenging himself on the Yeehats, he has killed the noblest game of all—man. Most importantly, the death of John Thornton has freed Buck to follow the call from the place whence it came. "The last tie was broken. Man and the claims of man no longer bound him" (*CW*, 206).

Buck hears the call, "sounding more luringly and compelling than ever before." He meets the wolf pack in the clearing, and "they were awed, so still and large he stood" (*CW*, 207). Buck swiftly breaks the neck of the first wolf to challenge him and bloodies the three others who "tried it in sharp succession" (*CW*, 207). The whole pack joins in the challenge, and Buck holds them off for half an hour, when they fall back exhausted. At this point one wolf separates himself from the pack and approaches Buck, whining softly. Buck recognizes "the wild brother with whom he had run for a night and a day." They touch noses, and then an old wolf, patriarch of the tribe, comes over, also sniffs noses with Buck, and then points his nose at the sky and breaks into "the long wolf howl" (*CW*, 208). The tribal song is taken up by the whole pack, and Buck joins in. "Then, acting as one body, the pack sprang away into the woods. And Buck ran with them, side by side with the wild brother, yelping as he ran" (*CW*, 209).

Buck has been initiated into the tribe and restored to his rightful kingdom. No more does he submit himself to the rule of man.

Whereas once he pursued his desire for mastery within an industrial order prescribed by human masters, he now runs by the side of his wood brother. His consciousness has undergone several revolutions: from his initial kingly pretensions, which hid from himself his actual dependency on Judge Miller's largesse, Buck came to realize his true position; his education proceeded dialectically as he first asserted his leadership over the dog pack and then totally submitted to John Thornton out of love. In his final apotheosis, Buck achieves the reconciliation of his desire for mastery and the desires aroused by the old call from the forest. His desire to be king is wedded to the radical egalitarianism implied by his relationship with his wood brother. In the last sentence of the tale, Buck leaps into our memories, serene and triumphant. "When the long winter nights come on and the wolves follow their meat into the lower valleys, he may be seen running at the head of the pack through the pale moonlight or glimmering borealis, leaping gigantic above his fellows, his great throat a-bellow as he sings a song of the younger world, which is the song of the pack" (*CW*, 210–11). Buck's integration of himself is achieved by going back in time to a "younger world." The kidnapped king has been restored to his tribal community.

Like Cooper's hero, Leatherstocking, Buck moves from age to golden youth. His discovery of his wood brother, like the Deerslayer's pact with Chingachgook, puts him in touch with a natural community, and through this bond, he is immortalized. The body will die, but the consciousness that has been rooted in a community will live with that community and its traditions. In *The Call of the Wild* London resolves the terrible choice between self-advancement and solidarity in such a way that neither must be sacrificed. Buck is the canine equivalent of a street-gang leader, and *The Call of the Wild* is a mythic affirmation of the author's working-class origins, of a solidarity that is strength. But in order to make this affirmation, the story must be taken back into the "womb of time," into a tribal, precapitalistic world. The lyric intensity and beauty of this work arise from the deep satisfaction that author and reader experience at having the contradictions of our society mythically resolved.

If Buck is at peace with himself, he remains at war with the human society he once counted himself privileged to be part of. The Yeehats tell of a Ghost Dog who cunningly robs their traps and defies their bravest hunters. "Hunters there are who fail to return to the camp, and hunters there have been whom their tribesmen found with throats slashed cruelly open and with wolf prints about them in the snow greater than the prints of any wolf" (*CW*, 209–10). Buck has not forgotten John Thornton. Like Melville's Indian-hater, he is destined for the rest of his days to demand ritual atonement for the death of the beloved father. And each spring he returns to the place where "the smiling timber land" gives way to "an open space among the trees. Here a yellow stream flows from rotted moose-hide sacks and sinks into the ground, with long grasses growing through it and vegetable mould overrunning it and hiding its yellow from the sun; and here he muses for a time, howling once, long and mournfully, ere he departs" (*CW*, 210).

THE SEA-WOLF,
OR, "THE TRIUMPH OF
THE SPIRIT"

If *The Call of the Wild* is about remembering, *The Sea-Wolf* is about forgetting. London turned from a mythic story of self-integration to a Victorian farce of sentiment and repression. John Thornton, the good father of *The Call of the Wild*, is replaced by the bad father of *The Sea-Wolf*, Wolf Larsen. The most striking of the obvious differences between the two books is that of the consciousnesses that separately inform them. *The Sea-Wolf* purports to be the narrative of a literary critic and author of a recent article on Edgar Allan Poe, one Humphrey Van Weyden. The savagery of the wild is replaced by the quintessence of civilization. But not quite. Van Weyden's consciousness and the bourgeois idealism that characterize it do not dominate the book. Rather, London pits it against the competing consciousness of Wolf Larsen, self-made man and seer of the industrial system in which he has made himself a tyrannical king. Wolf Larsen sees that terrible vision Jack London had seen when he imprudently snatched the veils away and looked upon Truth naked; his materialistic philosophy reflects his vision of life within capitalist society, typified in the novel by the tyrannical organization of work aboard the sealing ship of which he is captain. It is the business of the novel to repress that vision, just as London had resolved to forget what he had seen when Truth stood unveiled before him.

The problems London had in forgetting are embodied in the structural problems of the novel, for the familiar plot he sets out with suggests just the opposite of this movement: an upper-class hero is kidnapped, introduced into a rugged, hostile environment, and made to learn a new code in which the exigencies of survival replace middle-class morality. This plot, if it works as it does in *The Call of the Wild*, implies the triumph of the primitive and the resurgence of old memories. But in *The Sea-Wolf*, Humphrey Van Weyden survives and Wolf Larsen dies. Instead of the triumph of the primitive, we have, as Richard Watson Gilder wanted to entitle the story, "The Triumph of the Spirit." For "Spirit," one could substitute "Illusion," for *The Sea-Wolf* is very like an extended conversation with London's White Logic, in which the secondary truths that make for life—the "lies"—are deliberately and unhappily married to a plot that tends in the other direction.[1] *The Sea-Wolf* may be thought of as a struggle between London's "sick" consciousness (Wolf Larsen and his primary truths) and his "well" consciousness (Humphrey Van Weyden and his secondary truths). The terrifying mode of Wolf Larsen's death suggests the costs of London's "cure."

The novel opens with an allusion to Nietzsche and Schopenhauer, whom Van Weyden's gentleman friend, Charley Furuseth, reads "to rest his brain." This allusion suggests that the context for this tale is London's "long sickness," which indeed Wolf Larsen will reenact with startling psychosomatic symptoms. When the ferry Van Weyden is taking to Charley Furuseth's summer place collides and sinks, Van Weyden is rescued by the sealing ship captained by Wolf Larsen. Short-handed because of the death of his first mate, Larsen inducts Van Weyden into his service as cabin boy and promotes a crew member, Johansen, to first mate. Like Buck, Van Weyden has been pampered and sheltered by his middle-class life. Aboard the *Ghost* he is awakened to the realities of life within industrial society. But in its consciousness this book is more like *The People of the Abyss* than *The Call of the Wild*. Whereas Buck is initiated into the realities of *his* estate, Van Weyden is initiated into the realities of life for the working class, of which he is not *really* a part; he witnesses the degradation of men aboard the *Ghost*, but he is always removed from that condition, even as he describes his adaptation to it. He is pretending to be a sailor, just as Jack London pretended to be "Sailor Jack" when he descended into the slums of East London.

The way in which Van Weyden's consciousness is withdrawn from that of the other crew members may be illustrated by some incidents that rather directly parallel London's experiences in the East End of London, as told in *The People of the Abyss*. In the first place, Van

Weyden's experiences begin with an immersion in the sea, through which he is transformed into a member of the industrial working class. It will be recalled that London described his descent into the English slums in nautical metaphors: the people of the East End were a "sea" into which he slipped and from which he escaped to his "port of refuge." Significantly, the first crew member with whom Van Weyden has intimate dealings is Thomas Mugridge, a cockney.[2] Van Weyden is given some of Mugridge's clothes to wear while his dry out, and his tender skin "creep[s] and crawl[s] from the harsh contact" with the "rough woolen undershirt." But London goes beyond Van Weyden's physical revulsion from the cockney's clothes—so like his own experience in *The People of the Abyss*—to describe Van Weyden's revulsion from the cockney himself: "I had taken a dislike to him at first, and as he helped to dress me this dislike increased. There was something repulsive about his touch. I shrank from his hand; my flesh revolted" (*SW*, 18). Mugridge is dirty and unpromising in appearance, but Van Weyden's repulsion is largely a reaction to Mugridge's unconscious posture of "hereditary servility" (*SW*, 18). Endowed with the unctuousness of Uriah Heep, he fawns and smirks and looks after Van Weyden's needs with a solicitousness that "comes only of generations of tip-seeking ancestors" (*SW*, 16). When Van Weyden tells him he will not forget the kindness of his clothes, "a soft light suffused his face, and his eyes glistened as though somewhere in the deeps of his being his ancestors had quickened and stirred with dim memories of tips received in former lives" (*SW*, 19). This reads like a parody of the ancestral memories that quickened Buck in *The Call of the Wild*, and it is characteristic of the transformation in London's stance as he turns from the world of animals to the world of men caught in a class structure. Just as in *The People of the Abyss*, a change of clothes effects an immediate change in status. No longer does Mugridge fawn and smirk and say "sir" to him, but neither does he treat him as an equal. "Servile and fawning as he had been before, he was now as domineering and bellicose. In truth, I was no longer the fine gentleman with a skin soft as a 'lydy's' but only an ordinary and very worthless cabin boy" (*SW*, 33–34). Now Van Weyden is subject to the petty tyrannies that Mugridge, as cook, inflicts on his new cabin boy.

Van Weyden's sheltered middle-class life has fostered a belief in certain ideals that, though they may seem to describe his condition,

do not reflect the reality of life for the working class. These ideals—
his belief in the soul, immortality, humanity, love—are exposed as
illusions in the brutal society of Wolf Larsen's sealing ship. Van
Weyden's first shock is the degrading death and burial at sea of
Larsen's first mate. The mate's character is unknown to Van Weyden
and to the reader; all we are told of his life are the "sordid" details of
his death, brought on by a drunken debauch on shore: the stiffening
of his legs, the rolling of his head from side to side, the relaxation of
his muscles, and the dropping of the jaw, which exposes "two rows
of tobacco-discolored teeth" (*SW*, 21). These physical details are
meant to sum up the meaning of the man's existence: he is nothing
but a heap of disintegrating flesh. Wolf Larsen's attitude underscores
this grim naturalistic judgment; he curses wrathfully when the mate
dies, just as a team driver in the Klondike might curse at the death of
one of his dogs. The mate's death is meaningful to Larsen only as a
loss of labor power. His valuation of human life is evident in the
funeral service he provides.

> "I only remember one part of the service," he said, "and
> that is, 'And the body shall be cast into the sea.' So cast it in."
> He ceased speaking. The men holding the hatch cover
> seemed perplexed, puzzled no doubt by the briefness of the
> ceremony. He burst upon them in a fury.
> "Lift up that end there, damn you! What the hell's the matter
> with you?"
> They elevated the end of the hatch cover with pitiful haste,
> and like a dog flung overside, the dead man slid feet first into
> the sea. [*SW*, 32][3]

Shorn of all but a mocking remnant of tradition, this death is indeed
less dignified than that of a dog like Dave, who was appreciated and
respected by his masters and given consideration far beyond that afforded this dead man. Van Weyden is "inexpressibly shocked" by this
performance, but he is possibly more shocked by Larsen's oaths—
"vile language of any sort had always been repellent to me," he
informs us—than he is by Larsen's lack of humanity. He is also dis-
turbed by the "sordid" and physical nature of this death, for to him
death "had been peaceful in its occurrence, sacred in its ceremonial"
(*SW*, 22). While Van Weyden protests this treatment to the reader,
his protests are fastidious rather than humanistic. The reader is asked

to choose between Van Weyden's Victorian prudery and Larsen's savagery. Like London himself, we are made to choose between the companionship of Tennyson's poetry or the brutalities of a street gang. What is missing is the humanistic vision that informs London's description of the death of the dray horse and makes *The Call of the Wild* a powerful myth of self-integration. What he achieved by journeying into the "womb of time" was not possible in a novel that dealt with the capitalist society of the present. *The Sea-Wolf* is about master-slave relations in an industrial workplace and about the fragmentation of consciousness that class divisions foster.

Humphrey Van Weyden's education on board the *Ghost* takes place within the confines of these limited choices, so that while it parallels Buck's experiences in the wild, it does so only up to a point. *The Sea-Wolf* is firmly within the realm of "reason." The reality into which Van Weyden is initiated is a creation of Wolf Larsen, whose view of man is a direct reflection of the value placed upon workers in capitalist society. " 'Life is a mess,' " he believes. " 'It is like yeast, a ferment, a thing that moves and may move for a minute, an hour, a year, or a hundred years, but that in the end will cease to move. The big eat the little that they may continue to move, the strong eat the weak that they may retain their strength. The lucky eat the most and move the longest, that is all' " (*SW*, 45). The industrial organization aboard the *Ghost* validates Larsen's "piggish" world of social Darwinism and laissez-faire capitalism. The chain of command gives the captain power over his crew, just as it gives the cook, Mugridge, power over the cabin boy, Van Weyden. The abuses of that power are the subject of the first half of *The Sea-Wolf*.

One of the most dramatic of these incidents occurs when Harrison, a green hand, is sent up the rigging, eighty feet above the deck, to make an adjustment that could more easily and safely have been made by lowering the foresail. The danger of this operation is increased by the uncertain breeze, which causes the halyards to alternately slack and jerk taut. Harrison is afraid, but he is forced to climb up and cling to the rigging as the sails are whipped by the wind. When one of the crew members protests the gratuitous nature of this dangerous command, Larsen responds, " 'The man's mine, and I'll make soup of him and eat it if I want to' " (*SW*, 55). Humphrey Van Weyden is appalled by the "callousness of these men, to whom industrial organization gave control of the lives of other men. . . .

I, who had lived out of the whirl of the world, had never dreamed that its work was carried on in such fashion. Life had always seemed a peculiarly sacred thing, but here it counted for nothing, was a cipher in the arithmetic of commerce" (*SW*, 55). When Van Weyden challenges Larsen's "piggish" view of a Darwinian world in which the big eat the smaller and suggests that that does not give him carte blanche with other people's lives, Larsen responds:

> "Why should I be parsimonious with this life which is cheap and without value? There are more sailors than there are ships on the sea for them, more workers than there are factories or machines for them. Why, you who live on the land know that you house your poor people in the slums of cities and loose famine and pestilence upon them and that there still remain more poor people, dying for want of a crust of bread and a bit of meat—which is life destroyed—than you know what to do with. Have you ever seen the London dockers fighting like wild beasts for a chance to work?" [*SW*, 59]

Larsen's perception of the cheapness of life derives directly from London's vision of the Social Pit. Larsen is what London might have become had he not resolved to climb out of the Pit: a beast of prey, a wolf, "a man of whom to be always afraid" (*SW*, 69), because he was determined, in a world in which the strong ate the weak, to be one of the strong. He is like one of the "garmented bipeds" that London saw along the English docks in his "Vision of the Night"—an ape-like man who would not hesitate to rend and tear the limbs of human prey. Within the proletariat, the only road to mastery was the degradation of the "city savages." Wolf Larsen's character illustrates the logic of industrial capitalism taken to its extreme.

The character of Wolf Larsen is strangely appealing to Humphrey Van Weyden, and to understand their relationship is perhaps to comprehend the mysteries of this troublesome and self-contradictory novel. Larsen's character may be analyzed in three parts: his philosophy, already outlined; his magnetic physical presence; his authority and power. Humphrey Van Weyden is alternately attracted and repelled by all of these characteristics. To begin with the last first, Van Weyden seems to tolerate the master-slave relationship that links him to Larsen—in a way that he does not tolerate that relationship with Mugridge, his immediate superior. Whereas Van

Weyden chafes under Mugridge's petty flourishes of power in the ship's galley and successfully challenges him in a showdown, he shows no such inclination to challenge Larsen's authority. Larsen's extraordinary physical strength seems to rule out the possibility of a successful challenge, but Van Weyden does not even register indignation over his treatment. He simply records it, as he does at the beginning of chapter 10. Larsen, having discovered in Van Weyden an intellectual peer capable of discussing philosophy and poetry—as the rest of his crew cannot—regularly commands his presence when he feels like talking about books. Van Weyden writes, "My intimacy with Wolf Larsen increases, if by intimacy may be denoted those relations which exist between master and man, or better yet, between king and jester. I am to him no more than a toy, and he values me no more than a child values a toy" (SW, 78). This is simply a fact; Van Weyden registers no emotion, no outrage at this affront to his manhood, his reduction to a fool and jester.

That other reactions to Larsen's tyranny are possible is illustrated by the mutiny of Johnson. Possessed of a "straightforwardness and manliness" and a quiet bearing that suggest not timidity but the "courage of his convictions, the certainty of his manhood" (SW, 51), Johnson is from the beginning set up to be the sacrificial lamb, as the mulatto was in the Erie County Penitentiary. Larsen needles him by calling him "Yonson," and each time he mispronounces his name, Johnson quietly and firmly corrects his captain. When Johnson grumbles about the quality of the oilskins provided the men, Larsen takes this opportunity to provoke the inevitable confrontation. He calls Johnson to his cabin. With him are Van Weyden and Johansen, the first mate, who, like Larsen, has a grudge to settle with Johnson. Larsen insults him by calling him "Yonson" and implies that as an immigrant he has an imperfect grasp of the English language. Johnson stands up to these insults squarely, and when Larsen asks him if he knows why he has sent for him, Johnson replies, in his slow and ponderous way, "'I know you have it in for me. . . . You do not like me. You—you—. . . . You do not like me because I am too much of a man, that is why, sir'" (SW, 92). This is indeed Johnson's crime. He is "too much of a man for ship discipline," and his punishment is a brutal beating administered by both Larsen and Johansen while Van Weyden watches. It is extremely painful to read, precisely because Johnson is a man and not a degraded brute. Because he cannot give up, because "by the manhood that was in him he could not cease from fighting for that manhood" (*SW*, 94), the beating goes on for an extended period, and all that time Van Weyden is watching. For the first and only time in *The Sea-Wolf*, London's humanistic consciousness emerges and allows strong reader identification with the manly Johnson. But all that this humanistic consciousness brings to the reader is pain and suffering, just as all Johnson's manhood will bring him is suffering and death. One begins to see why London kept this humanistic consciousness carefully locked away.

The painfulness of this episode is increased by the care with which London has prepared us for it, and the cold deliberateness with which Larsen proceeds. In the midst of this confrontation he takes pains to make of Johnson an object lesson for Van Weyden. "'Look at him, Hump,' Wolf Larsen said to me, 'look at this bit of animated dust, this aggregation of matter that moves and breathes and defies me and thoroughly believes itself to be compounded of something good, that is impressed with certain human fictions such as righteousness and honesty and that will live up to them in spite of all personal discomforts and menaces. What do you think of him, Hump? What do you think of him?'" (*SW*, 93) Van Weyden, "impelled somehow with a desire to draw upon [him]self a portion of the wrath" about to break on Johnson's head, replies to Larsen's taunt, "'I think that he is a better man than you are.'" But Larsen refuses to cooperate with Van Weyden's attempted alliance with Johnson. Instead, he agrees with him, and freely admits that, unlike Johnson, he himself has "'no fictions that make for nobility and manhood.'" He believes only that "'a living dog is better than a dead lion.'" "'My only doctrine is the doctrine of expediency, and it makes for surviving. This bit of the ferment we call "Johnson," when he is no longer a bit of the ferment, only dust and ashes, will have no more nobility than any dust and ashes, while I shall still be alive and roaring'" (*SW*, 93). He forces Hump to witness what happens to people like Johnson who insist upon their manhood. At one point during the beating, Van Weyden, unable to bear the violence, makes a break for the door. Larsen stops him and forces him to stay and witness the punishment. "And when he could no longer rise they still continued to beat and kick him where he lay" (*SW*, 94). Johnson survives this beating, appears "abject before Wolf Larsen and almost groveled to Johansen," but beneath this appearance of submission Johnson's manhood and mutinous in-

tentions are as strong as ever. Later he and Leach, a cabin boy who
allies with him out of outrage at Larsen's treatment, attempt to escape; when they fail to reach freedom, they are deliberately drowned
by Larsen (*SW*, 102).

Van Weyden is appalled by Larsen's brutality, but at the same time
he is so attracted to his strength and the logical consistency of his
world view that he cannot challenge him in the outright way of
Johnson and Leach. The ambivalence he feels toward Larsen is like
that of a child toward a bad father. His first encounter with Larsen
establishes Larsen's parent-like authority. Larsen offers Van Weyden
the job of cabin boy as a means of making a man of him. " 'Now what
do you say? And mind you, it's for your own soul's sake. It will be
the making of you. You might learn in time to stand on your own legs
and perhaps to toddle along a bit' " (*SW*, 26). Like a son, Van Weyden
tries hard to prove himself to Larsen. He admits, "I felt somehow a
wild desire to vindicate myself in Wolf Larsen's eyes" (*SW*, 126).
Indeed, this self-proclaimed sissy and literary dilettante does learn to
stand up for himself, and he becomes a reasonably competent sailor
in the process. Wolf Larsen is responsible for this growth, and yet
Van Weyden's reactions to him remain strongly ambivalent. "As for
Wolf Larsen and myself," he writes, "we got along fairly well, though
I could not quite rid myself of the idea that right conduct for me lay
in killing him. He fascinated me immeasurably, and I feared him
immeasurably. And yet I could not imagine him lying prone in death.
There was an endurance, as of perpetual youth, about him" (*SW*,
139).

The role of this bad father is to educate his son into the realities of
life among the industrial proletariat. This is not a pretty picture, but
Larsen knows it is necessary to look at Truth with her veils snatched
away if one is to mature and grow up. He insistently holds up to Van
Weyden's reluctant scrutiny a vision of life in which the reality of
absolute power makes the notion of manhood absurd. The more Van
Weyden is confronted with the power relations in the industrial
organization of the *Ghost*, the more plausible does Wolf Larsen's
materialistic philosophy become. It is not accidental that Van Weyden's reaction to the death of Larsen's mate, in the opening chapters,
is to have a glimpse of the world as Wolf Larsen saw it: "Then it was
that the cruelty of the sea, its relentlessness and awfulness, rushed
upon me. Life had become cheap and tawdry, a beastly and inarticu-

late thing, a soulless stirring of the ooze and slime" (*SW*, 33). Van Weyden's education proceeds according to schedule, as he steals five cans of milk and trades them for a dirk with which to protect himself from Mugridge's aggravations. His progress is noted by Larsen at various points in the narrative. For example, when Van Weyden brings up the question of what is "right" in a certain situation, Larsen, "with a wry pucker of his mouth," remarks, " 'Ah . . . I see you still believe in such things as right and wrong' " (*SW*, 67). Later on, in response to Larsen's mocking taunts, the following exchange occurs between him and Van Weyden:

> "I may have learned to stand on my own legs," I retorted.
> "But I have yet to stamp upon others with them."
> He looked at me insolently. "Your education is only half completed then," he said dryly. [*SW*, 154]

Van Weyden is aware of the explanatory power of Wolf Larsen's philosophy and he is frightened by its implications and by the changes taking place in his own consciousness. After brutality follows brutality, Van Weyden reflects on his former sheltered life and laughs bitterly to himself that he "seemed to find in Wolf Larsen's forbidding philosophy a more adequate explanation of life than I found in my own" (*SW*, 99). As the death of Johnson and Leach approaches, Van Weyden finds himself "afflicted with Wolf Larsen's repulsive ideas." He wonders: "What was it all about? Where was the grandeur of life that it should permit such wanton destruction of human souls? It was a cheap and sordid thing after all, this life, and the sooner over the better. Over and done with! I too leaned upon the rail and gazed longingly into the sea, with the certainty that sooner or later I should be sinking down, down, through the cool green depths of its oblivion" (*SW*, 124). Van Weyden is in danger not only of adopting Larsen's philosophy but of falling prey to the suicidal moods that accompany it. He is slipping willy-nilly into the long sickness. But on the other side of this depression are the moments of elation when life is tasted to the full. The vitality of Larsen's consciousness is dramatized in the violent storm that challenges the *Ghost*. As the storm approaches, Van Weyden notices that Larsen is radiant with expectation. "It struck me that he was joyous in a ferocious sort of way, that he was glad there was an impending struggle, that he was thrilled and up-borne with knowledge that one of the great moments of living, when

the tide of life surges up in flood, was upon him" (*SW*, 127–28). Van
Weyden himself will experience something of this during the storm,
as he expertly assists Larsen with the management of the *Ghost*. As
they set out to pick up the men in the sealing boats, which are in
imminent danger from the high waves, he finds that in his concern
for the men he is able to forget himself. Just after this experience,
in which Van Weyden feels his expanding competence and power
under Larsen's rough tutelage, Van Weyden has his first thoughts
about the necessity of killing Larsen. And the plot takes a step in this
direction when, at this critical point in Hump's education, Maud
Brewster is introduced to shore up Humphrey Van Weyden's en-
dangered consciousness.

Before we plunge into the sentimentalities of Maud and Humphrey, it is important to look at the third way in which Wolf Larsen
exercises a strong attraction for Humphrey Van Weyden. Humphrey's attraction to Larsen's vitality and power expresses itself in
a frank admiration of his male body. In the beginning of the book
he indulges in long and loving descriptions of Larsen's physical
appearance—of his strong body and his deep gray eyes—"eyes that
masked the soul with a thousand guises." Among his powers are
sexual potency, for these eyes—already Humphrey knows this—
"could warm and soften and be all adance with lovelights, intense and
masculine, luring and compelling" (*SW*, 25).[4] As impressed as Van
Weyden is by his initial sight of the captain, his breath is "quite taken
away" when Larsen stands before him naked, while Van Weyden
doctors the wounds he has incurred in the recent attempted mutiny.
"I had never before seen him stripped, and the sight of his body
quite took my breath away. It has never been my weakness to exalt
the flesh, far from it; but there is enough of the artist in me to appreciate its wonder" (*SW*, 115). Van Weyden is qualified to pass
judgment, for he has made a careful study of the bodies of the crew
members:

> I must say that I was fascinated by the perfect lines of Wolf
> Larsen's figure and by what I may term the terrible beauty of it.
> I had noted the men in the forecastle. Powerfully muscled
> though some of them were, there had been something wrong
> with all of them, an insufficient development here, an undue
> development there. . . . Oofty-Oofty had been the only one

whose lines were at all pleasing, while, in so far as they pleased, that far had they been what I should call feminine.

But Wolf Larsen was the man type, the masculine, and almost a god in his perfectness. As he moved about or raised his arms, the great muscles leaped and moved under the satiny skin. [*SW*, 115]

This male body, exuding virility and potency, is permitted no outlet for its sexual energies in *The Sea-Wolf*. Sexuality is part-and-parcel of what must be repressed, along with Wolf Larsen's materialism and Larsen himself. Each time Larsen appears to be making a sexual overture, Humphrey Van Weyden interferes. The first time this occurs in a rather disguised way. Mugridge, it will be remembered, enjoys exercising his power over Van Weyden, the cabin boy. It turns out that the reason for the great airs Mugridge puts on "is that Wolf Larsen seem[ed] to have taken a fancy to him." Van Weyden reflects: "It is an unprecedented thing, I take it, for a captain to be chummy with the cook, but this is certainly what Wolf Larsen is doing. Two or three times he put his head into the galley and chaffed Mugridge good-naturedly, and once this afternoon he stood by the break of the poop and chatted with him for fully fifteen minutes. When it was over and Mugridge was back in the galley, he became greasily radiant and went about his work humming coster songs in a nerve-racking and discordant falsetto" (*SW*, 51). Humphrey's determination to challenge Mugridge's insolent power may be seen as an expression of his jealousy of Mugridge's relationship with Larsen. Van Weyden replaces Mugridge in Larsen's affections, such as they are, as he becomes the one to whom Larsen turns for his chats.

A more obvious challenge to Humphrey's relationship with Larsen occurs when the *Ghost* picks up another shipwrecked passenger, who turns out to be Maud Brewster, New England poet. Now Humphrey has competition, for Maud too knows her Browning and can quote to Larsen long purple passages of Victorian poetry. While the other crew members are reduced to adolescent giggles by the presence of this woman in their midst, Larsen turns on her the full power of his alluring eyes. Van Weyden watches this with alarm. As she quotes to Larsen a beautifully rendered version of Dowson's "Impenitentia Ultima," Van Weyden confesses, "I watched not her, but Wolf Larsen. I was fascinated by the fascinated look he bent upon

Maud" (*SW*, 196). Larsen and Maud become quite carried away by the passages of poetry they alternately recite to each other, and as they part for the evening, Humphrey notices the way in which Larsen's eyes, "golden and masculine, intensely masculine and insistently soft, [flash] upon Maud at the door." That night, Humphrey tells us, "For some unknown reason, prompted mysteriously" (*SW*, 198), he goes to bed fully clothed. He awakens with alarm and springs from his bunk to find Larsen in the act of embracing the struggling Maud Brewster. Humphrey rushes to the rescue, but this Gothic farce is interrupted not by Van Weyden's puny and ineffectual punches but by the onset of one of Larsen's mysterious headaches, the first symptom of the illness that will kill him. Instantly he is transformed from a dominant male to a frightened and helpless child. He calls out—to Van Weyden—for help, and Humphrey gently lowers him into a chair. Larsen keeps muttering, " 'I am a sick man, Hump.' " Larsen seems almost to have expected that he would be afflicted at the moment in which he attempted to give expression to his sexual energies. " 'Hump,' he said at last, 'I must get into my bunk. Lend me a hand. I'll be all right in a little while. It's those damn headaches, I believe. I was afraid of them. I had a feeling—no, I don't know what I'm talking about. Help me into my bunk' " (*SW*, 200). What Larsen suspects but is afraid to say is that, like a proper Victorian wife, he develops sick headaches at the very thought of conjugal love. Larsen, uncompromising seer of the "piggish" industrial society, cannot bear to face genital love with a middle-class woman. That reality is too much; better that Truth should retain a few shreds of clothing so that the illusion of Love may remain intact.

Larsen's weakness becomes Van Weyden's strength, as the latter becomes Maud's gallant and utterly sexless protector. Humphrey, whose realization that he loved Maud came in the moment he saw Larsen looking at her warmly, seems motivated by the desire to protect her (and Larsen) from the brutalities of sex. The sentimental hero and heroine make a virtue out of the sexual repression that causes Larsen's downfall. This is one of many instances in which Larsen and Van Weyden share a strange set of attitudes pertaining to their social and sexual relationships, attitudes that work to Larsen's detriment and Van Weyden's advantage.

Their common attitude is best reflected in their detachment. Neither Larsen nor Van Weyden is emotionally engaged in their social relationships; each remains a detached observer of the antics of others. This attitude arises in the first place from their perception that they are socially and intellectually superior to their associates, who, for the purposes of the novel, are the crew of the *Ghost*. Van Weyden's repugnance to the lower-class Mugridge has already been noted. He reveals his condescension to the entire crew in his analysis of their reasoning powers, as evidenced in their debate about whether or not seal pups can swim at birth:

> Childish and immaterial as the topic was, the quality of their reasoning was still more childish and immaterial. In truth, there was very little reasoning or none at all. Their method was one of assertion, assumption, and denunciation. They proved that a seal pup could swim or not swim at birth by stating the proposition very bellicosely and then following it up with an attack on the opposing man's judgment, common sense, nationality, or past history. Rebuttal was precisely similar. I have related this in order to show the mental caliber of the men with whom I was thrown in contact. Intellectually they were children, inhabiting the physical forms of men. [*SW*, 38]

Van Weyden's conclusion that intellectually the crew members are children exactly parallels Larsen's attitude toward them, as observed by Van Weyden: "They are more like children to him, even the hunters, and as children he treats them, descending perforce to their level and playing with them as a man plays with puppies" (*SW*, 64). This is the most benign expression of Larsen's detachment: Van Weyden goes on to describe another of his moods, in which he

> probes them with the cruel hand of a vivisectionist, groping about in their mental processes and examining their souls as though to see of what soul-stuff is made.
>
> I have seen him a score of times at table insulting this hunter or that with cool and level eyes and, withal, a certain air of interest, pondering their actions or replies or petty rages with a curiosity almost laughable to me who stood onlooker and who understood. Concerning his own rages, I am convinced that they are not real, that they are sometimes experiments, but that in the main they are the habits of a pose or attitude he has seen fit to take toward his fellowmen. [*SW*, 64]

We recognize in Larsen the public pose that London adopted after his long sickness. Larsen, an emotionless stage manager, works the machinery and gives the actors their cues. But of special interest here is the posture of Van Weyden, who, as observer of Larsen observing the crew, is *twice* removed from social reality. Van Weyden himself adopts Larsen's scientific experiments and uses them on Larsen, as in the discussion he has with him about Spencer's philosophy. "[Larsen's] brows drew in slightly with the mental effort of suitably phrasing thoughts which he had never before put into speech. I felt an elation of spirit. I was groping into his soul-stuff as he made a practice of groping in the soul-stuff of others. I was exploring virgin territory. A strange, a terribly strange, region was unrolling itself before my eyes" (*SW*, 68). The intimacy we feel when we are permitted to witness the formation of "thoughts which . . . ha[ve] never before [been] put into speech" becomes for Van Weyden the occasion for a cold exploration of "virgin territory." This defloration elates Van Weyden and causes him to grow "overbold." He begins passing "stiff strictures" on Larsen's life and philosophy. "In fact," he writes, "I was vivisecting him and turning over his soul-stuff as keenly and thoroughly as it was his custom to do it to others" (*SW*, 71). Larsen becomes enraged and turns on Van Weyden, physically mastering him in his powerful grip. This is no doubt the reaction Van Weyden wanted to provoke. Perfectly calm and cool himself, Van Weyden has successfully maneuvered Larsen into the expression of genuine feelings. He has won. He has fumbled with the soul of another without exposing his own. He has mastery of the situation and temporary mastery over his tyrannical captain.

Van Weyden's penchant for detached analysis acts as a check on his emotional engagement. It works even to cool off his rhapsodic appreciations of Larsen's body. After his long and detailed description of Larsen standing stripped before him, Van Weyden concludes with a lame adaptation of Larsen's materialism, "I had seen the mechanism of the primitive fighting beast, and I was as strongly impressed as if I had seen the engines of a great battleship or Atlantic liner" (*SW*, 117). Van Weyden experiences no sexual feelings toward Maud; his sexuality is aroused only by Larsen, and he is able to turn off these feelings. Larsen, on the other hand, is still able to experience sexual feelings, even if he cannot express them. Humphrey Van

Weyden, the "healthy" consciousness who triumphs over the "sick" Larsen, is actually a much sicker man. He is further removed from social reality and from the expression of his feelings. So emotionally dead is he that he is not even aware of paying a price for his detached stance, whereas Larsen suffers for his loneliness.

Humphrey, immune to such feelings himself, is a good observer of these feelings as they affect Larsen. He notes that Larsen is "an individualist of the most pronounced type" and that "he is very lonely. There is no congeniality between him and the rest of the men aboard ship. His tremendous virility and mental strength wall him apart" (*SW*, 64). The qualities that "wall him apart" will contribute to his strange illness, the growth of which may be followed in the metaphors that are used to describe him. As "the loneliness of the man is slowly . . . borne upon [Van Weyden]," he remarks of Larsen, "He seems consuming with the tremendous power that is in him and that seems never to have found adequate expression in works" (*SW*, 79). His consciousness, removed from his men by their fear and his scorn, is walled apart; it has nothing to feed on but itself, and so it is self-consuming. This completely self-contained and self-sustaining consciousness is described by Larsen himself when he tells Van Weyden that he has no roots. Van Weyden, impelled by his overwhelming curiosity, asks Larsen one day why he has never made anything of himself; why, in spite of his superior intelligence and broad reading, he remains only the captain of a sealing ship. Larsen responds with a parable: " 'Hump, do you know the parable of the sower who went forth to sow? If you will remember, some of the seed fell upon stony places, where there was not much earth, and forthwith they sprung up because they had no deepness of earth. And when the sun was up they were scorched, and because they had no root they withered away. And some fell among thorns, and the thorns sprung up and choked them'" (*SW*, 82). When Hump asks him the point of the parable Larsen replies, "I was one of those seeds." He goes on to describe his meager childhood and early work life.

> "In the English merchant service. Cabin boy at twelve, ship's boy at fourteen, ordinary seaman at sixteen, able seaman at seventeen, and cock of the forecastle, infinite ambition and in-

finite loneliness, receiving neither help nor sympathy, I did it
all for myself—navigation, mathematics, science, literature,
and what not. And of what use has it been? Master and owner
of a ship at the top of my life, as you say, when I am beginning
to diminish and die. Paltry, isn't it? And when the sun was up
I was scorched, and because I had no root I withered away."
[*SW*, 83–84]

He contrasts his career with that of his brother, Death Larsen, who is
"a lump of an animal without any head," and "is all the happier for
leaving life alone. He is too busy living it to think about it. My mistake was in ever opening the books" (*SW*, 84). We recognize in
Larsen's saga of "infinite ambition and infinite loneliness" the general
pattern of Jack London's life. He even uses phrases almost verbatim
from London's letters of the period of his early success: "receiving
neither help nor sympathy, I did it all for myself" echoes his letter of
1898 to Mabel Applegarth. "My mistake was in ever opening the
books." He had written this to Cloudesley Johns in 1902.

    These passages are revealing of both Wolf Larsen and Jack London,
and, as usual, the revelation that comes indirectly, through the metaphor, is the most significant. Larsen finally addresses Van Weyden's
question directly when he tells him that he failed not for want of
ability but for lack of opportunity. In this regard Larsen's career
departs from that of his fabulously successful author. But the failed
Larsen and the successful London share the same loneliness, and
both their lives are described in the parable of the sower who went
out to sow. Significantly, this is a parable about the kingdom of
heaven. Larsen was one of the seeds that fell on rocky ground, and
thus, for lack of root, did not blossom. This failed seed was Jack
London, successful author who gained the world and lost his soul.
In seeking success he was seeking the kingdom of heaven; he was
seeking immortality, but he found only death and disintegration. The
immortality he sought was achieved by Buck, who linked his life
with past generations and ran side by side with his wood brother.
But the lonely individualist had no such roots. His consciousness,
being perfectly self-contained, would die with him. Larsen argues
that the "only value life has is what life puts upon itself." This is true
and consistent for a consciousness that is not rooted in anything
outside of itself. With death comes the death of the consciousness,

for it has not disseminated itself. With analytic precision, Larsen describes what death means to him, as he reflects on the fate of Harrison, the green hand whom he sent up the rigging:

> "He held on as if he were a precious thing, a treasure beyond diamonds or rubies. To you? No. To me? Not at all. To himself? Yes. But I do not accept his estimate. He sadly overrates himself. There is plenty more life demanding to be born. Had he fallen and dripped his brains upon the deck like honey from the comb, there would have been no loss to the world. He was worth nothing to the world. The supply is too large. *To himself only was he of value, and to show how fictitious even this value was, being dead he is unconscious that he has lost himself.* He alone rated himself beyond diamonds and rubies. Diamonds and rubies are gone, spread out on the deck to be washed away by a bucket of seawater, and he does not even know that the diamonds and rubies are gone. He does not lose anything, for with the loss of himself he loses the knowledge of loss."
> [*SW*, 59–60; my emphasis]

If one is of value only to oneself, then to die, or to forget oneself, is to completely lose oneself. Thus self-consciousness becomes existence. The self keeps the self in existence by a self-reflexive act of will. The need for self-forgetfulness, so strong in London's periods of depression, grew in proportion to the insatiable, unrelenting demand of his consciousness to be aware of itself, or otherwise die. Unable to invest his consciousness in others, London was tormented by the self-consuming demands of that consciousness. Like Melville's Ahab, whose tightly clenched fists made his fingernails pierce his palms, he was self-crucified.

What this meant for London is dramatized in the self-consumptive death he reserves for Wolf Larsen. Afflicted with a brain tumor, "a thing that devours and destroys," Larsen becomes blind, deaf in one ear, and paralyzed on one side. The progressive deterioration of his five senses dramatizes the withdrawal of his consciousness from dialogue with the world. " '[T]he curse of it is,' " he says, " 'that I must lie here, conscious, mentally unimpaired, knowing that the lines are going down, breaking bit by bit communication with the world. I cannot see; hearing and feeling are leaving me; at this rate I shall soon cease to speak; yet all the time I shall be here, alive, active, and powerless'" (*SW*, 267). As Humphrey Van Weyden reflects on "the awfulness of Wolf Larsen's living death," he concludes: "The man of him was not changed. It was the old, indomitable, terrible Wolf Larsen, imprisoned somewhere within that flesh which had once been so invincible and splendid. Now it bound him with insentient fetters, *walling his soul in darkness and silence, blocking it from the world* which to him had been a riot of action" (*SW*, 268; my emphasis). Like the narrator in Poe's "The Cask of Amontillado," Van Weyden presides over the walling up of his double: the king dies and the jester survives. Indeed, Van Weyden is to Larsen like the rational narrator of many a Poe tale, who observes the dying antics of a mad and self-destructive alter ego; and Larsen is, in Van Weyden's words, "buried alive," which reminds us of Poe's penchant for premature burials. (Perhaps this is the significance of Van Weyden's recent article on "Poe's place in American literature" [*SW*, 8]).

Larsen loses his voice, and, when he writes down on a pad of paper what he wishes to say, Van Weyden remarks, "It was like a message from the night of the grave, for this man's body had become his mausoleum. And there, in so strange sepulture, his spirit fluttered and lived. It would flutter and live till the last line of communication was broken, and after that who was to say how much longer it might continue to flutter and live?" (*SW*, 274). The horror of Larsen's death is that it does not come soon enough. Before death comes, Larsen's last line of communication is broken: "The last line was down. Somewhere within that tomb of the flesh still dwelt the soul of the man. Walled by the living clay, that fierce intelligence we had known burned on; but it burned on in silence and darkness. And it was disembodied. To that intelligence there could be no objective knowledge of a body. It knew no body. The very world was not. *It knew only itself and the vastness and profundity of the quiet and the dark*" (*SW*, 277; my emphasis). Larsen is more fortunate than Jack London in that he dies soon after the last line is down. Immediately upon his death, Maud and Humphrey are rescued by a U.S. revenue cutter, and the novel is concluded. The business of the book has been the killing of Larsen; once he is dead, the book can end.

London's life did not end with his long sickness, but went on in the sentimental consciousness typified by Humphrey Van Weyden. If Wolf Larsen's tragedy is his loneliness and his final inability to communicate at all, Humphrey is emphatically not alone. He has his Maud, and they communicate to one another—at greater length than the reader would wish—the banalities of their sentimental love. Just as Charmian Kittredge helped London dispel the clouds of his long sickness, so Maud Brewster's "bewitching," "sweetly spiritual, if not saintly" presence dispels the power of Wolf Larsen's "cold explanation of life" and renders it "truly ridiculous and laughable" (*SW*, 176). But the real horror, as suggested earlier, is that the consciousness of Van Weyden, the survivor, is actually sicker than that of the dead Larsen. There are several ways in which this pale survivor has circumvented the therapeutic process. In the first place, it should be clear that for London, his art remained his last "line of communication"; as long as that line was intact, he was not yet immured in his own flesh. But the sentimental consciousness heralded the death of London's art, which depended on looking squarely at social reality and measuring it against his inner needs. When Maud Brewster is introduced into *The Sea-Wolf*, the stark, realistic descriptions of life aboard the *Ghost* are replaced by mawkish conversations between Humphrey and Maud. London's crisp prose degenerates into sentimental simpering, as Maud makes "a *moue* of disappointment" at Humphrey (*SW*, 204), and Humphrey "avers" that he is unafraid (*SW*, 210). If the language is elegant and insufferable, so too is the portrait of Maud, whom Humphrey must render "goddesslike and unapproachable" so that he can make the delightful discovery of "the little traits that proclaimed her only woman after all, such as the toss of the head which flung back the cloud of hair, and the search for the [hair]pin." She is his "mate-woman," he her "mate-man," terms Jack and Charmian applied to one another (*SW*, 206).

If the sentimental consciousness killed London's art, it also denied the basic movement of the plot that structures *The Sea-Wolf*. Up to the point at which Maud Brewster is introduced, Van Weyden develops his sea legs, and it has been the business of the novel to educate him into the realities of capitalist society so that he can truly grow up. That is to say, the movement of the novel has been toward self-integration. This process is interrupted by the sentimental heroine, and, instead of self-integration, we have self-repression, dramatized by the dominance of Van Weyden's consciousness and the burial of Wolf Larsen's. The failure of self-integration is further dramatized in Van Weyden's regression as he and Maud become more like children at play than sexually mature adults. On the open boat, as Maud and Humphrey escape from the *Ghost*, Maud learns to steer, and then, like a good little mother, she insists that Humphrey go to sleep. She even tucks him in. Humphrey's response is ecstatic: "I experienced a positive sensuous delight as I crawled into the bed she had made with her hands. The calm and control which were so much a part of her seemed to have been communicated to the blankets, so that I was aware of a soft dreaminess and content and of an oval face and brown eyes framed in a fisherman's cap and tossing against a background now of gray cloud, now of gray sea; and then I was aware that I had been asleep" (*SW*, 208). When Larsen and the *Ghost* return to haunt them, Maud and Humphrey play hide and seek with the blind Larsen: "And so we dodged about the deck, hand in hand, like a couple of children chased by a wicked ogre" (*SW*, 257). This vignette captures the infantile fantasy that was London's cure for the long sickness.

If London can be condemned for retreating to sentimental illusions, in another sense he did not retreat in *The Sea-Wolf*. He simply wrote his story within the limitations created by the society in which he lived. The contradictions of *The Sea-Wolf* are the contradictions of his society, and in this sense he was reflecting, not evading, that society. According to London's perceptions, to write a story of self-integration actually achieved within capitalist society would have been to lie. Larsen, the bad father, puts Van Weyden in a double bind: he initiates him into manhood by showing him that in his society manhood is punished. To truly become a man is to choose death, like the manly Johnson. Humphrey Van Weyden desires to live. He tells Maud: " 'Mine is the role of the weak. I remain silent and suffer ignominy, as you will remain silent and suffer ignominy. And it is well. It is the best we can do if we wish to live' " (*SW*, 165). To this extent, London told the truth in *The Sea-Wolf*. It is the truth of a dependent people. The kingly heritage of Buck has been exchanged for the bells of jesters who "must dissimulate, and win, if win we can, by craft." He tells Maud that they must provoke no scenes with Larsen and must hide their mutinous alliance behind "smiling faces" (*SW*, 165). The child-like, sentimental posture is a defense against the absolute power wielded by Larsen. There were obvious gains to be made by the sentimental pose. It allowed Van Weyden to forget that terrible vision of life aboard the *Ghost*, in which master oppressed hunters and hunters ravaged and destroyed the seals, "flinging the naked carcasses to the shark and salting down the skins so that they might later adorn the fair shoulders of the women of the cities" (*SW*, 125). In a stroke, the "piggish" world view of Larsen was replaced by the "spiritual" world of Maud Brewster, whose body, like her verse, is "sublimated" (*SW*, 168). The reality of industrial capitalism was blotted out by the force of Love. This repressive solution worked just as long as those participating in it were able to repress their own sexuality and adult identity. It was imperative that Love did not degenerate into love.

The sentimental pose seemed to work for Maud and Humphrey—although it is doubtful that they would have escaped Larsen had it not been for his debilitating illness. What worked when the ogre of industrial capitalism was slain did not work as well for Jack London, who lived in a society that, he believed, might die of its own illness—but not within his lifetime. The problem he faced after his initiation into the working-class world of shop and prison was how to preserve his kingly heritage beneath the posture of the "meek and lowly" ex-prisoner. That kingly self, unless fed by ancestral memories and fostered by a living tribe of like-minded subjects, was bound to remain a fictitious self, one whose consciousness was validated only by itself. In *The Sea-Wolf* London moves his bourgeois narrator into a sentimental, not a political, alliance. The limitations of this stance have already been suggested. The gravest damage done by the sentimental pose is that it further removed Van Weyden from his emotional life. By attenuating the lines of communication between the inner self and the world, the sentimental alliance made it all the more difficult to keep alive that inner self. Worse, the sentimental posture deliberately gave the lie to the emotional life: it served up warmed-over Victorian poetry and called it intimacy. "Poor inner self!" London wrote to Charmian in a mood of self-analysis, "I wonder if it will atrophy, dry up some day and blow away."[5] Without a robust inner self, manhood and kingly pretensions are swallowed up by the demands of the dissimulating public self. The king becomes the slave of his jester.

EIGHT

DOMESTICITY:
THE FUTURE OF
AN ILLUSION

Jack London's life imitated his art: soon after he finished *The Sea-Wolf* he married his answer to the long sickness—Charmian Kittredge. In their happiest moments, they enjoyed a sentimental relationship very like Humphrey and Maud's. In darker hours, London withdrew into a Larsen-like persona: he smoked and drank and put on gloves and boxed with his wife. From his disillusionment at age twenty-seven to his death at age forty, this woman was London's chief palliative.

Six years older than Jack, Charmian Kittredge was a reasonably independent woman with several accomplishments: she was an excellent horsewoman and a promising pianist. She lived in Glen Ellen with her aunt and uncle, Ninetta and Roscoe Eames. On a typical day she practiced the piano for several hours, took a ride through the hills on her favorite horse, went into San Francisco to shop, and did some sewing. She also read broadly, but there seems to have been no particular pattern to her reading, nor does she ever, in her rather detailed diary entries, reflect on its significance. For example, on September 5, 1901, she read part of Charlotte Perkins Gilman's *Women and Economics*:[1] such a book, read with an eye to its significance for the life of a woman like Charmian Kittredge, could have been cause for a revolution in consciousness. But for Charmian, it is just another item to be recorded, along with the amount of sewing she had completed. Her accomplishments and her expectations were conventional and middle class: she expected to be an adornment for a man rather than purposive in her own right. In spite of this, she pursued her interests with vigor and discipline, at least in the early years of her relationship with Jack. If she was less conventional than Bess Maddern, it was because she had been on her own for a number of years and had a frank appreciation for the joy of sex.

From January until the beginning of August 1904, Jack was out of the country reporting on the Russo-Japanese War. On August 2, the day of his return, Charmian Kittredge made no comment in her diary save for a string of exclamation points. Their intimacy had begun before his trip abroad, and now they discreetly resumed it. As often as she could, Charmian spent part of the day with Jack, and she began the task that would be hers until his death: typing the manuscript pages that flowed ceaselessly from his pen. This was only one of the ways in which she went about making herself indispensable to Jack London.

The copy of *The Abysmal Brute* that London gave to Charmian bears this inscription:

> Dear My-Woman:
> The years pass, we live much, and yet, to me, I find but one vindication for living, but one bribe for living—and the vindication is you, the bribe is you.[2]

The way in which London's emotional dependence on Charmian grew until she stood between life and giving up life may best be understood by turning to those months in the spring of 1905, when their relationship blossomed out of the depths of London's long sickness. His months in Korea and Manchuria had only postponed the reckoning: so much on one side of the ledger for Jack London, author; so much on the other side for Death. As he struggled to see what could give life significance in the face of certain death and dissolution, he came to the conclusion that one must affirm the "secondary truths," the ones that made for life, even if one knew that at bottom these were lies. This repressive solution was intimately connected with his relationship with Charmian Kittredge.

Charmian first became aware of the black mood into which Jack had sunk when, on March 8, 1905, he arrived in Glen Ellen on horseback, tired and lame from an accident. She notes in her diary, "I realize Mate's sad condition, and try to get him out of it. My growing sorrow and hopelessness over him." But instead of getting him out of his mood, Charmian began to slip into his. They spent several days in the blues, London reading Conrad's "The End of the Tether."

Then London departed, promising Charmian that he would return on April 1. She notes on March 16, "Life getting full of hope again. Things clearing." But she is not certain of Jack's commitment to her. She worries that he may not come as promised. In the meantime she visits him frequently in Oakland. Her primary concern, as reflected in her diary, is not the saving of Jack London's soul. Whether or not he succeeds in giving his life a meaning that will redeem his mortality is not, to Charmian, the issue of moment. She worries more about whether or not she will catch her man (and so redeem *her* life, in the conventional way). In this she was successful, and she was aided by the forces of mortality. London developed piles (in his morbid imagination, a malignant tumor), which necessitated surgery and a week's recuperation at Shingle Sanitorium. Charmian came to his bedside every day, and in contrast to Bessie and in the face of scandalous attacks on Charmian by the "crowd" (the bohemian friends that London had collected since his rise—friends that included Carrie and George Sterling), Charmian proved herself "too good to be true." Her willingness to stand by him, to mold herself to his needs, to be a soothing presence when he was sick, led Jack to believe that she was the only person worth a damn. As he turned down a page on his past, his false friends and his first wife, he elevated Charmian to a place of special worth. She notes, "these days (during Mate's illness before and after operation) are the turning point in the lives of Mate and me. We are more truly learning each other, our worth to each other."[3] Just as she stood with Jack against the bitterness of Bess, Jack had come to Charmian's defense when the "crowd" had attempted to discredit her reputation, and Charmian basked in the splendid isolation of their loyalty to one another: "Jack London (my Mate!) says that the pleasure I take in my new saddle (his gift) is more joy to him than all he has ever done for the ungrateful ones."[4]

Charmian cannot distinguish clearly between the state of her relationship with Jack and the state of his emotional health: to her, they ripen hand-in-hand. She writes on May 20: "It seems too beautiful to be true, that Jack London, my own Mate, is at the Glen Ellen end of the San Francisco trip. To find him waiting my returns from the city makes me appreciate the change from the sad, unnatural winter." Before the year was out they would be married, and even before that, the illusions that would structure the rest of Jack London's life would be in place: Charmian, horses and dogs, the land, the adventure of the *Snark*—these were all new projects into which London threw his energies in a desperate attempt to shackle himself to life, and the chiefest of these was Charmian. The restoration that proceeded during the spring and summer of 1905 involved London's absorption of Charmian's values and country way of life.

While he was recovering from his operation in April, Charmian bought Jack a horse ("Ban") and dreamed about their summer plans. In May Jack and Charmian began looking at ranch properties, and on the back of one of her diary leaves Charmian directly connects this new interest of Jack's with his recovery: "Jack's madness over 'Sierra Vista' one of the biggest joys of my life. His 'Long Sickness' (Nietszche) is over, and *he* feels that a new, happy life is before him."[5] On August 19 they consummated this new life (and symbolically linked the woman and the land) by making love at Sierra Vista. "These are [the] happiest days of my life, I think," Charmian confided to her diary.[6] On June 7 they put down a deposit on a ranch and on June 26 London began writing *White Fang*. Conceived while London was in the process of settling down with Charmian, *White Fang* appropriately enough tells of the domestication of a wild animal. Here London consciously reverses the plot of *The Call of the Wild*, and, in less conscious ways, he betrays his art and his politics. A brief look at the ending of this story reveals much about London's new allegiances.

White Fang ends where *The Call of the Wild* had begun: at Judge Scott's estate in the Santa Clara valley. Here the wolf-hero must learn what Buck had to unlearn: respect for the laws, established by men, regarding property. At first White Fang responds as he did in the Northland: when he sees a chicken, he tears into it and eats it. But after he goes on a rampage and kills fifty chickens at once, earning both the ire and the admiration of his master, Weedon Scott, he learns that chickens are off limits. This was a law decreed by the "god," and to please his "love-master" he obeys his laws punctiliously. White Fang is not only very smart, he is extremely adaptable, and this is his strength. "Life had a thousand faces, and White Fang found he must meet them all . . ." (*WF*, 301). In the Santa Clara valley life is more complex than it was in the Northland, and "the chief thing demanded by these intricacies of civilization was control, restraint—a poise of self that was as delicate as the fluttering of gossamer wings and at the same time as rigid as steel. . . . Life flowed past him, deep and wide and varied, continually impinging upon his senses, demanding of him instant and endless adjustments and correspondences, and compelling him, almost always, to suppress his natural impulses" (*WF*, 301). This suppression of his natural impulses goes hand in hand with the canine equivalent of marriage. One day White Fang deserts his master to follow Collie, a rather shrewish female, into the woods: "The master rode alone that day; and in the woods, side by side, White Fang ran with Collie, as his mother, Kiche, and old One Eye had run long years before in the silent Northland forest" (*WF*, 314). The language closely parallels the ending of *The Call of the Wild*, but the lyric beauty of that book is replaced in *White Fang* by a coy sentimentality. Collie presents White Fang with "a half-dozen pudgy puppies," and the book ends as they come "sprawling toward him . . . he gravely permitt[ing] them to clamber and tumble over him" as "he lay with half-shut, patient eyes, drowsing in the sun" (*WF*, 326, 327).

This betrayal of genuine emotion for the furry feeling of a Hallmark greeting card is paralleled by London's betrayal of his political commitments. As we have seen, in *The Call of the Wild* he transformed his prison experiences into the story of a dog's growing consciousness of his colonization. For London and for Buck, captivity fostered a political awareness, the growth of which meant the intensification of that essentially human capacity of beings to become conscious of themselves. In Emily Dickinson's succinct line, which condenses Hegel's theory of master-slave relationships into three words, "Captivity is consciousness."[7] In *White Fang* London introduces a convict, Jim Hall, seemingly for the sole purpose of making the opposite point, that captivity brutalizes: "He was a ferocious man. He had been ill-made in the making. He had not been born right, and he had not been helped any by the moulding he had received at the hands of society. The hands of society are harsh, and this man was a striking sample of its handiwork. He was a beast—a human beast, it is true, but nevertheless so terrible a beast that he can best be characterized as carnivorous" (*WF*, 315). San Quentin further degraded him through the agency of a guard who "was almost as great a beast as he." One day Jim Hall "sprang upon the guard . . . and used his teeth on the other's throat just like any jungle animal." For this he is "buried alive" in an isolation cell, and his punishment recalls the manner of Wolf Larsen's death. "For weeks and months he never made a sound, in the black silence eating his very soul. He was a man and a monstrosity, as fearful a thing of fear as ever gibbered in the visions of a maddened brain" (*WF*, 316).

If one is to live with any comfort in the sunny ease of the Santa Clara valley, it is important to kill consciousness, or at least to kill the characters who embody consciousness. In *White Fang* this imperative becomes mixed with the defense of the master and his laws. Judge Scott had sentenced Jim Hall to life imprisonment, and when the convict escapes and enters the judge's house to take revenge, White Fang proves both his wolfish ancestry and his loyalty to his master by slaying the intruder. Besides ridding London of specters from his working-class past, this improbable elaboration of plot accomplishes the important work of nullifying the power of death. White Fang has sustained massive injuries in his set-to with the convict: three broken ribs, a punctured lung, internal injuries, and three bullet holes that have caused him to lose "nearly all the blood in his body." London is taking no chances. Having done everything but totally obliterate his hero, in three pages he brings him back to life ("'The Blessed Wolf!'"), and, with the arrival of the pudgy puppies a page later, establishes him as a wise-eyed patriarch. (The man who supervises White Fang's recovery is a "Doctor Nichols," an approximation of the name of the man who performed the operation on Jack London's piles, Dr. Nicholson.) London patronizingly forgives the local surgeon, who allowed White Fang less than one chance in ten thousand to live.

> [He] was not to be censured for his misjudgment. All his life he
> had tended and operated on the soft humans of civilization,
> who lived sheltered lives and had descended out of many
> sheltered generations. Compared with White Fang, they were
> frail and flabby, and clutched life without any strength in their
> grip. White Fang had come straight from the Wild, where the
> weak perish early and shelter is vouchsafed to none. In neither
> his father nor his mother was there any weakness, nor in the
> generations before them. A constitution of iron and the vitality
> of the Wild were White Fang's inheritance, and he clung to
> life, the whole of him and every part of him, in spirit and in
> flesh, with the tenacity that of old belonged to all creatures.
> [*WF*, 323]

London's own fear of death, aroused by the mysterious growth on his rectum, is now laughed to scorn; the power of the Northland to educate man to his puniness and mortality is here transformed into an illusion of eternal life. And London's blood-and-struggle beginnings in the Oakland proletariat are similarly reduced to a tonic that fortifies him in his new surrounding by setting him apart: "[White Fang] remained somehow different from other dogs. He knew the law even better than did the dogs that had known no other life, and he observed the law more punctiliously; but still there was about him a suggestion of lurking ferocity, as though the Wild still lingered in him and the wolf in him merely slept" (*WF*, 305). He is lonely, but if death is denied, in such loneliness there is strength: "He never chummed with other dogs. Lonely he had lived, so far as his kind was concerned, and lonely he would continue to live" (*WF*, 305).

London wrote *White Fang* at his characteristic pace, and within five months it was finished and successfully marketed. On November 11 he telegraphed Charmian, "Wild Mate, I have no fancy for dying just yet. *White Fang* sold to *Outing*."[8] Eight days later Jack and Charmian were married. This summer and fall of 1905 marked London's first attempt to employ in his life the sentimental formula of his art, and, judged by the ordinary criteria of success, the formula worked. London was saved from the long sickness.

The problem with illusions is their unreliability. They seem to work, but their very working intensifies the problem they are meant to cover up, so that bigger and better illusions must be put in their place. Until three or four years before his death, London's ranch in the Sonoma valley proved a useful illusion, because it so readily gave itself to expansion, first of the acreage, and then of the quality of improvements: eugenically bred livestock, scientific farming, a cash crop (eucalyptus trees), and a stone mansion followed one another in a succession of enthusiasms that had the practical effect of chaining London to the production of daily potboilers. London's farming efforts foundered on what should have been for him the embarrassing problem of the laziness and deceit of his hired help. Far from proving a self-sustaining cash crop, eucalyptus trees proved a bust; there was no market for them. And London's mansion, Wolf House, burned to all but a mocking shell before he ever lived in it. He was never even to have a home of his own.

Charmian on horseback, Jack looking on,
at the Beauty Ranch
(Reproduced by permission of The Huntington Library, San Marino, California)

Seeming to sense the unreliability of illusions, London supplied himself with half a dozen. The same summer that spawned his engagement with Charmian and the land also gave birth to the adventure of the *Snark*. "Planning our trip around the world," Charmian gleefully notes on August 9. London planned to build a yacht and spend seven years sailing about from port to port. That this nomadic existence was completely at odds with his plan to invest himself in the hills of California did not faze him. The *Snark* trip was a grand gesture, designed to make life worth living and, perhaps, to recapture some of the romance and adventure that the books had promised London as an overworked and miserly newsboy. Built in the aftermath of the San Francisco earthquake, which sent the cost of labor and materials skyrocketing, the *Snark* cost a fabulous sum and was so poorly constructed that it would not heave-to.[9] The man Jack had chosen to captain the vessel, Charmian's uncle, Roscoe Eames, turned out to be lazy and insolent. The crew was devastated by physical ailments ranging from seasickness and impacted teeth to tropical fevers. One man died, another went crazy, and Jack London ended up in a hospital in Sidney, Australia, with a rare disease that made his skin puff up and flake off and so debilitated his nervous system that he could not maintain a standing position. He held out, incredibly, for two years before he tacitly admitted the failure of the voyage by turning his face toward California.

As each of his brave schemes broke down or threatened to break down, London hedged his bets. He drank. In *John Barleycorn* he says that he was not, during his long sickness, tempted by alcohol. Whether or not this is true, it is certain that alcohol was a mainstay of his recovery. A little more than a year after they were married, Charmian wrote in her diary, "Mate not looking well; drinks cocktails, takes no exercise. I feel bad about him."[10] A few weeks later she writes "Mate takes 3 cocktails before dinner, all by himself. I cry."[11] Though he already is drinking by himself—a development that his account in *John Barleycorn* would lead us to believe came later than this—he drank more heavily whenever he left the ranch for the city. The months he spent in New York in 1912 prior to the voyage on the *Dirigo* were for Jack one long debauch and for Charmian a waking nightmare. Even short trips to Oakland, where Jack and Charmian spent quite a bit of time during the building of the *Snark*, had the same effect on his drinking. "Mate went out with

Socialists . . . came home very late, *full*; I had nervous chills, slept not at all."[12] She writes the next day, "Thank God, I don't have to live in a city always. I almost think that such a life would in the end kill that otherwise imperishable thing—the love of Jack and me."[13] London embroidered Charmian's sentiment in *Burning Daylight*, one of the "domestic" novels, which, like *The Valley of the Moon*, he wrote at a time when he was rebounding from world travels and was homesick for the ranch. The advantage of having several illusions was that, when one failed, there was another to fall back on. And when all failed, there was the bottle.

Nick Carroway, the sympathetic observer of the career of Fitzgerald's hero in *The Great Gatsby*, distinguishes between the corruption of Gatsby's life and the purity of his "incorruptible dream" (pp. 154–55). A similar distinction should be made between the tawdriness of London's illusions and the significance of the emotion from which they had sprung. London's illusions were all attempts to root himself in an existential reality. That they were miscalculated attempts does not change the impulse behind them, a large and deep impulse to connect himself with the earth and his fellow creatures, in order that his existence would be touched by larger currents flowing behind him and through him. This is the impulse of mortal life toward immortal life.

One can see that impulse operating in his hopes for his ranch. Biographers understandably have seen his extravagant venture as London's attempt to live the life of a California magnate.[14] London wrote to his publisher, "it is dreadfully hard for me to get my friends to understand just what the ranch means to me. It does not mean profit, at all. . . . The ranch is to me what actresses, race-horses, or collecting postage stamps, are to some other men."[15] But his ranch was more than a gentlemanly hobby and a badge of his new social status. It was an attempt to create a *home* on a scale grand enough to overcome his loneliness and rootlessness. Writing to George Sterling of his plan "to buy land in the woods, somewhere, and build," he explained, "for over a year, I have been planning this home proposition, and now I am just beginning to see my way clear to it. I am really going to throw out an anchor so big and so heavy that all hell could never get it up again. In fact, it's going to be a prodigious, ponderous sort of anchor."[16] But like his attempts to buy his way into the lower-class subculture of the Oakland gangs, this attempt to invest himself in the land failed because in the end it was only his money, not himself, that was sown into the earth. The incongruous mixing of metaphors here—"land" and "woods" suggestive of shore values, "anchor" suggestive of sea values—points to the contradictory impulses in London's consciousness. Although he desired to root himself in the soil, he—like Melville's Ishmael and Twain's Huck Finn—was happiest when floating free of all the complications of society. How to plant himself in an uncongenial soil: that was the problem London struggled with and never satisfactorily resolved.

One common way of satisfying the impulse toward immortality is to recreate oneself through one's progeny. To an artist the offspring of his mind and heart are as important as the offspring of his loins, and in the next chapter we shall see what happened to London's attempts to achieve immortality through his writing. But because biographers have made much of London's desire to have "seven sturdy Saxon sons and daughters," it is important here to examine London's relationship to fatherhood. With Bess Maddern he had two daughters, Joan and Bess. With Charmian he had one daughter, Joy, who lived only thirty-eight hours. Subsequently Charmian had a miscarriage, and thereafter she either did not conceive or did not carry the fetus beyond the first month.[17] It is tempting to conclude that London's failure to produce a litter of children, and especially his failure to produce a son, was a bitter blow to his patriarchal illusions. This interpretation has a certain explanatory power, but it is not consistent with the picture that emerges from Charmian's diary. That document suggests that it was primarily Charmian, not Jack, who wished to have children.

Five months after they were married, Charmian, who recorded her menstrual periods with scrupulous accuracy, noted that she was late: "I almost began to worry—and—*almost* to *dream*."[18] A year later she has apparently resolved her conflicting feelings, for she expressed her desire for a baby to her husband. But when she broached the subject of babies London's response was, "I did not know how much I needed you myself."[19] He made strenuous demands on Charmian and recognized that motherhood would divert her attention from him and his work. Besides typing his manuscripts, Charmian mothered him quite a bit. She always accompanied him to the dentist, where, owing to the neglect of his teeth in his youth, he spent many hours. On one occasion she remarks on his "agony in the dentist's chair, and how he clings to me."[20] Again, when London was suffering aboard the *Snark* with a strange tropical disease, Charmian records, "Mate miserable and weak. I put him to sleep. Crazy over me."[21] Their relationship seems to have been strengthened by illness, and one recalls that their love was forged during London's recuperation from surgery. This was not a reciprocal arrangement, however, for when Charmian was ill, with rare exceptions Jack was incapable of coming to her support. When she came down with the grippe on their voyage, she complained, "Wretchedly ill these days. J's vaporings about taking care of me go glimmering and I spend my hours in loneliness and sleeplessness and tears and pain. . . . I think J is sick sometimes, mentally, or he wouldn't do as he does."[22] To Jack, Charmian represented a healing peace and repose, and it was not appropriate for *her* to get sick. After his long sickness, Charmian remembers him saying, " 'You did it all, my Mate Woman. You've pulled me out. You've rested me so. And rest was what was needed— you were right.' "[23] She quotes a letter from Jack, written presumably around the time of their marriage: " 'You, just you—with strength and surety and power to hold me to you for that old peace and rest which you have always had for me.' "[24] Jack once told her, " 'You don't know what you mean to me. It's like being tossed in the Paumotus and coming into a safe harbor at last!' "[25]

Charmian claims that Jack drew on his love for her and the nature of their relationship as he wrote the stories collected in *Love of Life*. As evidence of this, she quotes the ending of one of these stories, "Negore the Coward," in which the hero dies in the arms of a woman. "And as even the memories dimmed and died in the darkness that fell upon him, he knew in her arms the fulfillment of all the ease and rest she had promised him. And as black night wrapped around him, his head upon her breast, he felt a great peace steal about him, and he was aware of the hush of many twilights and the mystery of silence."[26] The editor to whom London first submitted this manuscript "comment[ed] with surprise and delight upon the intangible 'new touch' in Jack's work."[27] Art now imitates life.

Making love and writing books were intimate expressions of Jack London's emotional life, and both were so shaped by his notions of what was proper for men and women to say to one another that sometimes love and art dissolved into a tepid bath of Victorian sentimentality. As he courted Charmian and pulled himself out of the long sickness, he read Tennyson's *Idylls of the King*, and lamented that he had grown up without Charmian's knowledge of the gnomes and fairies.[28] London's recovery involved a willful embrace of illusions that were to take the place of lost dreams, and, as we saw in *The Sea-Wolf*, a retreat from the literary realism that distinguished his best work.

The intimate relationship between London's marriage, his recovery from the long sickness, and the change in his art is symbolized by Charmian's role as London's typist and secretary. When there was talk of hiring a secretary to keep up with London's voluminous correspondence, Charmian wrote in her diary, "I hate the thought of a secretary. I love the intimacy of the correspondence. It keeps me so in touch with Mate's life."[29] She was the filter through which flowed the daily thoughts of her author-husband. Though they eventually did hire a secretary, Charmian continued to type London's manuscripts. From 1904 until 1916 hers were the first eyes to see what Jack had written and hers the first consciousness through which his stories passed. Charmian was his most constant and immediate audience. In 1912 she began to participate actively in the writing of his books. She supplied London with notes on women's culture—sewing, childbirth, and baby clothes—which he used in *The Valley of the Moon*.[30] Her role in the writing of *The Mutiny of the Elsinore* was even more direct: she copied out pages of her diary for Jack to use, suggested to him where he should end the book, and made notes on the heroine,[31] who, the reader is somewhat taken aback to discover in that book, has "the distressing attributes of the blind-instinctive race-mother," or, in another refrain, "the nest-making, planet-populating, female, human-woman" (pp. 100, 101).

This characterization of the heroine probably reflects Charmian's increasing preoccupation with motherhood and Jack's distancing of himself from it. The narrator of *The Mutiny on the Elsinore*, a disillusioned writer, confesses his dissatisfaction with women: "I had endured them, but I had been too analytic of the faults of their primitiveness, of their almost ferocious devotion to the destiny of their sex, to be enchanted with them" (p. 9). Charmian was at this time forty-two years old and facing menopause with only the painful memories of her short-lived "Joy-baby" and her dimming hopes of conceiving again. Her diary reflects an intense desire to have a baby, and as she brought pressure to bear on her husband, the baby question was always connected with the question of Jack's drinking. Their baby was born and died in June of 1910. A little over a year later, Charmian springs the first of her "baby propositions," which she will repeat on several occasions in the next few years. "I spring 3-drinks-a-day and baby proposition, and it looks as if it might go thro'," she records on November 9, 1911. On the next day she writes "Mate falls for the less drink and more baby. Takes me up on it." But this resolve meant little during the two months of the winter they spent in New York City, during which Jack's drinking was unusually heavy, even for a man to whom *moderation* meant three drinks a day. On their last day in the city before they sailed on the *Dirigo*, Charmian notes, "He drinks pretty steadily all morning. Throws up some of it."[32] She continued to want a baby very badly, and on May 23, 1912, promised herself to "have another serious confab with Mate concerning Land Alcohol." Shortly thereafter they tried to conceive, and by the time they returned to land in July, she was pregnant. At very nearly the same time, London finished *The Valley of the Moon*, the novel he had set aside in New York. In that novel, the heroine has a miscarriage during a violent workers' struggle in the city; when she and her husband move to the quiet California hills, she successfully gives birth. Charmian felt "blue and foreboding" as she typed the part of the manuscript that dealt with Saxon's miscarriage.[33] Her forebodings proved a more accurate oracle than the plot of *The Valley of the Moon*, for, on August 13, less than two months after their arrival in Glen Ellen, Charmian miscarried.[34]

Charmian continued to press her suit: "I tell Mate, 6 weeks on water, and then I'll try again," she writes on August 20, 1913. Despite London's decision, in February of 1914, to "turn down a page" on the baby matter—a decision that upset Charmian deeply—he reconsidered, and they continued to hope for a baby. In April she felt "pretty sure of {her} condition," and, marking ahead in her diary, counted the days until birth. But the following month she was puzzled and disappointed: "My waist-measure is lessening, I am all at sea, and look sadly at the penciled-ahead days in this diary."[35] What she took for pregnancy was in all likelihood evidence that she was getting beyond child-bearing age.

In a diary composed of massive amounts of trivia, Charmian's desire to have a baby evokes a few genuine and moving moments. Her account of the loss of her daughter, Joy, is particularly worth remark. In the days immediately following the baby's death, the restraint she exercised almost broke down when her milk came in: "After remaining dormant until they thought there'd be no trouble, my breasts rose up in protest, *beautiful* protest; and then came the strapping and binding of bandages, and the drying up of the surging milk. Alas and alack! I dare not *think* lest I weep and hurt my broken body."[36] All around her other women were giving birth, and she listened to the sounds of the newborn: "I learn their voices—some loud and strident, others soft and cooing, conciliatory, caressing. I love to hear them, and *still* I must not think."[37] Six days after the death, she allowed herself "the luxury of *letting down* a little from this iron control—of letting the tears run and run,—of thinking, and *daring* to think once more. I dare think now of my empty arms, and my unused breasts, and of the dear rotundity that was mine so many sweet months, in which lived and moved the little body that died in getting out."[38] Each day the nurses brought her various babies who had recently arrived, and she took some comfort in holding them next to her. Jack, too, was profoundly moved by the death of his daughter, but his way of dealing with his emotions was different from Charmian's. That night he got into a fight in a bar; he left the following night to cover the prizefight in Reno. When he returned he was full of news of the trial he was involved in as a result of his fight in the bar, and within a few weeks he was totally absorbed by his scheme to make "enormous profits" from his investment in a new lithography machine, the Millergraph.[39] London's way of dealing with disappointment was to hurl himself with frenetic energy at new schemes and to project away from himself the painful emotions of loss.

Motherhood would have given Charmian a sphere of work all her own, separate from the consuming demands of her husband. As it was, she expended what might have been maternal energies on catering to his needs. "I put him early to sleep every night now," she reports in 1911, "—tuck him in and leave him."[40] When he did not think of her as a "mother-woman," London thought of Charmian as a "kid-woman," a kind of playmate and, as he was fond of calling her, his "twin-brother," full of "grit" and always game for pranks and boxing matches and grand voyages.[41] She ruined her health trying to keep up with the multiple expectations put on her (she especially resented the amount of "hospitality" she was expected to extend to

Jack's friends), but no doubt she thought herself blessed to be a New Woman, quite freed from the restrictive roles of Victorian womanhood. Viewed from another perspective, Charmian missed the best the nineteenth century had to offer women—the satisfactions of motherhood—without finding anything substantive to put in their place.

Besides the vicarious role in which Charmian served as her husband's amanuensis, playmate, and hostess, she admirably fulfilled another role the twentieth century increasingly expected of women: that of consumer. She tells of discovering, early in their marriage, her husband's "delightfully medieval" attitude toward the management of the family purse:

> Having been myself independent, and believing that he would
> take this into consideration, I looked for him to make no
> matter of a separate bank account, or at least the "allowance"
> loved of wives, that I might not suffer a sense of bondage.
> But no—like the bulk of men his was the pleasure of spending
> his own money upon the "one small woman." Any other
> arrangement was frowned upon—at the suggestion a frost
> seemed to spread over his face. And, seeing that it was he,
> I found the bondage sweet.[42]

Since her husband was one of America's best-paid writers, and since he was an exceptionally generous man, the bondage was sweet, indeed. In the various ports they entered on the *Snark* trip, Charmian took great pleasure in the clothes she had made and the jewels she bought. She spent much time buying, sorting, and admiring opals, and her preoccupation with her "treasures" gradually eclipsed her work on her "diary" (a travelogue that eventually was published as *The Log of the Snark*). She had begun this latter venture with considerable enthusiasm and energy, but she was discouraged by her husband's harsh criticisms of her work. Near the beginning of the voyage she wrote, "Mate criticizes my diary; misunderstands my attitude, and I shed many tears. My eternal loneliness. I mold myself in-so-far as I can to him; but I cannot stand irritability, nor will I. I mold myself so far, and what of rampant individuality I have refuses to get down and mind as I might wish."[43] By contrast with London's disparagement of Charmian's literary efforts, her pursuit of her "treasures" received his open encouragement. A diary entry

written just before their return from the voyage is especially revealing: "Go out late in afternoon to spend my remaining $14.00.
Discover embroidered coat and silk lace bertha-collar-thing, etc. and
come home full of hopes. My mate cables for $200.00 more. He's so
in love with my love for my things."[44] The involuted and distanced
emotional relationship suggested in the last sentence recalls Charlotte
Perkins Gilman's analysis of the sexualization of economic functions.

Gilman did not find it surprising that men recoiled with loathing
from the women they had made, but London's loathing was always to
be a secret from himself. He acted out his hostility rather than face it
directly. Whatever his "irritability," Charmian continued to adapt
herself to his needs. She even tried to "innoculate" herself against his
heavy smoking by taking up smoking herself,[45] but no matter how
"good" she was, his moods continued: "Mate distant. Wonder when
I'll get hardened—there's only one way—try to love him less. But
he isn't himself when he's like this. It wears off without words—I
kiss him goodnight yesterday after it was over; and I was good today,
we boxed, 2 times . . . and lost a game of cribbage to him, and copied
52 pages, Chap. XXVII, and counted."[46]

On her second anniversary she notes that she has boxed with her
husband before breakfast: "Head sore, but feel fine."[47] These boxing
matches caused Charmian considerable pain, but her participation in
them was part of her attempt to mold herself to her husband's needs.
What dark and repressed desires this pummeling served is hinted at
in a diary entry in which news of the boxing match is sandwiched in
between comments on their love life. During a particularly trying
time when everything was going wrong on the *Snark* trip, Charmian
records that their attempt to make love was "nearly disastrous, as the
time before." She writes: "But I persist, and everything is different,
after. Box, and get awful bump on mouth. Almost hysterical; but
after looking at it, I went on boxing. But must have sustained shock,
as I hardly slept all night. Mate the lover."[48] In the complicated
depths of Jack London's psyche, a psyche shaped by "the books"
and their notions of "Love" as well as by his own unacknowledged
desires, love and violence were sometimes inextricably linked.

NINE

THE LITERARY
MARKETPLACE

In spite of its sentimental caperings *The Sea-Wolf* earned Jack London a lot of money and remains today one of his most popular fictions. Because he was grappling with the contradictions of his society, the struggle to the death between Wolf Larsen and Humphrey Van Weyden has relevance beyond the psychomachy of London's long sickness. His sentimental solution was not a unique and isolated private happening, although he felt it to be such, but a solution agreeable to all those who were unwilling to face the realities of their society. London was engaged in a covert alliance with his readers, who preferred the illusions of Van Weyden to the brutal truths of Wolf Larsen. His collaboration with his bourgeois audience, a consideration in all of the writing London did for the market, was especially marked in his writing of *The Sea-Wolf* because of the special circumstances that surrounded its composition.

London had written about half the novel, which Macmillan had contracted to publish, when the *Century* expressed interest in serializing it. George Brett, the editor at Macmillan, informed London that Richard Watson Gilder was willing to pay $4,000 for the serial right, but that he specified certain provisions designed to insure the marketability of the story. Gilder would take the story, Brett informed London, "provided you will give him permission to blue pencil it ad lib and provided you can give him a synopsis of the last half full enough for his purpose and he likes it, i.e. thinks the American public will stand it." Gilder also had some reservations about the part of *The Sea-Wolf* that he had read. "I may tell you that he was very doubtful about what he called the brutality of the first half and thinks that several of the incidents will have to be cut down for magazine publication," Brett wrote.[1] Within the week London had written to Gilder giving him permission "to blue pencil all he wishe[d]"; as for his other provision, London felt that it was "practically impossible to give any synopsis of such a novel as this," but, as he summarized his letter in another letter to George Brett, "I have striven to show him that the situation, because of the characters themselves, will not permit of anything offensive."[2] By "offensive" London meant sexually suggestive, and from what we know of Maud and Humphrey, he was justified in his statement that "the characters themselves" would not permit such indiscretion. The point was delicate in the negotiations with Gilder, however, because, as London wrote to Cloudesley Johns, "the only thing Gilder hesitates about is the last half (unwritten) wherein a man and woman are all by themselves on an island."[3] In separate letters London assured Johns, Brett, and Gilder "that the American prudes will not be shocked by the last half of the book."[4]

It meant a lot to London to have the *Century* serialize his novel. In the first place, it meant $4,000. (*The Saturday Evening Post* had paid him only $700 for *The Call of the Wild*.) London had recently made an arrangement with Macmillan whereby he promised them several forthcoming books, of which *The Sea-Wolf* was one, in exchange for a stipend of $150 a month for two years. London had suggested this arrangement as a way of buying time to write the kinds of books he wanted; he wished to be free of the magazine stories he wrote in order to meet the monthly bills. Although this arrangement was in place, because of the peculiar financial circumstances in which he found himself (which included his recent separation from his wife), London was not free of money worries. He wrote to Johns on July 11, 1903, that he was "letting [the] contracted work go and hammering away at hack in order to catch up with a few of [his] debts" and that he did not anticipate "getting even" with his work for a full year.[5] If *Century* refused the novel, London wrote to Johns, "I'll have to plunge into bookwork up to my ears to escape bankruptcy. If *Century* does take it, why then I can take a vacation."[6] And "outside of money considerations," he wrote Brett, "I should greatly like to see the novel serialized in the *Century*. It means much in the way of advertisement and of bringing me into the notice of the clique of readers peculiar to the *Century*."[7]

London was under a great deal of pressure to write the remainder of *The Sea-Wolf* in accordance with the tastes of the American public, as arbitrated by Richard Watson Gilder. It is impossible to say how much these pressures influenced London's selection of language, scene, and incident. Clearly the second half of the book is inferior to the first, and it was this half that the *Century* puffed in its ads. "A strong love interest develops in the latter part of the story," said its announcement of the serialization, "and the plot brings out most picturesquely the triumph of the ideal over the actual phases of force and matter."[8] London's willingness to submit to Gilder's blue pencil suggests that his artistic conscience was not as active as his calculations of profit. On the other hand, London insisted that in the synopsis he prepared for Gilder there was "no alteration in [his] original conception of handling the story." "I elected to exploit brutality with my eyes open, preferring to do it through the first half and to save the second half for something better."[9] The credibility of London's statement is reinforced by the fact that *The Sea-Wolf* is only one of many "broken-backed" novels that London wrote. In "roughly one-third" of London's novels, "the structure follows a single clear-cut and unusual pattern," Gordon Mills argues. "In this pattern, the story is broken approximately into halves. The first half is an adventure story, marked by numerous scenes of violence. Near the mid-point of the book a love theme is introduced, and thereafter this theme dominates the book, although adventure may continue. In every instance this love theme symbolizes an attack upon unrestrained individualism and brutality."[10] Not only is this a striking pattern in London's novels; as we have seen, the movement from social reality to illusion, from Truth naked to Truth re-veiled, was essential to London's recovery from the long sickness. It is more likely that London's own compulsion to put the veils back on Truth, rather than the preferences of the *Century*'s readers, produced the Victorian repression that characterizes the end of *The Sea-Wolf*.

It is not surprising, however, that the strategy London devised to deceive himself and make it possible for him to go on living in industrial America in 1903 was one that was profitable in the literary marketplace. London had made the reasoned decision that it was better to live than to die; to live, he had to adjust himself to the world in which he lived. Standing alone before the power of monopoly capital, he was weak. Survival dictated that he at least adopt the pose of one who submitted to the industrial discipline of his

society. The sentimental endings he constructed did not challenge
the dominant order, and yet they gave the illusion of resolving its
oppressive social relationships. In being true to his own illusions,
London was true to those of the mass of the people. The congru-
ence of his private illusions and those of the public has its basis in a
common bourgeois consciousness, in a common need to forget the
sordid reality of the class structure.

Unfortunately, the sentimental strategy distanced London from his
readers in the same way that it distanced Humphrey from genuine
emotional engagement. The bonds created by a mutual agreement to
ignore the most important issues cannot be as strong as the comradeship forged through mutual sharing of fears and woes. London's
sentimental alliance with his middle-class readers undercut real communication between author and readers. Before he came to write
The Sea-Wolf London articulated this problem in an essay entitled
"Again the Literary Aspirant." The "howling paradox" that faced the
artist was "how and in what fashion must he sing the joy of his heart
that the printed speech thereof may bring him bread?"[11] He begins
by explaining that this is not a paradox for the mere literary aspirant,
"nor does it so appear to the man with artist-soul and the full purse."
Nor is it a problem for the man who has already arrived: he has
"compassed the paradox" in some way. "But the man dreaming
greatly and pressed by sordid necessity, he is the man who must
confront the absolute contradiction." The contradiction arises out of
the commercial considerations of the mass market: editors will publish only what masses of people want to read because they need
a large circulation to sustain the advertisements that bring in the
cash. This mass market taste lowers the literary quality of what is
printed. London argues that this mass market "is the penalty of
democracy." It is the price of "admitting the mass into living, or of
being forced to admit the mass into living (which is the same thing);
of giving the mass good houses, good clothes, free public schools,
and civil and religious liberty." These "newly manumitted" people,
whom London later refers to as "our own peasants and serfs, our
villains and clouts and clowns," are "totally without art-concepts,"
and yet they determine "what manner of speech the business manager may permit the editor to print on the pages of his magazine."
They are the hands that feed the writers, "and whosoever feeds a
man is that man's master." The aspiring artist who "spill[s] his unsung

song on the typewritten page ... quickly finds that singing into a
typewriter and singing out of a magazine are quite unrelated per-
formances"; that his "soul's delights and heart's desires" do not necessarily please the mass of people who seek "immediate literature," not
literary masterpieces.[12]

London had written to Cloudesley Johns at the beginning of his
career, "If cash comes with fame, come fame; if cash comes without
fame, come cash," but he was not able to take such a hard-boiled
approach to his art as he sometimes projected. He found in his dealings with the magazines that "bread and glory are divorced." He
knew how to write stories that the *Black Cat* would buy; he knew
how to imitate formulas that sold well. But what London was not
sure about in 1902 was how to "compass the paradox": how to both
be true to his heart songs and bring in the bread: "where he dreamed
of serving one master he finds two masters. The one master he must
serve that he may live, the other that his work may live, and what the
one demands most of all the other has little or no use for."[13] London
illustrates the different standards of the two masters in a dialogue
between a critic, "ultimate appraiser" of the work, and a magazine
editor.

> "Truth alone endures," whisper the discerning. "Be a far-
> visioner and we shall remember you, and our children and
> our children's children shall remember you." And the artist-
> aspirant sits him down and gives form and substance to eternal
> and beautiful truth. "Too strong," says the editor. "Which is
> another way of saying 'too true,'" the artist-aspirant objects.
> "Quite true," the editor replies. "It would cost me a thousand
> subscribers. Learn, O bright-browed youth, that I want no
> far-visioning; my subscribers are loth to part with their
> honest money for far-visioning." "You ... don't ... want ...
> truth ... ?" the artist-aspirant quavers. "Not so," says the
> editor, "but it were well to learn that there be truth and truth
> and yet again truth. We do want truth, but it must be truth
> toned down, truth diluted, truth insipid, harmless truth,
> conventionalized truth, trimmed truth."

The strong truth of the clear-sighted Wolf Larsen must be repressed;
in its place the magazine editors, acting for the mass of people, en-
shrine the insipid, harmless, and conventionalized truth of Hum-

phrey Van Weyden. When the artist-aspirant objects that to trim his truth is to "clip [his] immortality," the editor brusquely informs him, "I do not run an immortality market."[14]

London did not want to choose between having life and having immortal life. He wanted both. He wanted to fill his belly each month from the cash receipts of his stories, and he also wanted to be a "far-visioner" who would be remembered by us and by our children and our children's children. Never, in a conscious way, did he work out a strategy to achieve this. Yet he intuited that there was a difference between what the public consciously clamored for and what they unconsciously desired. London believed that his own success came out of his insistence on fidelity to himself and his own heart-songs, his refusal to quit grappling with the paradox until he learned somehow to compass it. When George Brett cautioned him that publication of *The Road*, London's tramping reminiscences, was likely to damage the sale of his other books, London replied, "In *The Road*, and in all my work, in all that I have said and written and done, I have been true. This is the character I have built up; it constitutes, I believe, my big asset. As my character has developed through my work from time to time, there have been flurries of antagonism, attacks and condemnations; but I pulled through them all, and the consistent and true picture of myself is by that much more clearly limned."[15] In capital letters, London spelled out the generalization that he drew from all of his publishing experience: "IT WAS MY REFUSAL TO TAKE CAUTIOUS ADVICE THAT MADE ME":

> At the very beginning, had I taken the advice of the magazine editors, I'd have been swiftly made into a failure. *McClure's Magazine* gave me $125 per month and held the bread-and-butter lash over me. Phillips said, "Write such and such stories for our magazines. Quit writing the stories you are writing." In short, he wanted me to make an eunuch of myself; wanted me to write petty, smug, complacent bourgeois stories; wanted me to enter the ranks of clever mediocrity and there to pander the soft, fat, cowardly bourgeois instincts. It was because I refused his advice that I broke with *McClure's* . . . but in the end I pulled through and did better by far than if I had taken Mr. Phillips' advice.[16]

London contemplates this discrepancy in "Again the Literary Aspirant" as he puzzles over the names of those who have arrived, who have "compassed the paradox," even though sketches such as theirs, the editor had said, "were not at all in demand." As to how the artist manages to compass the paradox—"That, dear reader, as the editor told him, is his business. Yours to be grateful that he does compass it."[17]

Remaining true to his deepest inner needs was essential for the artist, and yet this alone would not sell his work. In order to compass the paradox, the artist had to work out a special language—analogous to that in which Buck and Thornton communicated—which involved an act of translation: Buck took Thornton's hand in his teeth and applied pressure, but Thornton understood that this was not the act of aggression it seemed but an act of love, and likewise for Buck's understanding of Thornton's rough way of shaking his head from side to side. Beneath the gesture or the language is a common emotional message, and things are not necessarily what they seem. As Ahab tells the sober-minded Starbuck, who is "not game" for Moby-Dick, "come closer . . . thou requirest a little lower layer."[18] "The problem of the 'language of the tribe,'" London wrote to a correspondent, "is more profound than you apprehend—also more disconcerting than you may imagine for the one who attempts to talk in the lingo of two different worlds at one and the same time."[19] Communication between artist and readers depends upon disguise, beneath which the heart-songs of the artist are apprehended as the heart-songs of the reader.

Why is this disguise necessary? In the first place, it is obvious that disembodied feeling cannot be communicated; it requires gesture, form, language, which inevitably creates a potential disjunction between emotion and its expression. But what London is talking about in "Again the Literary Aspirant" is not this primary and necessary separation of feeling and expression. He does not complain that he wrote down his heart-songs and they were not understood. They were understood all too well. "Too strong," said the editor, which, he admitted, was another way of saying "too true." The problem faced by London—and Hawthorne, Poe, and Melville—was not just to find words in which they could communicate—but words in which they could communicate deadly truth while seeming to communicate only truth insipid, truth diluted, truth conventionalized. They had to develop a language that would subvert the sentimentalities of the mass market at the very moment in which they seemed to be serving those interests. Truth of the human heart—humanistic truth—was at odds with the social organization of society, and yet that society, through the editor acting as middleman, arbitrated what passed for truth. Thus it was necessary to dissimulate and smile while passing to the reader a sugar-coated dagger.[20]

This strategy relied heavily on the power of unconscious suggestion. Hawthorne's poetic language, Poe's symbolic landscapes, Melville's rich allusions—these were the means by which a hidden cargo was slipped by the readers. London achieved his ends in similar ways through use of what Earle Labor has called his "symbolic wilderness."[21] Instead of writing about the city savages, London transformed his material into a story of the primordial savagery of a wolfdog, in which neither the actors nor the plot carry an overt social message. This artistic transformation of his material in *The Call of the Wild* is like the distancing effected for Hawthorne by his use of the past; his stories that take place in the present—like *The House of the Seven Gables*—see the oppression of the old families by the monied interests, but they are incapable of challenging this by anything more threatening than the sentimental marriage of Phoebe and Holgrave. By contrast, *The Scarlet Letter*, set in the seventeenth century, probes dark and dangerous realms of psychic and social oppression. He allowed himself to do this, and was allowed by his readers, because his immediate aim was not readily apparent; it emerged only in the symbolic texture of the language, whose implications for nineteenth-century America were less than obvious. The writer who would write about his present society was, in London's words, forced to make a eunuch of himself. He had to diminish his artistic power, to dilute his truth. On the other hand, if he appeared to be writing of a society safely removed from that of his editors and readers, he had more latitude. Like slaves singing songs about the kingdom of heaven and thinking about a much more immediate deliverance, the artist-aspirant sang mutinous songs and dreamed of freedom.

There were several problems with this method of compassing the paradox created by bourgeois society. In the first place, it was easy to be misunderstood. "I have again and again written books that failed to get across," London complained to Mary Austin:

Long years ago, at the very beginning of my writing career, I
attacked Nietzsche and his super-man idea. This was in *The
Sea-Wolf*. Lots of people read *The Sea-Wolf*, no one discovered
that it was an attack upon the super-man philosophy. Later on,
not mentioning my shorter efforts, I wrote another novel that
was an attack upon the super-man idea, namely my *Martin
Eden*. Nobody discovered that this was such an attack. At
another time I wrote an attack on ideas brought forth by
Rudyard Kipling, and entitled my attack, "The Strength of the
Strong." No one was in the slightest way aware of the point
of my story.[22]

The striking discrepancy between what London thought he wrote
and what readers understand him to write remains today. On the
conscious level he may have been attacking Nietzsche (and the long
sickness) in *The Sea-Wolf*, but his readers, attracted to the vitality of
Wolf Larsen just as Humphrey Van Weyden was, do not respond to
London's attack, but to the truth of London's character, who looks
unflinchingly at the industrial society in which he lives. What London
thought he was laying to rest is the very thing that remains with the
reader. It is of course nothing new to suggest that the author's unconscious purposes make his work compelling in ways unknown to
himself. But here is precisely the problem: the artist-aspirant, in
smuggling his deadly truths to the reader in sugar-coated packages,
may fool himself in the process. In order to communicate through a
shared network of unconscious associations, the author must, to a
certain extent, hide what he is doing from himself. Thus the result of
all of this surreptitiousness is a kind of half-aware dream-knowledge.
This is the best possible result: the other, more germane to *The Sea-
Wolf*, is out-and-out mystification of the true relationships between
people and their relationship to society. As London says through
Pathurst, the jaded playwright of *The Mutiny of the Elsinore*, "I had
come to be oppressed by what seemed to me the futility of art—a
pompous legerdemain, a consummate charlatanry that deceived not
only its devotees but its practitioners" (p. 9).[23] If the artist can communicate intimate knowledge only by seeming not to do so, then
after he has said it, he cannot be sure that he has been understood,
and his readers cannot be sure that he meant what he seems to be
saying. The effect of this uncertainty is that reader and author, even

though they participate in the same social reality and have heart-songs in common, have the impression of communing only with themselves. The literary marketplace in this way acts to keep a collective consciousness from forming.

This indirect method of communication also gives rise to a new occupational group—the literary critics—whose task it is to explicate to the masses the hidden meanings of the artist's work. London differentiates his reading audience into "the large number of people [who] demand literature that is immediate" and the "small number of people [who] make the ultimate appraisement." The small number of people are the critics. "The critic hammers, hammers, hammers, praising and blaming, interpreting, explaining, making clear and plain, on his own responsibility guerdoning the artist and forcing the large number of people finally to guerdon him."[24] Although the critic facilitates communication between author and the common reader, he may also substitute a hierarchical structure and elitist jargon for the common singing of heart-songs. In his very facilitating the critic reinforces the social structures that divide author and audience: the critic, in London's words, "stand[s] upon the heads and shoulders of the others."[25] He is the "discerning" one who instructs the clownish masses. By setting himself above the masses he strengthens the very class divisions that make an interpreter necessary. And often the literary critic is well represented by London's Humphrey Van Weyden, who was so distanced from the social reality and from his own emotional responses that all he could possibly add to the readers' understanding was another layer of mystification.[26]

In "Again the Literary Aspirant" London did not view the task of the literary critic in such a way. He felt allied with him as with one who saw the truth, and it goes without saying that there are perceptive critics. By hammering away—like schoolmasters in the classroom, London analogized—they ultimately determine what works will last and will be read by future generations. But the price of this ultimate appreciation is that one has a very limited audience of discerning people, and this audience may be one that in large part is not even born at the time of the work's publication. Although London desired very much the immortality created by the continued life of his work in future generations, he also wanted to live in the here and now. The delayed communication between author and future genera-

tions may in some ways diminish the perception of a collective consciousness. For the reader it may obscure the social reality that gives
rise to that consciousness. The specific historical and social setting—
and possible analogies to the present—may be swallowed up in the
generalities of what are taken to be "universal truths." For the author,
this delayed communication could be disastrous: the artist-aspirant
who goes unappreciated for a month of his life, "failing to live to-day
and this month, [is] unbenefited by any possible resurrection of
to-morrow and next month."[27] Just as his body dies without bread to
sustain it, his consciousness, failing to make immediate contact with
an understanding readership, may withdraw.

London's perception of this division of readers into the discerning
few and the uneducated masses undercut his own attempts to communicate through his art. In notes for a story entitled "Forty Horses
Abreast," London penciled his scorn for his audience. "He ran his 40
horses of thought abreast. They couldn't get it, it's rich. They write
mere one-horse philosophy."[28] His disdain for the masses, apparent
in the epithets he applies to them in "Again the Literary Aspirant," is
even more baldly stated in the notes he scrawled on the envelope
that contained the manuscript. The first phrase he noted thereon is
"art representative of an inartistic people." The artist, it is implied,
does not speak for the people; he is better than the people deserve.
"Clodhoppers do not understand," London noted. "Matthews' wrong.
Prove by Munsey's."[29]

The references to Brander Matthews and Frank A. Munsey suggest that London had specific experiences of his own in mind as he
wrote "Again the Literary Aspirant," experiences that informed the
essay but did not make their way into the final draft. *Munsey's Magazine*, which in 1907 boasted the largest circulation and earning power
in the world, represented the ultimate challenge to London. To sell a
story to *Munsey's*, and to have it be a good story besides, was to
"compass the paradox" in an irrefutable way. Frank Munsey, a self-
made man who turned $40 of his own and $240 of borrowed money
into a publishing empire capable of buying and killing dailies that
competed with his other publishing ventures, embodied the editorial
consciousness London had in some way to get around if he would
be read by the masses. Describing the editorial stance of Munsey's
journals, Oswald Garrison Villard writes:

There was in them no editorial illumination, or passion, or
power. He stood with the great capitalists, of whom he was one,
and his dailies safeguarded their interests. But they were also
clean and respectable (as well as dull) both in their news and
advertising columns. No salacious stories crept into them. It is
to his credit that he never stooped to the gutter to succeed;
he preferred to kill or sell a daily rather than to degrade it.
In other words, his newspapers reflected the viewpoint of the
average prosperous American concerned with his own affairs
and his own success.[30]

In a letter to Cloudesley Johns, London expresses his determination
to storm this citadel of publishing propriety: "Lucrative mediocrity—
I know, if I escape drink, that I shall be surely driven to it. By God! if
I have to dedicate my life to it, I shall sell work to Frank A. Munsey.
I'll buck up against them just as long as I can push a pen or they can
retain a Ms. reader about the premises. Just on general principles,
you know."[31] Several months later he writes again to Johns, "Say, I
think I have stuck *Munsey's* with a thirty-two hundred word essay.
I wonder if it can be possible."[32] London never did sell work to
Munsey's, but his friend Cloudesley Johns did, and it was the occasion
of much private mirth on London's part. Johns had enough money so
that he did not have to rely on income from his writing, and London
envied him his immunity to the marketplace. London took great
pleasure in seeing his fellow aspirant seduced by filthy lucre, as he
recounts in his letter to Anna Strunsky:

> I have a friend who scorns such {hack} work. He writes for
> posterity, for a small circle of admirers, oblivious to the world's
> oblivion, doesn't want money, scoffs at the idea of it, calls it
> filthy, damns all who write for it, etc., etc.,—that is, he does all
> this if one were to take his words for criteria. But I received a
> letter from him recently. *Munsey's* had offered to buy a certain
> story of him, if he would change the ending. He had built the
> tale carefully, every thought tending toward the final consum-
> mation, notably, the death by violence of the chief character.
> And they asked him to keep the tale and to permit that char-
> acter, logically dead, to live. He scorns money. Yes; and he
> permitted that character to live. "I fell," is the only explanation
> he has vouchsafed of his conduct.[33]

The remarkable career of Johns's character, who, "logically dead," was permitted to live, is apropos of London's own stance after he pulled himself out of the long sickness.

London had studied the market long enough to know that endings were critical. Before Johns sold this story to *Munsey's* he had facetiously advised him that, if he really wanted to place "The God That Failed," he could simply change the ending so that the hero's prayers were answered. "Then a myriad of Sunday School papers would have clamored for it. You might even have had it printed as a tract and sold several hundred thousand. It's all in the ending you see."[34] London's awareness of manipulating his own plots to suit the tastes of readers of pulp fiction like the *Black Cat* increased his contempt for the masses. He was less aware of the way in which he was being manipulated and shaped by the forces he was manipulating, of the way in which his own psyche was fragmenting under the pressure of his divided allegiance. That process may be inferred from *John Barleycorn* and *The Sea-Wolf*. The forces that were brought to bear on him, through his art, are clear in his correspondence with his editor, George P. Brett of Macmillan Company.

Brett expressed his understanding of the relationship between editor and author when he wrote, "we are . . . engaged in a sort of partnership which will tend to make your name and work increasingly better known through the coming months and years."[35] Brett patiently schooled London on the best way to bring renown to himself and profits to the company. Of the hero in "The Game," Brett wrote: "I should be sorry, I think, to see him made the hero of a book of similar stories, if you should decide that it is possible to do such a book, because his ending is not only tragic but very mournful under the circumstances, and the public likes, as I think I have told you before, to have its endings cheerful wherever it is possible to do so."[36] This rule of thumb applied even to documentary writing like that of *The People of the Abyss*, of which he wrote: "Now the great fault of this manuscript in my opinion, that is to say as far as its possible sale to the public is concerned, is this, that the manuscript is pessimistic in tone throughout, and that the natural audience for such a manuscript on the other hand is an optimistic one, an audience believing in the betterment of conditions and indeed in the roseate view of all existing institutions."[37] It was Brett's opinion that an "optimistic roseate view" could be included without making the book "less true to the actual facts." He suggested that the last chapter be "an optimistic chapter, a chapter pointing out the possibilities of amelioration of the terrible conditions that you set forth." He assured London that "there are literally thousands of people" ready to right these conditions if only they were shown the way.[38] The likely effect of such an optimistic view, of course, would be to reinforce the middle-class readership's belief in the goodness of the Way Things Are. Whatever pain they might have experienced through reading about the degraded lives of the slum dwellers would be anesthetized in the pious thought that this might be changed—thus sparing the reader any further thought or effort on the matter. London summarized the revisions he made in response to Brett's suggestions: "I have wholly cut out the references to the King of England in the Coronation chapter, have softened in a number of places, made it more presentable in many ways, and added a preface and a concluding chapter. In this concluding chapter I have surely been optimistic (as I really am), though I have seriously challenged the political managing class of England."[39]

The function that popular literature serves is clearly suggested in a letter Brett wrote to London during World War I, at which time London was trying to market two new dog stories. Brett found the first of these, entitled "Jerry" [*Jerry of the Islands*], "to be one of the best and most truthful of dog stories ever written." But he thought it unfortunate that the story was so bloody, because "the public is getting its surfeit of gory incidents from the daily press," which was reporting the war news. If the story could be marketed after the war, he felt "Jerry" would be "a much better proposition in the way of sale from a business standpoint." To make sure his point had not miscarried, he summarized it in another letter: "Perhaps my understanding of the psychology of the reading public of the moment is wrong, but as I see it what they are looking for now is something the exact reverse of what they are getting in the daily press, which of course, is full of the suffering and sudden death which goes with this great European war."[40] Popular fiction, in Brett's view, allowed escape from the pain of social reality. Of course, he would not have expressed it that way; he was only in the business of giving the public what they wanted. By extending his logic, we can infer that during peacetime bloody novels are needed to stimulate in the overfed and lazy populace the illusion of martial adventure. This logic goes a long way toward explaining the popularity of the naturalistic novel of blood and struggle during the affluent decade of 1896–1906.

By presenting an alternate view of social reality, marketplace fictions hamper the development of class consciousness, which must develop out of an awareness of one's relationship to social reality. The most direct example of American naturalism's mystification of this process was its championship of the blond beast. This pseudo-racial type was a direct response to the social reality of the urban beasts, about whom, as London saw in the East End, there was nothing magnificent or heroic. When the ghetto people kill, London wrote, "they kill with their hands, and then stupidly surrender themselves to the executioners. There is no splendid audacity about their transgressions. They gouge a mate with a dull knife, or beat his head with an iron pot, and then sit down and wait for the police" (*PA*, 222). One can compare this with the "splendid audacity" of a Wolf Larsen or, as London does, with "the great blonde beasts" who, "in the old time . . . rode in the battle's van and won their spurs by cleaving men from pate to chine. And, after all, it is far finer to kill a strong man with a clean-slicing blow of singing steel than to make a beast of him, and of his seed through the generations, by the artful and spidery manipulation of industry and politics" (*PA*, 168–69). Naturalism's glorification of primitive, Viking heroes was a disguised protest against the limiting conditions of twentieth-century urban life, a reactionary protest that presented in racial guise the possibility of recreating the self-made individual of the 1860s. Thus energies that might have been channeled into class consciousness were diverted into a pseudo-racial consciousness that gave the illusion of class identity and strength. These blond-beastly fictions purveyed fantasies of violence to feed an inner conviction of impotence and rage.

In manipulating formulas that pleased his readers and put money in his pocket, London succumbed to the paradox rather than compassed it. To compass the paradox the artist had to be willing to live in a state of tension between what was and what his heart told him should be. This was not a comfortable state, yet out of such a "sickness" came *The Call of the Wild*, which both sold millions of copies and expressed the deepest truths of London's art. In order to do this London had to consciously embrace the paradox and the pain that that awareness brought with it. He had to be willing to face death and oblivion, and he had to believe in himself enough to do it. It was London's flaw that he loved life too much and believed in himself too little. Loving life, he killed himself emotionally so that he would not have to experience the pain. His "healthy" consciousness was distanced from the pain, distanced from the social reality, distanced from other people. All that was left to this consciousness was the sense of power and control that comes to those who consciously manipulate the emotions of others without involving their own.

London's accommodation to his society created in him the psychic satisfactions of a prostitute, satisfactions that are described with great awareness by Roberta Victor, the hooker whom Studs Terkel interviewed in *Working*:

> As a call girl I got satisfaction, an unbelievable joy—perhaps perverted—in knowing what these reputable folks were really like. Being able to open a newspaper every morning, read about this pillar of society, and know what a pig he really was. The tremendous kick in knowing that I didn't feel anything, that I was acting and they weren't. It's sick, but no sicker than what every woman is taught, all right?
>
> I was in *control* with every one of those relationships. You're vulnerable if you allow yourself to be involved sexually. I wasn't. They were. I called it. Being able to manipulate somebody sexually, I could determine when I wanted that particular transaction to end. 'Cause I could make the guy come. I could play all kinds of games. See? It was a tremendous sense of power.
>
> What I did was no different from what ninety-nine percent of American women are taught to do. I took the money from under the lamp instead of in Arpege. What would I do with 150 bottles of Arpege a week?
>
> You become your job. I became what I did. I became a hustler. I became cold, I became hard, I became turned off, I became numb. Even when I wasn't hustling, I was a hustler. I don't think it's terribly different from somebody who works on the assembly line forty hours a week and comes home cut off, numb, dehumanized. People aren't built to switch on and off like water faucets. . . .
>
> The overt hustling society is the microcosm of the rest of the society. The power relationships are the same and the games

are the same. Only this one I was in control of. The greater
one I wasn't. In the outside society, if I tried to be me, I wasn't
in control of anything. As a bright, assertive woman, I had
no power. As a cold, manipulative hustler, I had a lot. I knew
I was playing a role. Most women are taught to *become* what they
act. All I did was act out the reality of American womanhood.
[pp. 102–3]

London pandered to the tastes of society's pillars without Roberta
Victor's awareness of the psychic cost. Yet in asides and passing
remarks and notes for unwritten stories London allied himself with
the role of the prostitute. Writing to Mabel Applegarth of his lonely
battle to succeed, London capped his self-explanation with the retort,
"if I were a woman I would prostitute myself to all men but that I
would succeed—in short, I will."[41] In 1911 an article on Gaby Deslys,
Parisian sex symbol, caught London's eye in the *American-Examiner*.
Her success story was very like London's, and she had no reticence
in expressing her goals in life:

> "I am mercenary! I do love money. I take all I can and I keep
> all I get. I give nothing back.
>   That is because I am just! Just to myself, which is the highest
> form of justice. There is no justice in that foolish sentiment
> which prompts some women to sacrifice themselves. Once
> sacrificed, what are they? Slave or miserables! It is a weakness."

There were many men who wished to be seen with such a glamorous
and well-known woman, and Gaby Deslys tells with a mixture of
relish and contempt of the many offers from would-be escorts. These
foolish men who think she will leap at their invitations to dine with
them are told that she will come—but not for free. "There are few
men whose company could compensate me for my loss of time!" In
her bald statements of the logic of a commercial society, Gaby Deslys
is reminiscent of the clear-seeing Wolf Larsen. She summarizes her
philosophy succinctly: "The world will take all a woman has and will
give her nothing in return if she asks for nothing. But let her fix the
price for it and stand by it and the world will give her all she wants
and ask to give her more." London wrote at the top of this clipping,
"I can make a great woman character of her."[42]

Had London been able to write a story about such a woman, and had he faced squarely and consciously the implications of such a woman character, he might have overcome the ambivalence he felt toward middle-class women, whom he unconsciously took to be prostitutes disguised as saints. If he could have looked honestly at the reality of women's situation and seen in it a paradigm of his own, he might have found a true comrade, and banished, from his fiction and his life, the sentimental mate-woman. Instead, London harbored the ambivalence. His attitude toward women is the cornerstone of his walled-up consciousness, the stumbling block to awareness of self. While Humphrey Van Weyden embraced the saintly and sexless Maud Brewster, he secretly desired Wolf Larsen, who embodied both a materialistic philosophy and an unabashed sexuality. Had London been able to face the sexual exploitation of women—instead of preserving them as a saintly refuge from the commercial world— had he been able to look at Truth naked and ready to trade her favors for bread, he might have been empowered by that truth rather than helplessly enthralled by it. He might have joined with other women and men and turned their chains into their common strength. But this kind of truth-seeing character and clear-sighted alliance was not fostered by the fiction of the magazines.

TEN

LONDON'S SOCIALIST FICTION

After London established his literary reputation, he had more latitude in the material the editors would accept, and he experimented, especially in the period between 1905 and 1909, with stories that had a political point of view. It is fair to wonder if London did not bring a different consciousness to bear in the stories he wrote not for the literary marketplace but to further the cause of socialism. Three of these stories are especially revealing of London's relationship to the working class. They are "The Apostate" (1906), "The Dream of Debs" (1909), and "South of the Slot" (1909). A fourth, "The Strength of the Strong" (1911), is notable for its eloquent expression of the goal of a cooperative commonwealth.

Much can be inferred about London's relation to his material by the persona that he adopts in the telling of his stories. "The Strength of the Strong," like "South of the Slot," is an extraordinarily controlled and well-wrought piece. In it London adopts the parable form and with it a formal distance from his material. He employs a third-person narrator, but the events of the tale, which concern the rivalry between two primitive tribes, the Meat-Eaters and the Fish-Eaters, are told by Long-Beard, patriarch of the Fish-Eaters. This story-within-the-story technique further distances author and reader from the material, as does the story's unfolding in the dawn of human history. London's narrative stance in "The Strength of the Strong" is very like that characteristically adopted by Hawthorne in his allegories of the human heart: there is an evenhandedness in the portrayal of characters, and personality is subordinated to psychological and social types. This is appropriate to their exploration not of one person's consciousness but of the dynamics of social intercourse.

Long-Beard, speaking in "not exactly . . . the words recorded" but in "animal-like sounds . . . that meant the same thing," tells a story of human achievement and human frailty. His narrative begins with an incident through which a new tribal consciousness emerged. The Fish-Eaters, who numbered sixty men among their families, were attacked by ten Meat-Eaters from the neighboring valley. The Fish-Eaters all took to their trees and were overcome, family by family, by the Meat-Eaters. "Of the ten Meat-Eaters, each man had had the strength of ten, for the ten had fought as one man. They had added their strength together. But of the thirty families and the sixty men of us, we had had the strength of but one man, for each had fought alone."[1] In response to this incident, the Fish-Eaters held their first council, and in that council they formed their first tribe. For mutual protection against the Meat-Eaters, they adopted a social division of labor in which the lookouts posted on the divide acted as "the eyes of the tribe," and armed guards protected those who gathered food. Long-Beard then chronicles the events that disrupted the harmony of this tribe, and London's parable tells of the competition for wives, the rise of property and money, and, not least of all, the emergence of a bard who sings songs that justify the oppressive social order that emerges as a few members of the tribe gather to themselves the land, its natural products, and the fruits of the labor of others. The parable ends in the present, as Long-Beard expresses his conviction that "someday . . . all the fools will be dead," and people will no longer listen to the mystifying songs of Bug, who, "when a man rises up to go forward . . . sings that that man is walking backward to live in a tree." Then "all men will be brothers, and no man will lie idle in the sun and be fed by his fellows" (p. 286).

This is perhaps London's finest expression of his socialist con-sciousness. The distancing achieved by his formal devices allows him to deal forthrightly with the institutions of his society. The parable is a disguise of sorts, but it is an accepted literary device through which dangerous and seditious views may be expressed. In that it is an accepted and "public" device, it differs from the private dream-language that characterizes London's more covert attempts to sub-vert his readers. The "public" quality of London's narrative stance is responsible for the high degree of control he exercises on his material. With complete awareness of what it is about, "The Strength of the Strong" juxtaposes what is with what should be. Yet it must be said that, like Hawthorne's allegories, this parable appeals primarily to the intellect, not the emotions. It lacks the power of *The Call of the Wild* and does not seem to engage London's and the reader's desires on the deepest level. Still, it is a more humanistic vision than London ordinarily brought to his stories of human beings, which perhaps has to do with the fact that the Fish-Eaters are suspended between the animal world and the modern world of industrial capitalism.

"The Apostate" is the most directly autobiographical of the four stories. Though London is predictably closer to his material, he still exercises a high degree of control over his story. Perhaps because the factory life of Johnny, a "work-beast," so clearly represented an earlier, discarded self, London was able both to understand his character and to feel distant from him. The story begins with an effective and highly realistic scene in the domestic life of the working poor. Johnny's mother is engaged in waking Johnny up in the predawn hours so that he can eat his meager breakfast and walk two miles to the mills, where he has been employed since he was seven years old. She shakes him and pulls off his covers, and he does drowsy battle with her and makes a determined effort to hold on to his sleep. Although the psychology of the protagonists is very different, this morning scene reminds one of the opening of Richard Wright's *Native Son*, perhaps because the relationship of working-class mother to son is similar in both stories. The mother's consciousness, narrowed by the struggle to survive, sees only Work and Duty. She "[does] the best [she] can" (p. 223), but her vision does not extend beyond the borders of the factory gates. Johnny becomes an "apostate" to this consciousness, just as Bigger Thomas does through a very different set of actions. The mother is both self-sacrificing and dominant. (There is no father mentioned in either story.) She gives one of her slices of bread to Johnny that he may have a bit more food in his stomach to give him strength for the long day ahead. But she is also the immediate agent of Johnny's oppression, in that it is she who wakes him up and insists he hurry or else "be docked." And as the story develops, we learn that she has extracted much from Johnny in exchange for the bits of bread and half-cups of coffee she has denied herself. For Johnny is the oldest of the several children. At seven years old he became the male head of the family. At eleven, on the night shift, he was initiated into adolescence. At age twelve or thirteen, he is already an old man; his childhood is far behind him, and he feels "robbed of a large part of that playtime," for even as a young child he was pressed into duty as caretaker of his younger brother, Will. Will's robust and cheerful constitution is in contrast to that of the thin and apathetic Johnny, and he has been nurtured at Johnny's expense. His mother's plans for social advancement rest with Will, whom she hopes will remain in school and become a bookkeeper. Johnny must be sacrificed to that end.

In this story London aired some of his early resentments against his family and the demands that were made upon him in his childhood. He was twenty-one when John London died and he became the male head of the household; this meant that he had to take a factory job instead of continuing his college career. Long before this, his family relied upon his earnings, as London relates in the following letter to Mabel Applegarth:

> Duty—at ten years I was on the streets selling newspapers. Every cent was turned over to my people, and I went to school in constant shame of the hats, shoes, clothes I wore. Duty— from then on, I had no childhood. Up at three o'clock in the morning to carry papers. When that was finished I did not go home but continued on to school. School out, my evening papers. Saturday I worked on an ice wagon. Sunday I went to a bowling alley and set up pins for a drunken Dutchman. Duty— I turned over every cent and went dressed like a scarecrow.[2]

His specific resentments against his family come out in his memories of the times they asked him, not for his wages but for the nest egg that he had slowly accumulated by denying himself: "I remember how I was trying to save the money to buy a skiff—eight dollars. All that summer I saved and scraped. In the fall I had five dollars as a result of absolutely doing without all pleasure. My mother came to the machine where I worked [in the cannery] and asked for it. I could have killed myself that night. After a year of hell to have that pitiful—to be robbed of that petty joy." And again, he remembers the times that John London came to him at the high school where he worked in after-school hours as a janitor, to ask for "a half dollar, a dollar, or two dollars." He always gave it to him, even though he "had a place to put every bit of it" himself.[3]

London's character Johnny renounces the world of Work and

Duty that his family has enmeshed him in. He simply leaves his mother and brother and sisters to fend for themselves. He hops a freight train and exchanges the life of a work-beast for the life of a tramp, just as London did after his "orgy of work" in the Oakland power plant. But there remains a significant difference in the careers of author and character. London does not follow the career of his character past the point at which he breaks with his family and jumps the freight, yet, whatever lay in Johnny's future, we have no reason to suspect that he will educate himself and become a writer. Johnny's proletarian beginnings are in contrast to the lower-middle-class strivings of London's family. The social level to which the Londons aspired is aptly described in London's picture of what his life would have been like had he followed his sister Eliza's promptings:

> I would to-day be a clerk at forty dollars a month, a railroad man, or something similar. I would have winter clothes, would go to the theatre, have a nice circle of acquaintances, belong to some horrible little society like the W.R.C. [Women's Relief Corps], talk as they talk, think as they think, do as they do— in short, I would have a full stomach, a warm body, no qualms of conscience, no bitterness of heart, no worrying ambition, no aim but to buy furniture on the installment plan and marry.[4]

Johnny's life is closer to the bare necessities of life, and from the beginning his mind and body have been shaped by industrial rhythms. His mother was a mill worker, and Johnny was born right there in the mill, amid "the pounding, crashing roar of the looms . . . drawing with his first breath the warm, moist air that was thick with flying lint. He had coughed that first day in order to rid his lungs of the lint; and for the same reason he had coughed ever since" (p. 226). London's descriptions of Johnny are flat and without affect. He is the "perfect worker," yet London sets this down as a "commonplace," something that "didn't seem to mean anything to him anymore." There is no zest, no challenge in turning out more work than everyone else. Usually when describing work experiences, London mixes with the drudgery a note of challenge, whether he is writing of his own exploitation in the power plant or of Buck's toil in the traces. Even as he is aware of the exploitation of the worker, he pays tribute to the blond beast who can ride high on the shoulders of others. This dubious pleasure is denied Johnny, who "from the perfect worker . . .

had evolved into the perfect machine" (p. 226). London describes his experience in the glass factory: "The superintendent was very proud of him, and brought visitors to look at him. In ten hours three hundred dozen bottles passed through his hands. This meant that he had attained machine-like perfection. All waste movements were eliminated." London's focus shifts from Johnny's prodigious production to the effects of this work on his body: "Every motion of his thin arms, every movement of a muscle in the thin fingers, was swift and accurate. He worked at high tension, and the result was that he grew nervous. At night his muscles twitched in his sleep, and in the daytime he could not relax and rest. He remained keyed up and his muscles continued to twitch. Also he grew sallow and his lint-cough grew worse. Then pneumonia laid hold of the feeble lungs within the contracted chest, and he lost his job in the glassworks" (p. 231).

Johnny's work has shaped his spirit as well as his body. He has no strong desires. Up until his apostasy, he accepts his family and his job in an uncomplaining, listless way. "His consciousness was machine consciousness" (p. 234) and his life is circumscribed by industrial rhythms; he goes to work when it is dark and gets out of work after dark. London writes, "In the interval, the sun had made a golden ladder of the sky, flooded the world with its gracious warmth, and dropped down and disappeared in the west behind a ragged skyline of housetops" (p. 228). This description of nature's beauty is given an edge by the reader's awareness that such sights are outside the bounds of Johnny's consciousness. The factory whistle, not the sun's movement through the sky, punctuates Johnny's life, just as the memorable events in his life are the minute alterations in the industrial routine—like the occasional visits of the Factory Inspector (which strike terror in the hearts of the underage boys at the machines). The most memorable event in Johnny's work life was the day he was put to work on the starcher: "It was a colossal event. Something had at last happened that could be remembered beyond a night's sleep or a week's pay-day. It marked an era. It was a machine Olympiad, a thing to date from. 'When I went to work on the starcher,' or 'after,' or 'before I went to work on the starcher,' were sentences often on his lips" (pp. 233–34).

London has created a character who is almost totally the product of the machines upon which he works. He is not an actor but one who is acted upon; he has not shaped his destiny, it has shaped him—

and mangled him in the process. London gives Johnny the energy to break with this dehumanizing labor, but this ending does not counterbalance the portrait London has carefully constructed of a human being who has been turned into a machine. The humanizing power of the ending is also somewhat vitiated by Johnny's limited consciousness. The break comes almost as his body's protective reaction to the pace under which he labors. He falls ill with the grippe: "All his bones ached. He ached everywhere. And in his head began the shrieking, pounding, crashing, roaring of a million looms. All space was filled with flying shuttles. They darted in and out, intricately, amongst the stars. He worked a thousand looms himself, and ever they speeded up, faster and faster, and his brain unwound, faster and faster, and became the thread that fed the thousand flying shuttles" (p. 235). Johnny recovers from the grippe, but the week-long rest from work that the illness afforded him changes his consciousness. He decides he will never work again. This decision appears as a symptom of insanity to his mother, who hurriedly calls the doctor again. Her main concern has been that Johnny not lose his job through this illness, and when the foreman tells her that his job will be held for him, she "anxiously" urges Johnny to thank him. The reader experiences Johnny's refusal to work as a victory over his mother, not a victory over the oppressive system within which he labors.

London could not have described Johnny's working-class life in such convincing detail had he not experienced the same mind-and-body-destroying factory rhythms; yet London attributes to his character a consciousness more limited than his own, and this discrepancy distances London from his creation. London's detachment is apparent in his description of Johnny as he walks away from his home and his job, never to return: "He did not walk like a man. He did not look like a man. He was a travesty of the human. It was a twisted and stunted and nameless piece of life that shambled like a sickly ape, arms loose-hanging, stoop-shouldered, narrow-chested, grotesque and terrible" (pp. 238–39). This description comes as a shock, even though the distortion of Johnny's body by his work has been completely accounted for. The reader can believe that the industrial labor has extorted a terrible human price; what is unacceptable and disturbing about London's description of Johnny as "a twisted and stunted and nameless piece of life" is that it seems to totally deny him humanity; he lacks even the glimmering illusions that made London's dray horse labor on. He is only a piece of flesh. In London's reduction of his character to this material basis he makes him less than human in the very moment that he asserts himself against the system that has dehumanized him. London can empathize with Johnny in his victory over his mother, but in this story neither Johnny nor his author break through to a fully human consciousness. Neither does the story transcend the immediate power relationships of the family to mount a critique of the social relations of capitalist production.

The remaining two stories, in contrast to "The Apostate," portray the workers in class-conscious revolt. In "The Dream of Debs" a general strike has paralyzed the whole country. James McClintock describes this as the only one of London's stories that "dramatiz[es] collectivist triumph."[5] Given this focus we might expect the story to be informed by a collective consciousness markedly different from the lonely, walled-up self of a Wolf Larsen. What we have in fact is an upper-class narrator like Humphrey Van Weyden, who witnesses the events of the strike in San Francisco—and even his own physical discomfort—with perfect detachment. The major difference between this story and others in which London has portrayed the working class is that here they are superbly organized and disciplined, and, far from being beastly and degraded, they take destiny into their own hands and bring capital to their terms before the strike is over. As Philip Foner has observed, the details of the strike are carefully worked out, and London's descriptions suggest that he "had done considerable reading on the tactics of a general strike" (p. 106). But the emotions that London might have brought to this collective struggle are singularly absent. London's use of an upper-class narrator who is victimized by the strike denies the reader direct participation in the working-class victory, and his dead-pan narration kills much of the vitality of the story. Clearly, as McClintock has suggested, London intended to satirize the limited consciousness of this Mr. Cerf, whose final comment on the events is that the "tyranny of organized labor is getting beyond human endurance," and "something must be done."[6] But it is significant that London was unable to imagine himself part of this working-class struggle. In this dream of working-class triumph, London allied his consciousness with that of a deposed upper-class victim.[7]

Contrary to McClintock, "The Dream of Debs" was not the only story London wrote that dramatized collectivist triumph. Although a strike plays a smaller role in "South of the Slot," it triggers emotions the story has built toward, and it truly suggests the birth of a new, collective consciousness. This story may be thought of as "The Dream of Jack London," for in it he takes a character divided between the middle class and the working class, and he transforms him into "Big" Bill Totts, labor leader. In "South of the Slot" London creates an alternative to the scenario he had worked out in *The Sea-Wolf*. In that novel the bourgeois narrator triumphed over Wolf Larsen by refusing to look at the reality of capitalist society. In "South of the Slot," the working-class persona triumphs over the middle-class Freddie Drummond, and, because Bill Totts is engaged in a collective struggle, he is associated not with the pessimistic materialism of Wolf Larsen but with unity, strength, and emotional wholeness. It is perhaps the only happy ending London ever wrote that was not sentimental and false, with the notable exception of *The Call of the Wild*.

The story takes its title from the iron cable line that divided Old San Francisco. North of the Slot were the theaters, shopping district, and businesses. To the south lay the factories, slums, and working-class homes. "The Slot was the metaphor that expressed the class cleavage of Society, and no man crossed this metaphor, back and forth, more successfully than Freddie Drummond. He made a practice of living in both worlds and in both worlds he lived signally well" (p. 258). Freddie Drummond is a sociology professor at the University of California, and he has built his academic reputation on his books about the working class. In order to write these books, Drummond assumes the clothes and identity of a working-class man, "Bill Totts," and simulates a working-class life south of the Slot. Then, in his "real" identity as Freddie Drummond, he analyzes the experiences that Bill Totts has had and writes books like *The Unskilled Laborer*, "a book that was hailed everywhere as an able contribution to the Literature of Progress and as a splendid reply to the Literature of Discontent. Politically and economically, it was nothing if not orthodox. Presidents of great railway systems bought whole editions of it to give to their employees. A manufacturers' association alone distributed fifty thousand copies of it. In its preachment of thrift and content it ran Mrs. Wiggs of the Cabbage Patch a close second" (p. 258).

London's stance is satirical, after the manner of Dickens. Whereas in "The Apostate" and "The Dream of Debs" London distanced himself from the working class by virtue of his middle-class consciousness, in "South of the Slot" London achieves artistic control by distancing himself from his middle-class character. London was often capable of vitriolic denunciations of "bourgeois pigs," but he seldom achieved such a measured assessment of a bourgeois character. This is all the more remarkable in that Freddie Drummond is engaged in precisely the sort of incognito research among the working class that London himself engaged in for *The People of the Abyss*.

In Drummond we recognize familiar traits of the London persona. "Before he arose to the surface from that first plunge into the underworld," London writes, "he discovered that he was a good actor and demonstrated the plasticity of his nature. He was astonished at his own fluidity" (p. 260). As Bill Totts, he is in the working class but not of it. He "kept notebooks, making a scientific study of the workers' slang or argot until he could talk quite intelligibly," but he does not use this language for real communication. "This language . . . enabled him more intimately to follow their mental processes and thereby to gather data for a projected chapter in some future book which he planned to entitle 'Synthesis of Working-Class Psychology' " (p. 260). London satirizes Drummond's "natural inhibition" and academic detachment. "He had but few friends. He was too undemonstrative, too frigid. He had no vices, nor had any one ever discovered any temptations. . . . When a freshman he had been baptized Ice-Box by his warmer-blooded fellows. As a member of the Faculty he was known as Cold-Storage" (pp. 260–61). This absence of emotion is, as we have seen, typical of London's middle-class characters. It should also be noted that Drummond's inhibitions are not unlike those of the working-class Johnny, who "from the perfect worker . . . had evolved into the perfect machine." Drummond was known as an amateur boxer, "but he was regarded as an automaton, with the inhuman action of a machine judging distance and timing blows, guarding, blocking and stalling" (p. 261).

Bill Totts is as graceful and warm as Freddie Drummond is cold and unbending. He drinks and swears and flirts with girls in an open and easy way and is "an all-around favorite." "Everybody liked Bill, and more than one working-girl made love to him." Drummond comes to enjoy the free and easy life south of the Slot, and his engagement triumphs over his academic detachment. In significant juxtaposition to the statement that more than one working-girl had made love to Bill Totts, London writes, "At first he had been merely a good actor, but as time went on simulation became second nature. He no longer played a part" (p. 262). Bill Totts's sexual and emotional life causes the crisis that upsets the nice double identity Freddie Drummond has sustained so well.

Drummond's crisis of class identity, as well as his journalistic experiences, place him at that point in London's career just before he went from the East End of London into his long sickness. Although Drummond discards the bourgeois identity that London decided to maintain at great personal cost, on a conscious level Drummond makes the same decision London had:

> It was while gathering material for Women and Work that Freddie received his first warning of the danger he was in. He was too successful at living in both worlds. This strange dualism he had developed was, after all, very unstable, and as he sat in his study and meditated he saw that it could not endure. It was really a transition stage; and if he persisted he saw that he would inevitably have to drop one world or the other. He could not continue in both. And as he looked at the row of volumes that graced the upper shelf of his revolving bookcase, his volumes, beginning with his Thesis and ending with Women and Work, he decided that that was the world he would hold on to and stick by. Bill Totts had served his purpose, but he had become a too-dangerous accomplice. Bill Totts would have to cease. [pp. 263–64]

Drummond plots the death of his double, just as in *The Sea-Wolf* London had plotted the death of Larsen. Just as Larsen's headaches began with his overtures to Maud Brewster, which signaled the danger of this man to Van Weyden, so Bill Totts appears a real threat to Drummond when he falls in love: "it was this fact that had given Freddie Drummond his warning." To protect himself from Bill Totts's love for Mary Condon, Drummond determines to go no more to the working-class world, and, to make sure that he is "entirely safe," he coolly plans marriage to Catherine Van Voorst, a woman of his class whose inhibitions rival his own. "All seemed well with him," London writes, "but Freddie Drummond could not quite shake off the call of the underworld, the lure of the free and open, of the unhampered, irresponsible life South of the Slot" (p. 266). London's language resonates with *The Call of the Wild*, his own fictional response to the crisis of class identity that Drummond is experiencing.

Giving in to the impulse to "have but one wild fling more" before "he settled down to gray lecture-rooms and sober matrimony," and lured on by the need of "a trifle more of essential data which he had neglected to gather" (p. 267), Freddie Drummond once more assumes the identity of Bill Totts. Inevitably he meets Mary Condon, and, from Freddie Drummond's point of view, he behaves "abominably": he treats her to oysters and walks her home and kisses her "repeatedly." Mary, the outspoken president of the International Glove-Workers' Union No. 974, is obviously in love with Bill Totts, and he with her. They share similar class backgrounds and work together in the labor movement, and they enjoy a comfortable physical relationship with each other. Freddie Drummond shudders as he recalls the events of that night. London writes, "he saw the pit yawning before him" (p. 267). London's next sentence suggests that Drummond's horror stems from his imminent danger of polygamy, but it is significant that London should invoke the image of the "pit"; more than anything else, his own horror of slipping into the lower orders of society impelled him to embrace marriage and middle-class respectability. London protected himself against the slippery slope by his books and by his safe marriage to Bess Maddern. This story suggests that he also protected himself from a truly intimate union and a spontaneous physical relationship.

Mary Condon's "graceful and sinewy" body and "amazing black eyes" are distasteful to Freddie Drummond:

> He detested women with a too-exuberant vitality and a lack
> of—well, of inhibition. Freddie Drummond accepted the
> doctrine of evolution because it was quite universally accepted
> by college men, and he flatly believed that man had climbed
> up the ladder of life out of the weltering muck and mess of
> lower and monstrous organic things. But he was a trifle ashamed
> of their genealogy. Wherefore, probably, he practiced his iron
> inhibition and preached it to others, and preferred women
> of his own type who could shake free of this bestial and regret-
> table ancestral line and by discipline and control emphasize

the wideness of the gulf that separated them from what their dim forebears had been. [p. 264]

The evolutionary man that London, through Drummond's consciousness, describes as "climb[ing] up the ladder of life out of the weltering muck and mess of lower and monstrous organic things" was Jack London, climbing out of the "muck and ruck of the forecastle," and out of communion with the "monstrous organic things" who did such primitive, biological acts as would ensure the continuation of the species. Entrance into the middle class involved sexual repression, just as it involved an artificial exaggeration of the evolutionary distance between man and his "dim forebears."

After Bill Totts's long fling, Freddie Drummond devotes himself single-mindedly to correcting proofs and courting Catherine Van Voorst. Their wedding is two weeks away when they chance to be riding down Market Street in an automobile. At the junction of Market with two other streets, they are suddenly stopped by a police escort. A meat strike is in progress, and the police are there to see that the scabs of the Beef Trust are not interfered with. A large crowd of angry workers has gathered for just that purpose. Freddie Drummond had been discussing settlement-house work with Catherine Van Voorst, but he breaks off in mid-sentence. "Nor did he resume it again, for the situation was developing with the rapidity of a transformation scene" (p. 268). The identity of Freddie Drummond is about to give way, once and for all, to that of Bill Totts.

London's description of the battle between the workers and the police is dramatic and exciting, and it engages the emotions of the reader in a way that the distanced narration of the general strike in "The Dream of Debs" cannot match. Drummond's auto is brought to a standstill when an Irish driver's rickety express wagon locks wheels with it. "On the other side a brewery wagon was locking with the coal wagon, and an eastbound Kearny Street car, wildly clanging its gong, the motorman shouting defiance at the crossing policemen, was dashing forward to complete the blockade." The police are trapped between the blockading wagons and the roaring crowd.

> The police were struggling to clear a passage. The driver of the coal wagon, a big man in shirt sleeves, lighted a pipe and sat smoking. He glanced down complacently at a captain of

police who was raving and cursing at him, and his only acknowledgment was a shrug of the shoulders. From the rear arose the
rat-tat-tat of clubs on heads and a pandemonium of cursing,
yelling and shouting. A violent accession of noise proclaimed
that the mob had broken through and was dragging a scab
from a wagon. The police captain was reënforced from his
vanguard and the mob at the rear was repelled. Meanwhile,
window after window in the high office-building on the right
had been opened and the class-conscious clerks were raining a
shower of office furniture down on the heads of police and
scabs. Waste-baskets, ink-bottles, paper-weights, typewriters—
anything and everything that came to hand was filling the air.
[p. 269]

As Freddie Drummond watches the fray,

somewhere in his complicated psychology one Bill Totts was
heaving and straining in an effort to come to life. Drummond
believed in law and order and the maintenance of the established; but this riotous savage within him would have none of
it. Then, if ever, did Freddie Drummond call upon his iron
inhibition to save him. But it is written that the house divided
against itself must fall. And Freddie Drummond found that he
had divided all the will and force of him with Bill Totts, and
between them the entity that constituted the pair of them
was being wrenched in twain. [p. 270]

Bill Totts, looking through Drummond's eyes, sees that the struggle
between the police and the teamster of the coal wagon is likely to be
decisive, for if the police can break through the blockade before the
crowd can tear the scabs from the trucks they will have won the day.
Struck by several riot clubs, the teamster hurls himself to the pavement, a prisoner. At this critical moment, the man sitting beside
Catherine Van Voorst "emit[s] an unearthly yell" and springs into the
coal wagon. He holds the fort, and the crowd, "recogniz[ing] its
champion," cheers him on with cries of "Bill! Oh, you Bill!" From
the sidewalk a woman warns Bill of an attack coming from the front
end of the wagon, and after he cleans out that flank with some well-
directed lumps of coal, Catherine Van Voorst, to her astonishment,
sees this same woman "with vivid coloring and flashing black eyes . . .

staring with all her soul at the man who had been Freddie Drummond a few minutes before" (p. 271). As the office workers in the
windows above erupt in applause, the police are routed, the scabs
are torn from their seats, and their horses are scattered. Catherine
Van Voorst watches curiously as her former escort is kissed on the
lips by the dark-eyed woman; then he disappears down the street,
"one arm around the woman, both talking and laughing, and he with
a volubility and abandon she could never have dreamed possible."
Together they "cross the Slot and disappear down Third Street into
the labor ghetto" (p. 272).

Just weeks before Freddie Drummond's staid middle-class identity
was to have been signed and sealed in marriage, his alter ego heard
the primitive call in the heart of the labor ghetto, and followed it to
the place from whence it came. The last paragraph of London's story
describes the result:

> In the years that followed no more lectures were given in the
> University of California by one Freddie Drummond and no
> more books on economics and the labor question appeared
> over the name of Frederick A. Drummond. On the other hand,
> there arose a new labor leader, William Totts by name. He it
> was who married Mary Condon, president of the International
> Glove-Workers' Union No. 974, and he it was who called the
> notorious cooks' and waiters' strike, which, before its successful
> termination, brought out with it scores of other unions, among
> which, of the more remotely allied, were the chickenpickers
> and the undertakers. [p. 272]

The crisis in the double life of Freddie Drummond was created by
his double's love life, but it is significant that Drummond's final
transformation into Bill Totts was precipitated, not by a kiss but by
a collective struggle in which Bill Totts and Mary Condon were
but two of a large group of class-conscious workers doing battle for
their common interests. Out of this struggle came, as a natural by-
product, the consummation of Bill Totts's love for Mary Condon.
Their relationship has less in common with the sentimentalities of
Humphrey Van Weyden and Maud Brewster than with the graceful,
free-swinging strides of Buck and his wood-brother. Bill Totts and
Mary Condon are truly comrades united around basic, life-defining
issues.

The movement of this story and the emotions it arouses directly parallel those of *The Call of the Wild*, and yet London is dealing not with dogs and a rugged Alaskan landscape but with human beings in the industrial present of San Francisco. "South of the Slot" does consciously what London achieved unconsciously in his story of Buck: he restores his hero to his kingly heritage; this movement coincides with the hero's self-integration through his membership in a pack, a tribe, a collective consciousness. This is a remarkable event in London's fiction. For him to deal with contemporary society and not slip into the class typing that so debilitated his characters and undercut his sympathy suggests the breakthrough of a new consciousness. Freddie Drummond and Bill Totts certainly *are* social types, but London's distance from them is the distance of a social satirist, whose vision is humanistic even as it is bemused and critical. The ending of this story, though it is like that of *The Call of the Wild*, is less lyrical. London's distance from Bill Totts keeps him from romanticizing his exploits. London emphasizes the concrete and specific and work-a-day nature of his achievements (that the chickenpickers and the undertakers joined the cooks' and waiters' strike) instead of making him into an Ernest Everhard, responsible, in *The Iron Heel*, for organizing an international revolution. In "South of the Slot" London affirms the joys of living and loving and working within the capitalist order. Collective consciousness breaks the spell that kept Wolf Larsen immured within his own psyche, condemned to watch never-ending replays of the same bad movie in which dog eats dog. It was a way of living now in the society of the future.

It is hard to explain why London should have been able to write this remarkable story when he did. The assumption that when he wrote "socialist" stories his consciousness was different from that which informed the stories he wrote for the literary marketplace is complicated by the fact that "South of the Slot" appeared originally in the May 22, 1909 issue of the *Saturday Evening Post*, organ of the newly prosperous middle class. And as we have seen, this is the only one of London's socialist stories in which he succeeds in both suggesting a collective consciousness and conveying the emotional gratifications of that consciousness. Under these circumstances, it is difficult to attribute a different consciousness to a genre called socialist literature, and it will readily be seen that this is not so much a genre as a convenient way of grouping those of London's stories that deal directly with the working class.

"South of the Slot" was written near the end of a period of sustained creativity, during which London produced some of his strongest and most authentic writing. Between 1905 and 1909 he was moving in on materials directly significant to him, drawing heavily on both his life experiences and his involvement in socialism. In addition to the socialist stories examined here, he wrote *The Iron Heel* and many political essays. His autobiographical writings include *The Road*, reminiscences of his tramping experiences told in London's best narrative style, and *Martin Eden*, an autobiographical novel and a major achievement. London's ability to deal directly with the materials of his life and with the political issues that engaged him testifies to his growing self-awareness and suggests that, as London approached his thirtieth birthday, he was moving toward a productive self-integration.

But the picture is changed somewhat if we look not at London's artistic life but at his personal relationships. London's intimate relationships may best be understood as sets of conflicting desires. In 1900 he had married Bess Maddern for intellectual reasons—while he was emotionally drawn to Anna Strunsky. His marriage to Bess was "safe," just as Freddie Drummond's to Catherine Van Voorst would have been. This marriage was dead by 1903, and during the following two years London's emotional life was divided between Charmian Kittredge, on the one hand, and George Sterling, on the other. The Bess/Anna relationship was played out again in the Charmian/George drama. In each case London was pulled between a love that was conventional and socially sanctioned and one that was forbidden and deeply alluring. Both times London chose the "proper" love and ignored the deeper call of his emotional life. Indeed, both marriages, to Bess in 1900 and to Charmian in 1905, appear designed to save him from the wild impulses of his authentic emotional life. He wrote two similar letters, one to Anna and another to George, explaining why their love could not be. He wrote despairingly of "the paradox of social existence" and "the tyranny of the crowd" to Anna: "What you have been to me? I am not great enough or brave enough to say. This false thing, which the world would call my conscience, will not permit me."[8] When George

Sterling felt betrayed by Jack's marriage to Charmian, Jack wrote him, "No, I am afraid that the dream was too bright to last—our being near each other. If you don't understand now, some day sooner or later you may come to understand. It's not through any fault of yours, nor through any fault of mine. The world and people just happen to be so made."[9] In both letters Jack blames the frustration of his true loves on the "world" and social convention, but the real reason lies elsewhere, in London's deep mistrust of his emotional life. Perhaps this was to him the same thing as the "world," for he believed that the world had taught him to value his intellect more highly than his feelings and to hide his emotions for fear of being laughed at. "Should you know me, understand this," he wrote to Anna:

> I, too, was a dreamer, on a farm, nay a California ranch. But early, at only nine, the hard hand of the world was laid upon me. It has never relaxed. It has left me sentiment, but destroyed sentimentalism. It has made me practical, so that I am known as harsh, stern, uncompromising. It has taught me that reason is mightier than imagination; that the scientific man is superior to the emotional man. It has also given me a truer and deeper romance of things, an idealism which is an inner sanctuary and which must be resolutely throttled in dealing with my kind, but which yet remains within the holy of holies, like an oracle, to be cherished always but to be made manifest or to be consulted not on every occasion I go to market. To do this latter would bring upon me the ridicule of my fellows and make me a failure. To sum up, simply the eternal fitness of things.[10]

As his imagination and emotions were repressed, they were also reified or idealized. No longer simply part of the felt process of human relationships, they became an "inner sanctuary," a "holy of holies," an "oracle." London seems to have guarded his feelings carefully so as not to lose them, but he only succeeded in cutting off his emotional life from the human relationships that are the nub of our humanity.

Sentimental love is the inevitable product of this repression, and it was sentimental love that drew London to Charmian and away from George Sterling. London's marriage to Charmian coincided with another love, that of the " PEOPLE," as if London's consciousness had an

imperious need to spawn contradictory desires. Charmian and the
"people" saved him from the long sickness brought on by his vision
of life in capitalist America. Paradoxically, London's affirmation of
this conventional, sentimental relationship may in fact have freed
him to pursue in his writings material that otherwise might have
been threatening and inaccessible. Just as Samuel Clemens's marriage to Olivia Langdon released a flood of early memories that
informed *Huckleberry Finn*, so London's marriage to Charmian com-
menced a very productive period in which he did some of his finest
autobiographical and socialist writing.[11] Distanced from real working-
class struggle by his safe marriage, he could afford to write of both
the struggle and the humiliation of working-class life.

ELEVEN

SEXUAL POLITICS
IN *THE IRON HEEL*

If "South of the Slot" was Jack London's most self-aware socialist story, his most ambitious contribution to socialist literature was *The Iron Heel*. Insofar as *The Iron Heel* is compelling, its energy comes from what Trotsky called the "powerful intuition of the revolutionary artist."[1] Ernest Everhard, the hero of this book, is able to see further than his contemporaries; before others are fully aware of the oligarchic tendencies of capitalism, Everhard prophecies the coming of the Iron Heel. London's power as a political visionary is the mainspring of a book that lacks novelistic interest yet deeply reveals the consciousness and identity of Jack London.

Written in 1906, *The Iron Heel* was the first of three novels that London wrote in rapid succession, each very different and each suggesting a different career for the London hero. In his next novel, *Martin Eden*, London's hero is an artist who, continually beset by visions of his past, transmutes them into literature. In *The Iron Heel* Ernest Everhard employs his visionary power not in the service of art but of political change. In *Burning Daylight*, written shortly after *Martin Eden*, London's hero is neither a revolutionary nor an artist but an extraordinarily successful capitalist. Ideologically and generically these three books move from revolutionary fantasy to bourgeois realism to capitalist fantasy. *Martin Eden*, by far the best novel of the three, is a flash of realism pressed on either side by contradictory fantasies. Martin Eden, the artist, was a projection of the social type London had become; Ernest Everhard, the revolutionary, and Burning Daylight, the capitalist, projections of social types London sometimes wished to be.

The Iron Heel, though a wish fulfillment, is not in the same category with *The Call of the Wild*: if the latter is a dark and wild dream, the former is a daydream, spun in the light of reason. As we might expect, the light of reason placed restrictions on London's consciousness, and it is these limitations that form the subject of this analysis of *The Iron Heel*. By calling attention to these limitations, I do not mean to devalue London's power as a political visionary: his strengths have already been observed, notably by Philip Foner.[2] Necessarily my discussion will give short shrift to those parts of the novel that are London's forte and will therefore not present a balanced view. But by focusing on the way *The Iron Heel* fails as a novel, we can perhaps better understand London's inability to integrate the political and the personal in his own consciousness. Better than any other single work, *The Iron Heel* reveals the radical disjunction between London's political insight and his emotional limitations.

The strengths of London's novel may be briefly suggested by quoting one of his most eloquent critics. Commenting on the book in 1937, Leon Trotsky wrote, "The book surprised me with the audacity and independence of its historical insights." This sentence captures the book's appeal: with bold strokes London extrapolates the future, building always on the bits of history he has lived through—the rise of populism and socialism, the violent suppression of dissent (Haymarket, industrial strikes), the powerful combinations of capital, the lessons of the Russian revolution. Of London's fantasy of the future Trotsky writes: "One can say with assurance that in 1907 not one of the revolutionary Marxists, not excluding Lenin and Rosa Luxemburg, imagined so fully the ominous perspective of the alliance between finance capital and labor aristocracy. This suffices in itself to determine the specific weight of the novel." And on London's prevision of fascism, Trotsky writes:

> In this picture of the future there remains not a trace of democracy and peaceful progress. Over the mass of the deprived rise the castes of labor aristocracy, of praetorian army, of an all-penetrating police, with the financial oligarchy at the top. In reading it, one does not believe his own eyes: it is precisely the picture of fascism, of its economy, of its governmental technique, its political psychology. The fact is incontestable: in 1907 Jack London already foresaw and described the fascist regime as the inevitable result of the defeat of the proletarian

revolution. Whatever may be the single "errors" of the novel—
and they exist—we cannot help inclining before the powerful
intuition of the revolutionary artist.[3]

But against London's penetrating ability to see into the future must
be weighed the limitations of his consciousness, as reflected in what
Earle Labor calls his "unfortunate choice of narrator."[4] London frames
his social prophecy in the consciousness of a woman (Avis Everhard)
who is unconsciously oppressed by the sexist assumptions of capitalist society. Thus the vigor and bite of London's political analysis is
at every point undermined by the sentimentality of his narrative
consciousness. This contradiction between content and form is identical to the one that, as we have seen, vitiates "The Dream of Debs."
In that story of a general strike, the working-class victory is per-
versely viewed through the eyes of an upper-class narrator; *The Iron
Heel* likewise filters revolutionary material through a bourgeois consciousness, this time of a woman brought up on the ideal of romantic
love, for a similarly muted and unsatisfactory result. In each case the
mode of narration neutralizes the force of the plot. The pairing of
virile, working-class struggle with a feminized, bourgeois narrator
produces emasculated prose. Form cancels content. These structural
flaws in London's art reflect not simply the failure of craft but also
deep-seated emotional limitations.

London provides an introduction to his novel in which, in the
guise of the editor, "Anthony Meredith," he excuses the "bias of
love" that distorts Avis's portrait of Ernest Everhard: "Yet we smile,
indeed, and forgive Avis Everhard for the heroic lines upon which
she modelled her husband. We know to-day that he was not so
colossal, and that he loomed among the events of his times less
largely than the Manuscript would lead us to believe" (*IH*, ix). The
"Manuscript" is the novel that follows, allegedly written by Avis
Cunningham Everhard as a journal of the events that took place
before and during the First Revolt against the oligarchy (The Iron
Heel) in 1932 and that was discovered seven centuries later in its
hiding place "in the hollow oak at Wake Robin Lodge" (Jack and
Charmian's retreat). Her narrative of the bloody events of the failed
revolt begins, improbably, with a "poetic" nature description very
like those with which Charmian London lards her *Book of Jack London*:
"The soft summer wind stirs the redwoods, and Wild-Water ripples

sweet cadences over its mossy stones. There are butterflies in the
sunshine, and from everywhere arises the drowsy hum of bees"
(*IH*, 1). This beginning may be excused, perhaps, by viewing it as a
convention of the naturalistic novel, which delighted in startling
contrasts between the world of bourgeois respectability and that of
blood, violence, and abrupt changes of identity. (Norris began *Moran
of the Lady Letty* by burlesquing this convention: "This is to be a story
of a battle, at least one murder, and several sudden deaths. For that
reason it begins with a pink tea and among the mingled odours of
many delicate perfumes and the hale, frank smell of Caroline Testout
roses.")[5] But it is impossible to excuse Avis's invocation, on the next
page, of her "Eagle":

> And then I am lonely. When I do not think of what is to come,
> I think of what has been and is no more—my Eagle, beating
> with tireless wings the void, soaring toward what was ever his
> sun, the flaming ideal of human freedom. I cannot sit idly by
> and wait the great event that is his making, though he is not
> here to see. He devoted all the years of his manhood to it,
> and for it he gave his life. It is his handiwork. He made it.
> [*IH*, 2]

As Earle Labor aptly remarks, "It is 1984 as it might have been penned
by Elizabeth Barrett Browning."[6]

But, as hinted in the introduction by "Anthony Meredith," London
does not permit Avis Everhard's remarks to remain unchallenged. In
a running series of footnotes, her editor, writing from the vantage
point of a socialist society seven centuries in the future, corrects her
bias, explains obsolete terms, and otherwise reveals the primitive
nature of life under capitalism. Philip Foner characterizes these comments as "devastating notes on conditions in Jack London's times . . .
set forth with so keen a satiric sense as to give them place among
the most brilliant indictments of capitalism ever written."[7] This
is perhaps overstating the effectiveness of the footnotes, but the
point to be made here is that London, through this textual device,
has formally split his voice in two: the sentimental consciousness of
the narrator, coming from the age in which London lived, is cor-
rected by another voice coming, as it were, from beyond the grave.
This split in narrative consciousness is like the split in *The Sea-Wolf*
between the sentimental narrator, Humphrey Van Weyden, and the

clear-sighted lord of capitalism, Wolf Larsen. Clearly London's sympathies in *The Iron Heel* are with the politically astute voice of the future, yet by telling his story through Avis Everhard he gives much more weight to her consciousness. Thus just as Wolf Larsen's consciousness is "walled up" under the pressure of Humphrey and Maud's romantic love, so too the voice of the editor is effectively buried by the sentimental consciousness of Avis Everhard. It is suggestive that London imagines this voice finding utterance seven centuries after his hero's death. That is a long time for a writer to go underground, and it suggests both the tenuousness and the pertinacity of London's emotional commitment to immortal life. That commitment was always in danger of being lost to the more immediate and insistent demands of a narcissistic ego that, in *The Iron Heel*, is of enormous dimensions.

The first scene in *The Iron Heel* is in outline precisely parallel to the opening scene of *Martin Eden*; the proletarian hero is brought to an upper-class home and introduced to the bourgeois heroine, who immediately falls in love with him. Both heroes make "a rather incongruous appearance." Avis notices Everhard's clothes: "He wore a ready-made suit of dark cloth that was ill adjusted to his body. In fact, no ready-made suit of clothes ever could fit his body. And on this night, as always, the cloth bulged with his muscles, while the coat between the shoulders, what of the heavy shoulder-development, was a maze of wrinkles" (*IH*, 4–5). The hero's powerful working-class physique exercises its fascination on Avis, as it does on Ruth Morse; but in *Martin Eden* the hero's loose clothes and muscular build are the source of acute embarrassment to him in the Morse's genteel home. Likewise "the process of getting into the dining room was a nightmare to him. Between halts and stumbles, jerks and lurches, locomotion had at times seemed impossible. But at last he had made it, and was seated alongside of Her. The array of knives and forks frightened him. They bristled with unknown perils" (*ME*, 12). The emotions associated with Ernest Everhard's entrance into the home of Avis Cunningham could not be more different. Seated at dinner in the midst of Avis and her father, who is a university professor, and his preacher friends, who are skilled metaphysicians, Ernest not only knows how to use a knife and fork, he effortlessly triumphs in debate, and does it without even alluding to humiliations inflicted on him by his working-class background. "On point after point, Ernest challenged the ministers. When they affirmed that they knew the working class, he told them fundamental truths about the working class that they did not know, and challenged them for disproofs. He gave them facts, always facts, checked their excursions into the air, and brought them back to the solid earth and its facts" (*IH*, 19).

Everhard is the scientific socialist, reasoning from the world to his ideas about the world; the ministers are the metaphysicians, reasoning from their consciousness to the world. But never does London suggest to his readers what some of these "facts" of working-class life were, for specificity would puncture the daydream. The purpose of this scene is not to enlighten the readers to the realities of working-class life but to impress upon them the superiority of Ernest Everhard. "How the scene comes back to me!" exclaims Avis. "I can hear him now, with that war-note in his voice, flaying them with his facts, each fact a lash that stung and stung again. And he was merciless" (*IH*, 19). The pleasure that we are meant to take in this triumph is covertly sado-masochistic. Everhard's intellectual battles with the capitalist class and their flunkies are repeatedly described in terms of physical violence ("sometimes he exchanged the rapier for the club and went smashing amongst their thoughts right and left" [*IH*, 95]), and the pleasure Ernest takes in these victories is fraught with unhealthy and seemingly very unsocialistic emotions. Here he is at the Philomath Club, pausing in his blows to scrutinize the expression of his victim, Col. Van Gilbert, a tough corporation lawyer: "Ernest paused for a moment and regarded him thoughtfully, noting his face dark and twisted with anger, his panting chest, his writhing body, and his slim white hands nervously clenching and unclenching" (*IH*, 92). Though we are privy to these scenes suggestive of repressed sexuality, nowhere do we see Everhard expressing tender and sexual feelings toward Avis. The closest he comes to it is the "bold" look he gives her at their first meeting: " 'You pleased me,' he explained long afterward; 'and why should I not fill my eyes with that which pleases me?' " (*IH*, 6). Avis is delighted to be the object of his will, but her pleasure in his mastery is destined to be vicarious; in her erotic fantasies she prefers to see him mastering other men—in debate— to being herself sexually overpowered:

> His masterfulness delighted me and terrified me, for my fancies
> wantonly roved until I found myself considering him as a
> lover, as a husband. I had always heard that the strength of men
> was an irresistible attraction to women; but he was too strong.
> "No! no!" I cried out. "It is impossible, absurd!" And on the
> morrow I awoke to find in myself a longing to see him again. I
> wanted to see him mastering men in discussion, the war-note in
> his voice; to see him, in all his certitude and strength, shattering
> their complacency, shaking them out of their ruts of thinking.
> [IH, 25]

Her vicarious enjoyment of Ernest's powers makes her a perfect
mate, for in the few scenes in which they are together, he is so exhausted from doing battle with the oligarchy that he is reduced
to infantile dependence. After a long passage in which Everhard
prophesies boldly of the events to come, which will culminate "after
the travail of the centuries . . . in the day of the common man," the
following scene takes place between Ernest and Avis:

> "I had thought to see that day; but now I know that I shall
> never see it."
> He paused and looked at me, and added:
> "Social evolution is exasperatingly slow, isn't it, sweetheart?"
> My arms were about him, and his head was on my breast.
> "Sing me to sleep," he murmured whimsically. "I have had a
> visioning, and I wish to forget." [IH, 228]

This scene implicitly points to the inverse relationship between Everhard's powers of political vision and the infantilism of his social
relationships. Reminiscent of the scene in The Sea-Wolf when Maud
tucks Humphrey into bed, this passage may also be compared to the
scene in Lady Chatterley's Lover, when Clifford, the impotent husband
of Lawrence's heroine, allows himself to be bathed and cared for by
Ivy Bolton. Clifford Chatterley, a gentleman-artist whose war wound
has not permitted him to be a real husband to his wife, has by this
late point in the novel transformed himself into a hard-driving indus-
trialist who achieves extraordinary production from his miners. His
wife has taken their gardener for her lover, and in her own place she
has installed Mrs. Bolton, a miner's wife who looks after Clifford's
needs. After being in charge all day at the mines, Clifford openly

becomes a child with Mrs. Bolton: he kisses her breasts with "the exaltation of perversity, of being a child when he was a man." This dependency allows Clifford to become "a real businessman." Lawrence writes: "It was as if his very passivity and prostitution to the Magna Mater gave him insight into material business affairs, and lent him a certain remarkable inhuman force."[8] The perverse and infantile emotional relationships that Lawrence ascribes to his capitalist are identical to the ones London, in a much less self-conscious way, ascribes to his revolutionary. Both Lawrence and London describe relationships in which sexual feelings are displaced onto work and then replaced by pregenital, narcissistic emotions. In this scenario women allow men to sink back into a state of blissful unawareness. Ernest Everhard, whose X-ray vision crowds his consciousness with more reality than ordinary men experience, has particular need of this escape from thought.

Thus London's revolutionary hero has a very unrevolutionary consciousness. The contradictions here are acute: Everhard builds his vision of a new society by pumping iron in the oppressive social relationships of the capitalist society he wishes to overthrow. London's awareness of the contradictions of manhood in capitalist society was neutralized by his ignorance of the contradictions of womanhood. Like Hemingway, he writes about "men without women." Even though London's heroes are sometimes with women, his understanding of them does not include their relationships with women. He is at his best when describing oppression in the male spheres of work, saloon, and prison. When he attempts to write about women's spheres, which he identifies with romantic love and the upper class, he is too aware of his own victimization to understand the peculiar ways in which women, too, are victims. Like Charmian London, Avis Everhard takes pride in her ability to make her husband happy: "I came into his stormy life, not as a new perturbing force, but as one that made toward peace and repose. I gave him rest. It was the guerdon of my love for him. It was the one infallible token that I had not failed. To bring forgetfulness, or the light of gladness, into those poor tired eyes of his—what greater joy could have blessed me than that?" (*IH*, 182). Ernest is simply too tired to extend the revolutionary struggle into the politics of his domestic life. But if we were to reply to Avis's rhetorical question—what greater joy could have blessed her than to provide her husband forgetfulness—we might suggest that she urge him to struggle with the politics of his own sexuality.

London was aware of having failed, somehow, even though he succeeded. He was also aware that his failure had to do with a failure of self-awareness; in his copy of Jung's *Psychology of the Unconscious*, he underlined the following phrase in Beatrice Hinkle's introduction: "the character and intelligence which makes it possible for him to submit himself to a facing of his naked soul, to the pain and suffering which this often entails."[9] But nowhere does he hint that he understood the specific area of conflict and self-repression to be that of his sexual identity. That remained a closed book to him.

If Ernest Everhard was too weary to take up this subject, he was doubtless also too threatened. The feelings associated with sexual politics are so intense as to require great personal courage to face. The intensity of London's feelings—in particular the intensity of his unconscious revulsion from women—may be suggested by a revealing slip of the pen. This occurs just after Ernest's initial triumph over the churchmen at the Cunningham's dinner table, in which Avis's father took great delight. "After the guests had gone, father threw himself into a chair and gave vent to roars of Gargantuan laughter. Not since the death of my mother had I known him to laugh so heartily" (*IH*, 22). Clearly Avis means "not since *before* the death of my mother," but the elision conflates the two incidents, the death of the mother/wife and the confounding of the bourgeois metaphysicians. In this unconscious association, both events give rise to one long laugh of triumph. This slip may be compared to London's comments in *The Road* about the stories he made up about his past, for the consumption of his "marks." Invariably he presented himself as an orphan, and he delighted in disposing of his mother through deadly disease: "Heart disease was my favorite way of getting rid of my mother, though on occasion I did away with her by means of consumption, pneumonia, and typhoid fever" (p. 21). London did not always wish death upon his mother figures, but, as Kevin Starr has observed, "The shaming of an upper class woman appears as a frequent motif in London's stories."[10]

London could not clearly distinguish between the oppression of class and the oppression of sex. In a common pattern of reaction, he blamed women and vented on them the anger and rage that had psychic roots in his own childhood, social roots in the roles prescribed for men and women, and political roots in the class structure of his society. The depth of London's unconscious revulsion from women touches matters primitive and biological: women were, one suspects, terrifying to him because of their close physical connection with the processes of life, as embodied in their sexual functions. He had a strong emotional need to purify them, to raise them above the muck of biology. Competing with this need was his intellectual honesty, his impulse to recognize sexuality as a material fact of life. These conflicting desires surface in the relationship between the proletarian hero and the bourgeois heroine.

Whereas Martin Eden awakens Ruth sexually, Ernest Everhard's primary influence on Avis is to awaken her politically. At Ernest's prodding, Avis investigates how Jackson, a worker in the mill in which her father is a stockholder, lost his arm and got no compensation from the company. A foreman in the mill explains to her that

> there were many accidents in the mills, and that the company's policy was to fight to the bitter end all consequent damage suits.
> "It means hundreds of thousands a year to the stockholders," he said; and as he spoke I remembered the last dividend that had been paid my father, and the pretty gown for me and the books for him that had been bought out of that dividend. I remembered Ernest's charge that my gown was stained with blood, and my flesh began to crawl underneath my garments. [*IH*, 51–52]

In this passage London expresses Avis's awakening to her oppressive social role in language suggestive of a biological, sexual awareness. If she realizes that the blood of the injured mill workers is on her hands, the stain on her gown that makes her "flesh [begin] to crawl underneath [her] garments" is suggestive of menstrual blood. The Bitch Goddess realizes that she is a bitch. This interpretation is made plausible by the number of other occasions on which London makes similar unconscious associations between awareness of class and awareness of sex, as in the Judy O'Grady allusions. Sexuality, in London's mind, partook of the rapacity of capitalism. Like class, sex was an evil of an unreformed system, and London projected his ambivalence about both onto women. Avis Everhard, in the above passage, is physically repulsed by that stain on her gown. The crawling of her flesh that London attributed to her is suggestive of male horror at the uncleanness and primitiveness of women's lunar rhythm, a horror stretching from biblical times (and perhaps before) to the present. One thinks of Joe Christmas, in Faulkner's *Light in August*, whose response to hearing for the first time about menstruation is to engage in a primitive and bloody sacrifice: he kills a sheep, plunges his hands into the warm blood, and somehow "forgets" the terrible knowledge. When his mistress reminds him of it, he hits her.[11] One suspects here that love and death are very closely related: to accept the physical, biological basis of sexuality—as frequently reified in women's sexual functions—is to accept the inevitability of death along with the power to create new life. To accept sexuality is to accept mortality. As we shall see more clearly in *Burning Daylight*, the idealization of women in London's ideology was a strategy for avoiding a confrontation with this scariest of truths.

In one further way *The Iron Heel* is suggestive of Jack London's consciousness and identity. Chapter 19 is entitled "Transformation," and here the common naturalistic device of a radical change in class identity is employed in the service of a guerilla war against the Iron Heel. Avis assumes the identity of a daughter of the oligarchy: she becomes Felice Van Verdighan. As a double agent, she gives secret signals to both the revolutionaries and the mercenaries of the oligarchy. "As agents-provocateurs, not alone were we able to travel a great deal, but our very work threw us in contact with the proletariat and with our comrades, the revolutionists. Thus we were in both camps at the same time, ostensibly serving the Iron Heel and secretly working with all our might for the Cause" (*IH*, 306). Her work "in both camps at the same time" is suggestive of the posture London maintained throughout much of his life, writing for the bourgeois press but attempting secretly to subvert their principles. In order to accomplish this, Avis is commanded by Ernest, "You must make yourself over again so that even I would not know you—your voice, your gestures, your mannerisms, your carriage, your walk, everything." Avis obeys. "Every day I practised for hours in burying forever the old Avis Everhard beneath the skin of another woman whom I may call my other self." She adds that "One must become so adept as to deceive oneself. . . . It was necessary for us to practise until our assumed rôles became real; until to be our original selves would require a watchful and strong exercise of will" (*IH*, 274, 275). So completely does Avis assume "her new automatic self" that when she is reunited with Everhard after a long separation, not only does he not recognize her but she has a hard time maintaining her old identity, "so automatically imperative had become the new personality I had created" (*IH*, 287). London even imagines surgeons trained in the revolutionary art of plastic surgery (*IH*, 304n). But if one must become the enemy in order to destroy him, is the game worth the candle? London seems never to have asked this question in *The Iron Heel*, but it drives his hero to suicide in *Martin Eden*.

TWELVE

MARTIN EDEN,
OR, PARADISE LOST

Messing about in boats had been an important part of Jack London's childhood. In 1907 he undertook a world cruise in a yacht whose building he had carefully supervised. The seven-year voyage he planned was an adult version of the childhood adventures he had had in the Oakland estuaries. The scale was proportionally larger: instead of a small skiff, London now sailed on the *Snark*, a $30,000 extravaganza. Five years earlier the contrast between his journey in a plush Pullman car and his memories of tramping and jumping freights gave rise to the conception that became *The People of the Abyss*. In 1907, on board the *Snark*, London began writing an autobiographical novel that was perhaps similarly inspired by the contrast between his current position as owner of the *Snark* and his early memories of sailing about in small boats. Then he had discovered the wonder and mystery of life; now he was one of America's most highly paid writers. What did it all mean?

As a portrait of Jack London's inner life, *Martin Eden* has a seamless logic and a terrifying honesty.[1] Its original title was "Success," and it is a story of personal failure. Although form and content cancel each other out in "The Dream of Debs" and *The Iron Heel*, in *Martin Eden* London consciously uses the contradiction between form and content—between cultural myth and subjective reality—to make an authentic statement about the way life was for Jack London. He casts his story in the familiar pattern of the Ben Franklin/Horatio Alger parable of success, only to break that paradigm by insisting on a close look at what was ordinarily not scrutinized in the parable of success: the inner self.[2]

Jack and Charmian aboard the *Snark*,
just before sailing, 1907
(Reproduced by permission of The Huntington Library, San Marino, California)

As in the Alger stories, opportunity comes through a lucky accident: Martin Eden, a sailor, has intervened in a brawl and saved the
middle-class Arthur Morse from a drubbing. Morse then brings
Martin Eden to his house, where he is introduced to his sister, Ruth,
and to the amenities of middle-class life. From this early point in the
novel, Martin aspires to the hand of Ruth and the perquisites of her
class. He even, at one point, follows her father around, hoping for an
opportunity to rescue *him*. But Martin does not rely on luck. With
extraordinary self-discipline and determination, he educates himself
to make himself worthy of Ruth. He is something of an anachronism,
for, in a period of the rapid expansion of higher education and an
increasing emphasis on the institutional legitimation of one's class,
Martin Eden pursues the methods of Ben Franklin. He relies not on
the University of California but on the Oakland Free Library. He
makes lists of the unfamiliar words he meets in his reading. He
studies the style of successful writers and elicits the principles on
which their prose is constructed, just as Franklin studied the mode of
expression that made the *Spectator Papers* so pleasing. Through these
methods, Eden becomes a successful writer.

Around this simple structure of the rise of a naive and industrious
hero, London tells a complex and tragic story. What makes the Ben
Franklin/Horatio Alger model anachronistic are the class relationships that complicate every step of the hero's rise to success. Because
of these class relationships, Martin Eden's rise is also a fall. In one
common pattern, the hero falls from innocence to experience.[3]
London's hero falls from innocence to class-consciousness. For London, this fall was associated with the hero's detachment from the
natural world—the animal kingdom—and his entry into an artificial,
civilized, domestic world. Early in their relationship, London had
written to Anna Strunsky, "Take me this way: a stray guest, a bird of
passage, splashing with salt-rimed wings through a brief moment of
your life—a rude and blundering bird, used to large airs and great
spaces, unaccustomed to the amenities of confined existence."[4] Such
a "rude and blundering" animal is Martin Eden on his first visit to the
Morse home. Even though this house is endowed with a "spacious
hall" and "wide rooms," in Martin Eden's consciousness "the wide
rooms seemed too narrow for his rolling gait, and to himself he was
in terror lest his broad shoulders should collide with the doorways to
sweep the bric-a-brac from the low mantel." As he passes by a table

covered with books, he is afraid his long, loosely swinging arm may brush them off, and he "lurche[s] away like a frightened horse" [*ME*, 1].

Ruth Morse perceives "something cosmic in him. He came to her breathing of large airs and great spaces" (*ME*, 63). The novelty of his animal vigor both draws Ruth to him and impels her to tame that wild thing; for his part, his eyes held the expression "such as wild animals betray when they fear the trap" (*ME*, 2). When this wild man is subjected to the yoke of class relationships, through his courtship of Ruth, he is irrevocably removed from what will in retrospect appear a paradise of unself-conscious being, in which there was a seamless flow between his inner and outer self. The animal kingdom from which Martin Eden emerges at the beginning of the tale is, by the end of the book, transformed in his consciousness so that it appears to be a world of "ox-minded bestial creatures" (*ME*, 376). The distinction between the "animal" and the "bestial" is significant in London's fiction: the former signifies an unself-conscious communion with the natural world, the latter, a self-conscious awareness of a social order characterized by class. These distinctions operate in London's fiction to characterize not different social realities but different *perceptions* of social reality. In other words, they characterize consciousness. As a sailor, Martin Eden certainly *was* involved in class relationships, but he was not aware of distinctions of social worth until he left the sea and entered the middle-class world of Ruth Morse.

Eden's fall into class-consciousness is also a fall into self-consciousness. As he enters the home of Ruth Morse, he is "overwhelmed with consciousness of the awkward figure he [is] cutting. This was a new experience for him. All his life, up to then, he had been unaware of being either graceful or awkward. Such thoughts of self had never entered his mind" (*ME*, 6). Seeing himself through the eyes of his new middle-class friends, Martin realizes that he is something of an oddity. "He watched the easy walk of [Arthur] in front of him, and for the first time realized that his walk was different from that of other men. He experienced a momentary pang of shame that he should walk so uncouthly" (*ME*, 1). Later, when he is in the Oakland Free Library, the librarian asks Martin if he is a sailor. Martin, still new to the world of distinguishing class traits, is puzzled by the man's perspicuity.

> Now, how did he know that? he asked himself as he went
> down the stairs.
>
> And for the first block along the street he walked very stiff
> and straight and awkwardly, until he forgot himself in his
> thoughts, whereupon his rolling gait gracefully returned to
> him. [*ME*, 41]

Martin's rolling gait, developed on the sea, is not in itself uncouth or
ungraceful. It becomes so only when he, seeing himself through
middle-class eyes, tries to adapt his natural walk to an imitation of
the walk of a man like Ruth Morse's brother.

Eden's self-consciousness extends to his manner of speaking, and
the difficulties he has in talking to Ruth Morse on his first visit exemplify the way differences of class frustrate communication. When
Ruth tries to draw him out by asking about the scar on his neck, he
responds with some blunt words about someone with a knife, a
Mexican who tried to bite off his nose. Meanwhile, "a rich vision of
that hot, starry night at Salina Cruz" passes before his eyes, and he
sees every detail of the adventure, down to the reflected light of the
stars on the knife. "But of all this no hint had crept into his speech."
Martin's failure to supply the necessary details to make the anecdote
come alive is an artistic failure, but it is born of his inhibition. As he
sees "the shock in her gentle face" at his mention of this sordid fight,
"a blush of embarrassment shone faintly on his sunburned cheeks. . . .
Such sordid things as stabbing affrays were evidently not fit subjects
for conversation with a lady. People in the books, in her walk of life,
did not talk about such things—perhaps they did not know about
them, either" (*ME*, 7).

The difficulty of talking is increased by Ruth's unfamiliarity with
Martin's language. When Ruth asks about a second scar, Martin
explains, " 'One night, in a calm, with a heavy sea running, the main-
boom-lift carried away, an' next the tackle. The lift was wire, an' it
was threshin' around like a snake. The whole watch was tryin' to grab
it, an' I rushed in an' got swatted.' " Ruth pretends to understand, but
"secretly his speech had been so much Greek to her and she was
wondering what a *lift* was and what *swatted* meant" (*ME*, 7). As she
is unfamiliar with the sailor argot of his class, he is unfamiliar with
the literary argot of hers. When Martin tries to draw her out by
asking her about the books on the table, he makes the blunder of

mispronouncing the poet's name. When Ruth corrects his "Swine-burne" to "Swinburne," he blushes again. On the other hand, Ruth is never discomforted by her ignorance of Martin's language and experience; in this encounter, as in the second occasion Martin comes to call, "the difference between them lay in that she was cool and self-possessed while his face flushed to the roots of his hair" (*ME*, 53). The conversational topics Ruth suggests to draw Martin out only increase his confusion, for they require him to talk rather personally. One wonders if Ruth would have opened conversation with a total stranger of her own class by inquiring about a scar on his neck. Arthur Morse has brought Eden home as a "novelty," a "wild man," in the hopes that his colorful stories will amuse his family, and they take privileges with him. Ruth's attitude toward him is at one point likened to the "unusual feelings" she had had "when she looked at wild animals in the menagerie" (*ME*, 63). The whole Morse family views Martin as a creature without feeling, while in fact, London writes, "he was keenly sensitive, and hopelessly self-conscious." When Arthur Morse casts an "amused glance" at the embarrassed sailor, it "burned into him like a dagger-thrust" (*ME*, 2).

Sam Baskett has pointed out that one of London's central purposes in *Martin Eden* is to draw a portrait of the artist.[5] It should further be pointed out that Martin's desire to become an artist has its inception in his newfound awareness of class and of the barriers that class rears between experiences and their expression. As for London, Eden's artistic impulses are aroused by visions, and these visions are stimulated by experiences rooted in class differences. Martin's first vision, in chapter 1, is aroused by the sound of Arthur Morse's voice as he introduces him as *Mister* Eden. As he compares this manner of address with the "Eden" or "Martin Eden" or just "Martin" he has heard all his life, "his mind seemed to turn, on the instant, into a vast camera obscura, and he saw arrayed around his consciousness endless pictures from his life, of stokeholes and forecastles, camps and beaches, jails and boozing-kens, fever-hospitals and slum streets, wherein the thread of association was the fashion in which he had been addressed in those various situations" (*ME*, 4). Throughout the novel, the contrast between his present and his past, between his immediate experience in the middle class and his former experience in the working class, evokes visions that become Martin's goal to express through art. The more obvious the class differences between

Ruth's world and his sailor past, the stronger the artistic impulse they
arouse. Thus when Ruth sits down at the piano and uses her music
"aggressively, with the vague intent of emphasizing the impassable-
ness of the gulf that separated them," it has the opposite effect of
inciting Eden's imagination. As she plays at him, "her music . . . a
club that she swung brutally upon his head," we witness the birth of
Martin Eden, artist:

> . . . before his eyes and behind his eyes shone a great glory;
> and then the scene before him vanished and he was away,
> rocking over the world that was to him a very dear world. The
> known and the unknown were commingled in the dream-
> pageant that thronged his vision. He entered strange ports of
> sun-washed lands, and trod market-places among barbaric
> peoples that no man had ever seen. . . .
>
> He was a harp; all life that he had known and that was his
> consciousness was the strings; and the flood of music was a wind
> that poured against those strings and set them vibrating with
> memories and dreams. He did not merely feel. Sensation in-
> vested itself in form and color and radiance, and what his imagi-
> nation dared, it objectified in some sublimated and magic way.
> Past, present, and future mingled. [ME, 21]

The impression that these recurrent visions convey is of a secret
self, locked, as London writes, behind "prison-bars," "inarticulate
and dumb because of those feeble lips that would not give it speech"
(ME, 22). Martin's desire to be a writer is an outgrowth of his conviction that he has a self, a soul, longing to be expressed. He is aware
"that he had led always a secret life in his thoughts. These thoughts
he had tried to share, but never had he found a woman capable of
understanding—nor a man" (ME, 48). Writing was a way, as Nathaniel Hawthorne once wrote, of achieving a kind of second-hand
communication, an intimate relationship for those who, out of tem-
peramental reserve or some other reason, were denied it in their
daily social intercourse. But by choosing to relate to people whom
he perceives to be above his station, Martin condemns his search for
intimacy to failure. In the end his self is still locked behind those
prison bars. The public who buy his books do so for the wrong
reasons. The real Martin Eden they do not know. Art founders on
the very class divisions it promised to overcome. And Martin Eden

was to find that there was a severe emotional cost to making love through books.

A frequent criticism of *Martin Eden* concerns what one reviewer called "the strange development of the heroine."[6] The prissy, narrow, and dogmatic Ruth, to whom Martin Eden is unaccountably attracted, and who is presented as the sole motivation for his struggle out of the working class, lacks credibility as a character; London does not extend to her the sympathetic understanding to make her come alive. Women readers may be especially outraged by London's stereotypical characterization of this woman, who wields the grammar book with the relish of a Miss Ratched in the psychiatric ward, and any reader is bound to stand back and question not only the hero's choice of women but the authenticity of the emotions behind that choice. But this seems precisely what *Martin Eden* is about: the inauthenticity of Eden's emotional life. The most important fact about Martin Eden, who prides himself on being a realist and on being true to his experience, is that he measures people above his social class, not against his own emotional responses but against what he has read in books. The books are responsible for his failure to make real contact with others, and finally "they [are] all the comrades left to him" (*ME*, 240).

London suggested more than once that his initial mistake was in "opening the books."[7] His reading of novels like *Jane Eyre* and *John Halifax, Gentleman* created an image of the middle-class world that shaped his perceptions of what he saw when he finally entered it himself. For a working-class youth, reading about the doings of proper middle-class people who were involved in the rituals of courtship was akin to reading about the romantic rituals of medieval knights and damsels, so far removed was it from his experience. Consequently, these doings were overlaid with an aura of romance and adventure quite in excess of the actual portrait of middle-class life, however idealized that portrait. In "What Life Means to Me," London writes about his early impression of the intellectual and spiritual fineness of the society "above" him: "Up above me, I knew, were unselfishnesses of the spirit, clean and noble thinking, keen intellectual living. I knew all this because I read 'Seaside Library' novels, in which, with the exception of the villains and adventuresses, all men and women thought beautiful thoughts, spoke a beautiful tongue, and performed glorious deeds."[8]

Similar literary models inform Martin Eden's perceptions of Ruth
Morse and her world. As he sits at the Morse dinner table for the
first time, Eden is "charmed" by the aesthetic and intellectual aura he
greedily breathes in:

> He was feasting his love of beauty at this table where eating was
> an aesthetic function. It was an intellectual function, too. His
> mind was stirred. He heard words spoken that were meaning-
> less to him, and other words that he had seen only in books
> and that no man or woman he had known was of large enough
> mental caliber to pronounce. When he heard such words drop-
> ping carelessly from the lips of the members of this marvellous
> family, her family, he thrilled with delight. *The romance, and
> beauty, and high vigor of the books were coming true.* He was in
> that rare and blissful state wherein a man sees his dreams stalk
> out from the crannies of fantasy and become fact. [*ME*, 15;
> my emphasis]

Eden marvels at the fact that he is sitting "shoulder to shoulder, at
dinner, with people he had read about in books. He was in the books
himself, adventuring through the printed pages of bound volumes"
(*ME*, 15–16). If Eden's relationship with Ruth is shaped by the
books he has read before he sees her, its development is intimately
bound up with the books that are part of her world. Martin's first act
upon entering the Morse household is to pick up a volume of Swinburne lying on the table. When Ruth enters the room he is so lost in
it that he is not at first aware of her presence. This intermingling of
his reading with his first perception of Ruth is a suggestive and highly
significant act, and it is responsible for "the strange development
of the heroine." It suggests that Ruth appears as an incarnation of
the poetic fantasies that Swinburne has sent flashing across Martin's
vision.

> She was a pale, ethereal creature, with wide, spiritual blue eyes
> and a wealth of golden hair. . . . He likened her to a pale gold
> flower upon a slender stem. No, she was a spirit, a divinity,
> a goddess; such sublimated beauty was not of the earth. Or
> perhaps the books were right, and there were many such as she
> in the upper walks of life. She might well be sung by that chap
> Swinburne. Perhaps he had had somebody like her in mind

when he painted that girl, Iseult, in the book there on the
table. [*ME*, 4]

It is also important that Martin's initial reason for taking the volume
of Swinburne off the table was to cover the severe embarrassment
and discomfort that he was experiencing as he entered this unfamiliar
middle-class world. He did not know what the book was about and
did not care; he simply used it to cover up the painful feelings that
came with being out of his class. In doing this, Martin is only following the cue of his middle-class host. For, moments earlier, Arthur
Morse had picked up a letter and silently read it, to give Martin time,
as he understood the act, to regain his bearings. Martin carefully
observes the manners of this new class in order to discover how he
should act. One of the things that Martin will learn is that strong expressions of emotion, enthusiasm, and reckless and colorful language
are not considered appropriate.[9] (Charmian remembers Jack saying,
"Don't mind my harshness. I always raise my voice and talk with my
hands; I can't help it.")[10] Learning the proper literary conventions in
which to express toned-down feeling is an essential part of Martin's
education in middle-class behavior, and it is appropriate that his
story should begin and end with Swinburne's poetry, which tells
Martin how he feels and acts to distance him from those feelings.

If Martin sees Ruth as an incarnation of a literary character, his
model for their relationship is explicitly that of Robert Browning's
courtship of the sickly Elizabeth Barrett. Ruth's frailty is in contrast to Eden's muscularity, and both have been fostered by their
respective class backgrounds. Ruth is attracted by Eden's vitality and
strength, even as her maidenly instincts are repelled by them. To
Eden, "Ruth's physical frailty was an added charm. . . . He read of
sickly Elizabeth Barrett, who for years had not placed her feet upon
the ground, until that day of flame when she eloped with Browning
and stood upright, upon the earth, under the open sky; and what
Browning had done for her, Martin decided he could do for Ruth"
(*ME*, 150).[11] Eden's tendency to relate to people through the media-
tion of literary models is exacerbated by his contact with the middle
class, in which expression is, for Martin Eden, a matter of knowing
how to pronounce the right words, how to use proper grammar and
the proper frames of reference. As a result, Martin is involved in a
cruel joke: he is impelled to become an artist in order to express well

that which he has experienced, but in the realm of emotional experience he is denied knowledge of that experience—by the very books that draw him on in the pursuit of Beauty. He thinks he loves Ruth Morse, but all he knows of love is what he has read about. The sexual encounters he has had with working-class girls are not love, and neither does the affection shown him by his sister Gertrude seem to him applicable in the elevated world of Ruth Morse: Martin is struck by the utter difference between the beautiful kiss exchanged between Ruth and her mother, and the sordid kiss, tasting of sweat and soapsuds, which he and his sister exchange in a moment of rare tenderness. Unable to trust his former experience in the working class, and innocent of love experience with middle-class people, Martin is forced to rely on what little he knows of that world from books. As a result, Martin makes a fatal mistake: he confuses aesthetic sensibility with love and the birth of himself as an artist with the birth of himself as a lover. This confusion is clear in the language London uses to describe Martin's love for Ruth, which is always heightened by their tête-à-têtes over a favorite volume of Tennyson's poetry:

> [Ruth] read to him much from "The Princess," and often he saw her eyes swimming with tears, so finely was her aesthetic nature strung. *At such moments her own emotions elevated him* till he was as a god, and, as he gazed at her and listened, he seemed gazing on the face of life and reading its deepest secrets. *And then, becoming aware of the heights of exquisite sensibility he attained, he decided that this was love* and that love was the greatest thing in the world. [*ME*, 62; my emphasis]

Riding on the wings of Ruth's emotion, Eden imagines he feels what he imagines she feels. Characteristically looking to someone more "cultured" than himself to tell him how he feels, Eden never experiences his own emotions, but he imagines himself feeling the emotions of a more cultured (i.e., more powerful) person. The exception to this is the recurrent emotion of shame he experiences during his initial entrance into the middle-class world. This is indeed his own emotion and not one imagined through a fictitious persona. Yet Eden rids himself of this uncomfortable feeling as rapidly as he can; aspiring to Ruth's coolness and power, he imitates the models of high culture as he becomes increasingly detached and unenthusiastic in his manner.

Eden's success in distancing himself from his own emotions is most evident in his relationships with people of his own class. Significantly, Eden is never portrayed as having perfect communion with the working class; even in flashbacks to his early life, before his meeting with Ruth, Eden maintains a psychic distance from them. Remembering a time in the East End of London, when he embraced a fifteen-year-old street urchin, he recalls the ambivalent emotions he experienced: "She had put her lips up to be kissed, but he wasn't going to kiss her. Somehow he was afraid of her. And then her hand closed on his and pressed feverishly. He felt her calluses grind and grate on his, and a great wave of pity welled over him. He saw her yearning, hungry eyes, and her ill-fed female form which had been rushed from childhood into a frightened and ferocious maturity; and he put his arms about her in large tolerance and stooped and kissed her on the lips" (*ME*, 34). As we saw in *The People of the Abyss*, London experienced a similar mixture of pity and terror in response to the poverty of the East End. At that time in his life he was already significantly removed from the class he was observing. That London does not imagine for his hero, Martin Eden, a time when he was at one with the working class suggests that London himself could not remember such a time. Eden's "flesh was crawling" at the remembrance of the street urchin even though "his heart was warm with pity." In London's fiction, the state of at-one-ness with other living creatures is a mythical state; it exists before history, before consciousness, in a dimly remembered paradise lost, to be reclaimed only in the "womb of time."

As distanced as Eden is from the young girl in the East End, the humanity of his response to her is richly felt in London's description of "her yearning, hungry eyes, and her ill-fed female form which had been rushed from childhood into a frightened and ferocious maturity." After he meets Ruth, his encounters with working-class people evoke an emotion that is increasingly closer to scorn than pity. Moreover, the physical repulsion that he had felt at the proximity of the fifteen-year-old girl grows into a shame of his sexuality. Though Eden does not know it, this is the beginning of the "sickness" that will lead to his suicide, and it takes hold of him long before Ruth's love fails him.

The progress of this emotional illness may be marked early in the story. Shortly after Martin's first visit to the Morse home, he goes to the theater in hope of seeing Ruth there. He does in fact see her, but his adoring contemplation of her is alloyed by the insistent overtures of a pair of working-class girls, one of whom is Lizzie Connolly. In the practiced way of the streets, they smile at him, expecting him to smile back and to get acquainted in the ways London and Louis Shattuck perfected on the Oakland streets. Eden does smile back, but only out of his "intrinsic kindliness" and his desire not to hurt them. "He was not flattered by [their attentions]; he even felt a slight shame at his lowliness that permitted it. He knew, did he belong in Ruth's class, that there would be no overtures from these girls; and with each glance of theirs he felt the fingers of his own class clutching at him to hold him down" (*ME*, 45). When the show is over Eden hurries outside, his cap pulled over his face, hoping for a glimpse of "Her." But the working-class girls, assiduous in their pursuit, are already outside waiting for him. When Eden sees them "he could have cursed that in him which drew women." Thinking that it would never do for Ruth to see him with these girls, Eden falls in with them with the idea of getting away from the theater crowd to a vantage point from which he can see Her without being seen. "Quite naturally, as a matter of course, he swung in alongside the dark-eyed one and walked with her. There was no awkwardness on his part, no numb tongue. He was at home here, and he held his own royally in the badinage, bristling with slang and sharpness, that was always the preliminary to getting acquainted in these swift-moving affairs" (*ME*, 45–46). Eden is "at home" and "he held his own royally"; the language might be applied to a king restored to his throne, but Eden is a most reluctant sojourner in his one-time kingdom. While he flirts with the girls, he has one eye on the theater crowd; and all the time he is taking the girls' measure in a careless, detached way. He "knew it all, and knew them well, from A to Z. . . . And while he exchanged the stupidities of stupid minds with them, before his inner sight towered the book-shelves of the library, filled with the wisdom of the ages. He smiled bitterly at the incongruity of it, and was assailed by doubts. But between inner vision and outward pleasantry he found time to watch the theatre crowd streaming by. And then he saw Her" (*ME*, 46, 47).

Eden is "afflicted by a sudden spiritual nausea" at the contrast
between Ruth and the two girls by his side. London's language implies that Eden's nausea is primarily a response to the sexuality
lurking in "the bold defiant eyes of the girl before him," so unlike
"Ruth's clear, luminous eyes, like a saint's, gazing at him out of unplumbed depths of purity." Eden's detachment from sexuality, from
emotion, and from the human presence of these working-class girls
is conveyed in a mechanistic metaphor that London employed frequently in *John Barleycorn* to describe his removal from human
society. "Behind those black eyes he knew every thought process. It
was like clockwork. He could watch every wheel go around" (*ME*,
48). The thoughts behind the black eyes are "of ice-cream and of
something else," London says euphemistically: "Their bid was low
pleasure, narrow as the grave, that palled, and the grave was at the
end of it. But the bid of the saint's eyes was mystery, and wonder
unthinkable, and eternal life. He had caught glimpses of the soul in
them, and glimpses of his own soul, too" (*ME*, 48). Eden equates the
working class with sexuality and the grave, the middle class with
purity and eternal life. The tragedy is that Eden, in choosing the
middle class, was in fact choosing not eternal life but the illusion of
eternal life: a living death.

Eden's inner life is squelched in other ways by his adoption of
Ruth's standards of speech and behavior. While he is on an eight-
month voyage, he studies a grammar book and mentally corrects the
language of his shipmates. This must have distracted him from what
they had to say, but when he returns to Ruth, she is delighted by the
change in his language. The only problem was that "when he grew
excited or enthusiastic . . . he dropped back into the old slurring and
the dropping of final consonants" (*ME*, 75). To prevent such slip-
page, London writes, "he was always on guard, keenly watchful"
(*ME*, 102). Spontaneity and enthusiasm were treacherous, for such
self-forgetfulness permitted the ghost of his working-class self to
intrude upon the bowers of books, art, and love. This self-repression
has paradoxical implications for Eden's own artistic aspirations, for,
as London suggests in the following passage from *The Call of the
Wild*, art involves a complete forgetfulness and abandon: "There is
an ecstasy that marks the summit of life, and beyond which life
cannot rise. And such is the paradox of living, this ecstasy comes
when one is most alive. This forgetfulness of living, comes to the

artist, caught up and out of himself in a sheet of flame" (*CW*, 83). Martin Eden finds himself burned by this sheet of flame. Once, caught up in a vision of "a world without end of sunlit space and starry voids," he is struck dumb by the magnificence of his vision and "the pitiful inadequacy of speech." Torn between his inner vision and his desire to communicate this vision to Ruth, he is silent until he sees her "regarding him with an amused expression." Without stopping to choose his words he says to her, "'I have had a great visioning.'" Instantly he is transported by the lofty expression that has come, unbidden, from his mouth. But this new-found gift of words is soon to betray him. As he becomes carried away by what he has seen and felt and by his desire to make Ruth see this, he involuntarily uses the expression, "'By God.'" When he hears this oath echoing in his ears, "The blood surged into his face, wave upon wave, mastering the bronze of it till the blush of shame flaunted itself from the collar-rim to the roots of his hair." He humbly begs Ruth's pardon, but the damage is done, and she is "withering and shrinking" under the blast of this rough oath, the first she had heard "from the lips of a man she knew." By forgetting himself in a moment of artistic creation, Eden has truly become himself. But in this act of self-forgetfulness, he expresses himself in improper working-class language. Art has betrayed him into being himself, and he feels the emotion associated with that authentic self—shame (*ME*, 82–84).

After he has achieved literary fame Eden comes to realize the manipulative role that Ruth has played. He charges her, "'You would have destroyed my writing and my career. Realism is imperative to my nature, and the bourgeois spirit hates realism . . . all your effort was to make me afraid of life . . . you wanted to formalize me, to make me over into one of your own class, with your class-ideals, class-values, and class-prejudices'" (*ME*, 364–65). This is all true, but the novel would be more satisfactory if Eden came to an awareness of his own part in this. It was he, after all, who came in frank humility and asked to be initiated into the middle-class holy of holies; he presented himself to Ruth as clay to be molded, and she greatly enjoyed giving herself to that project. London remarks that Ruth "knew her Browning, but it never sunk into her that it was an awkward thing to play with souls" (*ME*, 65). But has not Martin seduced Ruth into this role by playing the innocent little boy? London never suggests he may have been at fault; he seems unaware of the incestuous nature of Martin's love and joins him in his anger when the boy-hero inevitably grows up and smashes the parental idol.

Eden, unaware of the dependency needs that lead him into submissive relationships, can only revolt by asserting his own will to power. He is never at peace with himself, for he is tossed between the poles of submission and mastery, self-abasement and self-exaltation. His wildest dreams of power bloom like evil flowers from the conviction of his lowliness. In the Oakland Free Library he wanders through the shelves of books, "alternating between depression and elation." One moment "the books seemed to press upon him and crush him." But in the next moment he is resolving that he will "master" this knowledge, as other men "had mastered it" (*ME*, 40). Even his desire to be an artist, closely linked as it is with his need to express himself, is related to his desire for mastery. After Martin has read Ruth a story— which she found too horrible—Martin is secretly pleased with the effect it has had on her. "He noted her pale face, her eyes wide and tense, and her clenched hands, with secret satisfaction. He had succeeded. He had communicated the stuff of fancy and feeling from out of his brain. It had struck home. No matter whether she liked it or not, it had gripped her and mastered her, made her sit there and listen and forget details" (*ME*, 114). He has reversed the power relationship that prevailed when he made his initial blundering visit to Ruth's house; now he is making her feel hot and confused while he is cool and collected. By becoming an artist, Martin became "one of the eyes through which the world saw, one of the ears through which it heard, one of the hearts through which it felt" (*ME*, 70–71). In this way *he* determined what was "real" to those who read him; he shaped their seeing, just as his own perceptions had been shaped by the middle-class books. The humiliation of being told how to see and feel is replaced by the power of telling others how to see and feel. As the determination to write comes to him, he is "drunken with unguessed power and [feels] that he [can] do anything." Writing is a way to master Ruth's world. With this awareness, he feels "invincible" (*ME*, 71).

As Martin's mastery of books and grammar proceeds, he begins to take the measure of the middle-class world. "A Superior Court Judge!" he thinks scornfully of Judge Blount, frequenter of the Morse dinner table. "It was only several years before that he had looked up from the mire at such glorious entities and deemed them gods." He grows increasingly bored with Ruth's friends. "Foolishly, in the past, he had conceived that all well-groomed persons above the working class were persons with power of intellect and vigor of beauty. Culture and collars had gone together, to him, and he had been deceived into believing that college educations and mastery were the same thing" (*ME*, 234). He makes the discovery "that the difference between these lawyers, officers, business men, and bank cashiers he had met and the members of the working class he had known was on a par with the difference in the food they ate, clothes they wore, neighborhoods in which they lived." But this realization does not bring a recognition of the commonality underlying the superficial differences. It only reinforces Eden's conviction of his superiority to all of them: "Certainly, in all of them was lacking the something more which he found *in himself and in the books*" (*ME*, 235; my emphasis). The books are Eden's most enduring idol, and they remain to the end the arbiter against which he tests his reality. One evening, at the Morse dinner table, Eden sees a vision of his former self, the "self-conscious savage" who was apprehensive about the vast array of eating implements, and he is overcome by his great disappointment in this middle-class world. "He glanced at Ruth for reassurance, much in the same manner that a passenger, with sudden panic thought of possible shipwreck, will strive to locate the life preservers. Well, that much had come out of it—love and Ruth. All the rest had *failed to stand the test of the books*. But Ruth and love had stood the test; for them he found a biological sanction" (*ME*, 295; my emphasis). Martin comes to no self-knowledge through the crumbling of his middle-class idols, but only turns in search of worthier companions. He finds such a one in Brissenden. This tubercular poet is able to "[convey] to Martin's consciousness messages that were incommunicable to ordinary souls. . . . Here was the best the books had to offer coming true. Here was an intelligence, a living man for him to look up to" (*ME*, 256). Martin revels in the emotion Ruth's world can no longer evoke: "'I am down in the dirt at your feet,' Martin repeated to himself again and again" (*ME*, 256).

At the end of Martin Eden's story, the books do come true, but not in the conventional ways. The happy ending of the formulaic success story is preserved in Maria Silva, Eden's landlady, for whom he buys a milk ranch. "Few persons ever meet the fairy princes they dream about," London comments, "but Maria, who worked hard and

whose head was hard, never dreaming about fairy princes, entertained hers in the guise of an ex-laundry man" (*ME*, 341). Eden finds
his end in the books when, aboard the *Mariposa*, "Swinburne show[s]
him . . . the happy way out" (*ME*, 378). "Swinburne had furnished
the key . . . 'That dead men rise up never!' That line stirred him with
a profound feeling of gratitude" (*ME*, 379). In spite of its literary
inspiration, Martin Eden's suicide is perhaps the most authentic gesture he makes in the book, for it confirms his own feeling of emotional deadness. "He remembered that some one had said that a
ghost was the spirit of a man who was dead and who did not have
sense enough to know it; and he paused for the moment to wonder if
he were really dead and unaware of it" (*ME*, 317). He had become
"numb to emotions of any sort save the artistic ones" (*ME*, 316) after
Ruth, at her family's insistence, broke her engagement to Martin
after a newspaper printed a misleading story about an allegedly revolutionary speech he had made at a street corner meeting. It is appropriate that his relationship with Ruth foundered not on a real issue
but on a fictitious persona created by the newspaper, for Eden's
whole relationship with her had been a fictitious, literary affair.

A very limited range of emotions is available to Eden: as a working-
class sailor, the only real emotion he experienced was shame; as a
successful author, he felt nothing. London's achievement in this autobiographical story lies in the precision with which he describes Eden's
inner life. It took a great deal of courage and self-awareness and trust
of his feelings just to acknowledge Eden's shame and to know when
he was incapable of feeling. The most moving scenes in the book
occur when Eden tries to go back to the working class he has left
behind in his pursuit of "books and art and love." Aware that he is
lonely, he gravitates to a bricklayer's picnic; here he is hailed by the
"old crowd," and, amidst the drinking and dancing and scrapping
over girls, he "began to feel really human once more. . . . Everybody was glad to see Martin back. No book of his had been published; he carried no fictitious value in their eyes. They liked him for
himself. He felt like a prince returned from exile" (*ME*, 329–30).

He sees Lizzie Connolly, and "from the instant he spoke to her,
she was his. He knew it. She showed it in the proud humility of her
eyes, in every caressing movement of her proudly carried body, and
in the way she hung upon his speech" (*ME*, 330). Lizzie's readiness
to give herself to Martin Eden is not self-abasing or degrading; she

acts with "proud humility," and there is a dignity to her bearing that belies Eden's former assessment of working-class people. But Martin has nothing left inside him to give to her; he is a shell of proper speeches and correct grammar. When she says of her present escort, "'I'd throw 'm down for you any time,' Martin, looking at her averted face, knowing that all he had to do was to reach out his hand and pluck her, fell to pondering whether, after all, there was any real worth in refined, grammatical English, and so, forgot to reply to her" (*ME*, 332). She tells him that she has "kept straight all these years," but Martin tells her that he is "not a marrying man." Undaunted, Lizzie offers herself to Martin on any terms: "'I'd do anything for you. I'm just made that way, I guess.'" At this declaration, "Martin sat up. He took her hand in his. He did it deliberately, with warmth but without passion; and such warmth chilled her" (*ME*, 333). He tells her that she is "a great and noble woman," that he "should be proud to know [her]" and that she is "a ray of light . . . in a very dark world." These fancy compliments, learned in Ruth Morse's world, do not disguise to Lizzie Martin's rejection of her. Martin then offers to "make it easy" for her by giving her money to go to school or to business college. "'Anything you want, just name it, and I can fix it for you.'"

> She made no reply, but sat, gazing straight before her, dry-eyed and motionless, but with an ache in the throat which Martin divined so strongly that it made his own throat ache. He regretted that he had spoken. It seemed so tawdry what he had offered her—mere money—compared with what she offered him. He offered her an extraneous thing with which he could part without a pang, while she offered him herself, along with disgrace and shame, and sin, and all her hopes of heaven. [*ME*, 334–35]

The irony is that Lizzie is willing to accept what the world would perceive as the role of the prostitute in order to be true to her emotions, while Eden, in rejecting this arrangement and tendering money instead of intimacy, is *actually* in the role of the prostitute. As moving as this section is, London is careful not to attribute strong emotion to his hero. Whatever he experiences comes from his vicarious participation in Lizzie's heartache, "which Martin divined so strongly that it made his own throat ache" (*ME*, 334). The end and emotional finale of this chapter rests heavily on Lizzie's responses. At her doorstep Martin tells Lizzie to make up with the fellow she had been with earlier in the day.

"I can't—now," she said.

"Oh, go on," he said jovially. "All you have to do is whistle and he'll come running."

"I didn't mean that," she said simply.

And he knew what she had meant.

She leaned toward him as he was about to say good night. But she leaned not imperatively, not seductively, but wistfully and humbly. He was touched to the heart. His large tolerance rose up in him. He put his arms around her, and kissed her, and knew that upon his own lips rested as true a kiss as man ever received.

"My God!" she sobbed. "I could die for you. I could die for you."

She tore herself from him suddenly and ran up the steps.

He felt a quick moisture in his eyes. [*ME*, 336–37]

Wishing he could marry her, not for himself but to make her happy, he quotes from the books, "Life is, I think, a blunder and a shame" (*ME*, 337).

Eden himself becomes aware of his emotional sickness when Ruth, professing to love him still, offers herself to him. He will soon discover that her offer has the sanction of her bourgeois family, but at first he believes it to be a grand and desperate gesture. Nevertheless, he finds himself stirred "only intellectually. In what should have been a moment of fire, he coldly appraised her." He tells her " 'I am sick, very sick. . . . Life has so filled me that I am empty of any desire for anything' " (*ME*, 367). Realizing the danger of this "strange and comfortable state of mind" in which "he no longer cared" (*ME*, 341) and stirred by a "remote instinct for preservation" (*ME*, 373), Eden decides that he must go away. The visions that come to him now are of the tropical vegetation in the South Seas and of a particular valley and a bay in the Marquesas. He plans to buy this land and make it his headquarters. "He would build a patriarchal grass house like Tati's, and have it and the valley and the schooner filled with dark-skinned servitors. He would entertain there the factor of Taiohae, captains of wandering traders, and all the best of the South Pacific riffraff. He would keep open house and entertain like a prince. And he would forget the books he had opened and the world that had proved an illusion" (*ME*, 328). Jack London's patriarchal ranch in the Sonoma valley was among the last of the illusions he grasped in an attempt to hold on to life, but in *Martin Eden*, even this illusion is out of the hero's reach. As he sails for the South Seas on the *Mariposa*, he recognizes his despair and the vanity of his quest:

> Life was to him like strong, white light that hurts the tired
> eyes of a sick person. During every conscious moment life
> blazed in a raw glare around him and upon him. It hurt. It hurt
> intolerably. It was the first time in his life that Martin had
> travelled first class. On ships at sea he had always been in the
> forecastle, the steerage, or in the black depths of the coal-hold,
> passing coal. In those days, climbing up the iron ladders from
> out the pit of stifling heat, he had often caught glimpses of
> the passengers, in cool white, doing nothing but enjoy them-
> selves, under awnings spread to keep the sun and wind away
> from them, with subservient stewards taking care of their every
> want and whim, and it had seemed to him that the realm in
> which they moved and had their being was nothing else than
> paradise. Well, here he was, the great man on board, in the
> midmost centre of it, sitting at the captain's right hand, and yet
> vainly harking back to the forecastle and stoke-hole in quest
> of the Paradise he had lost. He had found no new one, and
> now he could not find the old one. [*ME*, 377]

In *The Call of the Wild*, the "kidnapped king" is restored to his rightful throne. This was Jack London's dream, but *Martin Eden* was his reality: the "exiled prince," unable to find his way back to the paradisiacal kingdom, eases himself through a porthole of the *Mariposa*, takes a deep breath, and dives down, too deep to be brought up again. "His wilful hands and feet began to beat and churn about, spasmodically and feebly. But he had fooled them and the will to live that made them beat and churn. He was too deep down. They could never bring him to the surface" (*ME*, 381).

THIRTEEN

FADING BEYOND

In his next novel, *Burning Daylight*, London resurrects his hero and gives him, instead of a kingdom, a ranch in the Sonoma valley, and, instead of subjects or dark-skinned servitors, a wife. *Burning Daylight* blithely reaffirms the illusion of love that *Martin Eden* exposes. Together the two books form the characteristic pattern in which the truth is first revealed and then concealed. In the copy of *Martin Eden* that London gave to his wife, Charmian, he wrote this inscription: "You see, Martin Eden did not have you!"[1] The romantic illusion that the right woman could save the London hero from the insidious emotional illness from which he suffered was enshrined in *Burning Daylight*. Kevin Starr has analyzed the relationships between this novel and the illusions London pursued during his Sonoma ranch years;[2] it should further be pointed out that the illusion of salvation through a return to the soil is related to the illusion of sentimental love. *Burning Daylight* has a plot that moves the hero from a desire for mastery to a desire for intimacy. But the promise is not fulfilled. Instead of functioning as an intimate, privy to the hopes and fears and weaknesses of her husband, Dede Mason is "a wall . . . athwart his consciousness." One of the truths from which this wall defends Elam Harnish is the knowledge that he will someday die.

Like *A Daughter of the Snows*, *Burning Daylight* is structured around the contrast between urban life and the Alaskan wilderness. In the Alaskan half of the novel Elam Harnish (or Burning Daylight, as he is called) engages in a series of contests that demonstrate his frontier vitality and his superiority to ordinary mortals. London writes, "desire for mastery was strong in him, and it was all one whether wrestling with the elements themselves, with men, or with luck in a gambling game" (*BD*, 61). London rather explicitly characterizes Burning Daylight as a Nietzschean superman: "Deep in his

life-processes Life itself sang the siren song of its own majesty, ever
a-whisper and urgent, counselling him that he could achieve more
than other men, win out where they failed, ride to success where
they perished. It was the urge of Life healthy and strong, unaware
of frailty and decay, drunken with sublime complacence, ego-mad,
enchanted by its own mighty optimism" (*BD*, 61). This man's flaw,
London seems to be saying, is that he does not believe in his own
mortality. "At the sharpest hazards of trail and river and famine,
the message was that other men might die, but that he would pull
through triumphant. It was the old, old lie of Life fooling itself,
believing itself immortal and indestructible, bound to achieve over
other lives and win to its heart's desire" (*BD*, 62). In the risky ventures of the first part of the book the Alaskan setting functions more
as a frontier of capitalism than as a wilderness frontier. Although we
are told indirectly of various exploits in which Harnish has challenged the wilderness, the book is more concerned with the killing
he makes through his entrepreneurial skill. Anticipating that the
spot where two rivers come together will be a natural town site when
the gold rush hits, Harnish buys into what will become Dawson.
Playing his hunch, he obtains stakes all over the gold creeks; he
rationalizes the mining of gold in a way that would have won the
heart of Frederick Taylor, and he becomes a millionaire many times
over. When, in the middle of the book, Harnish turns his face toward
civilization, he only exercises in an urban setting the business skills
he has developed in Alaska. The real change in the second part of the
book is that Harnish is no longer in the prime of youth and health.
London attributes this degeneration not to the natural erosion of
time but to the unnatural effects of city living.

The other change that comes upon Harnish in the second half of
the book concerns his attitude toward women. In the beginning his
condescension masks his fear. On the one hand women are "toys,
playthings, part of the relaxation from the bigger game of life" (*BD*,
10). But the blithe mastery of this statement is betrayed by his un-
controllable fear of the "apron string," as if the mere presence of a
domestically inclined woman could reduce his manhood to abject
submission. When a dark-eyed woman known only as the "Virgin"
pursues him, he is "dominated by [a] wave of fear and murder" and
he is like "a frightened tiger filled with rage and terror at the appre-
hension of the trap" (*BD*, 11). This reaction is explained in a lengthy

and revealing discussion of the difference between love of women
and true comradeship:

> He was a slave to himself, which was natural in one with
> a healthy ego, but he rebelled in ways either murderous or
> panicky at being a slave to anybody else. Love's sweet servitude
> was a thing of which he had no comprehension. . . . But com-
> radeship with men was different from love with women. There
> was no servitude in comradeship. It was a business proposition,
> a square deal between men who did not pursue each other,
> but who shared the risks of trail and river and mountain in the
> pursuit of life and treasure. Men and women pursued each
> other, and one must needs bend the other to his will or hers.
> Comradeship was different. There was no slavery about it; and
> though he, a strong man beyond strength's seeming, gave far
> more than he received, he gave not something due but in royal
> largess, his gifts of toil or heroic effort falling generously
> from his hands. [BD, 10]

The comradeship of the Alaskan trail appears all the more warm and
vital to Burning Daylight after he has been hardened by civilization.
"The grim Yukon life had failed to make Daylight hard. It required
civilization to produce this result. In the fierce, savage game he now
played, his habitual geniality imperceptibly slipped away from him,
as did his lazy Western drawl. . . . His tremendous vitality remained,
and radiated from all his being, but it was vitality under the new
aspect of the man-trampling man-conqueror" (BD, 162–63).

The softening influence of a woman is now required to save Daylight from the excesses of civilization. Her ministry is the more necessary, as Daylight finds himself pitted not against nature but against
other men. "His battles with elemental nature had been, in a way,
impersonal; his present battles were wholly with the males of his
species, and the hardships of the trail, the river, and the frost marred
him far less than the bitter keenness of the struggle with his fellows"
(BD, 163). Daylight has a poor memory, or he would recall that his
struggle in Alaska was not against the frost but was indeed a "struggle
with his fellows." During the gold rush he had developed "the taste
for power. It had become a lust with him. By far the wealthiest miner
in Alaska, he wanted to be still wealthier" (BD, 107). Daylight is now
convinced that "cities [do] not make for comradeship as did the

Alaskan trail" (*BD*, 274) but never, in Alaska, does he exemplify the virtues of comradeship; instead, he plays the king of the revels, hell-roaring through the saloons, "howling his he-wolf howl and claiming the night as his, bending men's arms down on the bars, performing feats of strength, his bronzed face flushed with drink" (*BD*, 121). In *Burning Daylight*, the Alaskan wilderness is reduced to a flat symbol of an earlier, more vital and manly age, and London is incapable of evoking the emotions and experience to make it work. Instead, the Alaskan experience is only an earlier stage of the same grab for money and power that Daylight continues in the city. Once the frontier of capitalism has passed into a higher stage of development, the nature of these processes is more exposed and hence more harsh, but not different in kind.

As capitalism has passed into a more mature stage, so too has Burning Daylight. He becomes aware of his physical decline when he is bested in an arm-wrestling contest. Awakened to his condition, he critically views his body in the mirror and discovers that "a rising tide of fat had submerged [his muscles]. . . . The lean stomach had become a paunch. The ridged muscles of chest and shoulders and abdomen had broken down into rolls of flesh" (*BD*, 316).[3] After he views his flabbiness, "through his mind drifted pictures of his youthful excellence, of the hardships he had endured over other men, of the Indians and dogs he had run off their legs in the heart-breaking days and nights on the Alaskan trail, of the feats of strength that had made him king over a husky race of frontiersmen." Reverting again to the present, Daylight reflects, "and this was age." But London's Nietzschean superman does not dwell long on his mortality nor allow it to compromise his masterful philosophy. The vision of his aging body is immediately replaced by the vision of an eighty-four-year-old farmer in the Sonoma valley, whose body is still hard and vigorous from his daily round of chores. Then, he thinks of a man named Ferguson,

> a weakling and an alcoholic, [who] had run away from the
> doctors and the chicken-coop of a city, and soaked up health
> like a thirsty sponge. Well, Daylight pondered, if a sick man
> whom doctors had given up could develop into a healthy farm
> laborer, what couldn't a merely stout man like himself do under
> similar circumstances? He caught a vision of his body with all

its youthful excellence returned, and thought of Dede, and
sat down suddenly on the bed, startled by the greatness of
the idea that had come to him. [*BD*, 317]

Daylight resolves to renounce the city and the pressures of moneymaking; when he adopts a simple life on a Sonoma valley ranch, he is
reborn in the image of his younger self. "Burning Daylight, the city
financier, had died a quick death on the ranch, and his younger
brother, the Daylight from Alaska, had taken his place. The threatened inundation of fat had subsided, and all his old-time Indian lean-
ness and litheness of muscle had returned. So, likewise, did the old
slight hollows in his cheeks come back. For him they indicated the
pink of physical condition. He became the acknowledged strong man
of Sonoma Valley" (*BD*, 346). This return to his younger Alaskan
self, through nature, is a denial of the very truth that London, in his
early fiction, perceived in the White Silence of the Alaskan landscape: man's finitude. As Daylight regains his youth, so America
becomes a new world of small farmers when the clock is turned
backwards. London's hero in effect refuses to see the implications of
the society in which he is living by pretending that he can live in the
past. Denial of death and denial of social reality go hand in hand.

Daylight has two anesthetics that dull his perceptions and allow
these illusions to cloud his consciousness. The first is alcohol, which
is part of his city experiences; the second is his wife, who is part of
his return to the soil. Daylight, who had indulged in drinking binges
in the Northland, finds that "his drinking became systematic and
disciplined" in civilization:

> It was an unconscious development, but it was based upon
> physical and mental condition. The cocktails served as an inhi-
> bition. Without reasoning or thinking about it, the strain of
> the office, which was essentially due to the daring and audacity
> of his ventures, required check or cessation; and he found,
> through the weeks and months, that the cocktails supplied this
> very thing. They constituted a stone wall. He never drank
> during the morning, nor in office hours; but the instant he
> left the office he proceeded to rear this wall of alcoholic
> inhibition athwart his consciousness. [*BD*, 163]

Daylight's reliance on alcohol increases until he is saved by a woman who serves the same anesthetic function. Daylight hardly notices his stenographer, Dede Mason, until one day she tells him that "I shall" is more proper than "I will." Daylight, for whom all the ladies of the Yukon held no charm, is instantly enthralled by this woman's command of grammar: "For the first time it struck him that there was something about his stenographer. He had accepted her up to then, as a female creature and a bit of office furnishing. But now, having demonstrated that she knew more grammar than did businessmen and college graduates, she became an individual. She seemed to stand out in his consciousness as conspicuously as the *I shall* had stood out on the typed page, and he began to take notice" (*BD*, 167). This is the only suggestion we are given that Daylight might have felt himself lacking in culture when he stormed the gates of civilization. Unlike Martin Eden, who blushed and perspired at his awkwardness, Burning Daylight only feels the challenge of the world of wealth and culture. "Nothing abashed him, nor was he appalled by the display and culture and power around him. It was another kind of wilderness, that was all" (*BD*, 123); *Burning Daylight* denies the emotions that *Martin Eden* explores, and the hero happily marries the symbol of culture whom Martin Eden rejects as a shallow vessel.

In spite of London's complete lack of interest in Burning Daylight's emotional life, his description of his "growing intimacy" with Dede Mason suggests that something is very wrong:

> Among other good things resulting from his growing intimacy with Dede, was Daylight's not caring to drink so much as formerly. There was a lessening in desire for alcohol of which even he at last became aware. In a way, *she herself was the needed inhibition*. The thought of her was like a cocktail. Or, at any rate, she substituted for a certain percentage of cocktails. From the strain of his unnatural city existence and of his intense gambling operations, he had drifted on to the cocktail route. *A wall must forever be built to give him easement from the high pitch, and Dede became a part of this wall*. Her personality, her laughter, the intonations of her voice, the impossible golden glow of her eyes, the light on her hair, her form, her dress, her actions on horseback, her merest physical mannerisms—all, pictured over and over in his mind and dwelt upon, served to take the

place of many a cocktail or long Scotch and soda. [*BD*, 244; my emphasis]

Just as Maud Brewster hid from Humphrey the brutal realities that Wolf Larsen embodied, Dede Mason acts as a wall between Daylight and the consciousness of what he spends his days doing. And like *The Sea-Wolf*, this novel reflects rather than challenges the options of London's society. Daylight views life as "a big gambling game" in which "'everybody tries to rob everybody else. Most of them get robbed. They're born suckers. A fellow like me comes along and sizes up the proposition. I've got two choices. I can herd with the suckers, or I can herd with the robbers'" (*BD*, 252). Neither of these is pleasant to contemplate, but Daylight makes the best of it, becomes one of the biggest robbers of all, and employs anodynes to deaden his consciousness to the limitations of his choices. London's hero is not the first nor the last to discover this way of coping with his society, but to call this anesthetizing function "intimacy" is to miss the mark. If it is intimacy, it is like the "dreadful intimacy" of John Barleycorn, in which the knower is the known. The wall that John Barleycorn and the sentimental woman rear athwart consciousness hinders true communication and self-realization, and it is a monument to "the shrine of self" where Burning Daylight continues his demonic obeisances.

London voted for women's suffrage because he believed that, given the vote, women would do away with saloons. In this connection he wrote, "The women are the true conservators of the race. The men are the wastrels, the adventure lovers and gamblers, and in the end it is by their women that they are saved" (*JB*, 336). Like a good mother, Dede Mason reforms her wayward lover, encourages him to give up alcohol, business, city life, moneymaking, and to retreat to a ranch and grow eucalyptus trees. She in fact refuses to marry him until he makes this change. In London's fiction, the attempt to escape death and limitation, the attempt to achieve a spurious immortality that was in fact a living death, is repeatedly associated with marriage to a woman of middle-class refinement and culture. In *Martin Eden*, the elevated social stratum of Ruth Morse is a realm of spirituality and eternal life. London came to see this as an illusion, but only in illusions was he able to entertain the notion of

Jack and Charmian in Vera Cruz, 1914
(Reproduced by permission of The Huntington Library, San Marino, California)

his life's significance after his death. The illusion of immortality was preferable to the finality of a lonely death, just as the illusion of love was preferable to the self-consumption of a man immured in his own flesh. According to Charmian London, the clouds of London's long sickness were dispelled by a trip the two of them took on horseback, over the trails of the Sonoma valley. Her account deserves to be read as an example of the sentimental approach to nature that, in *Burning Daylight*, replaces London's earlier tragic vision:

> As we forged skyward on the ancient road that lies now against one bank, now another, the fanning ferns sprinkling our faces with rain and dew, wild-flowers nodding in the cool flows of wind, I could see my dear man quicken and sparkle as if in spite of himself and the powers of darkness. The response to my own mood in the earth's enchantment, which had been so lamentably absent from him in the few days gone by, kept mounting and bubbling and presently was overflowing in the full measure I knew so gloriously of him. Truly, as the summit drew near, I do believe he still did not know that the crisis had been reached and passed in his Long Sickness for which the mad German philosopher had given him a name, and that he had staved off despair and death itself for many a splendid, fruitful year to come.[4]

If London had indeed succumbed to the sentimental illusions as irrevocably as Charmian's account suggests, his name would have faded like the names of so many once-popular writers. Rather, he was engaged in a constant struggle to keep the illusions in place. Truth always threatened to discard the veils in which he had draped her. London's recurrent bouts with the Long Sickness and the White Logic testify to the strength of his devotion to reality, to truth-seeing and truth-saying. In these bouts of "sickness" lay the health of his art, and London's struggle with the truth constitutes his lasting claim on our attention. If he was capable of writing *Burning Daylight*, with all of its denials, he was also capable of writing, in *John Barleycorn*, of his self-consciousness of this process. "Healthful, and wholesome, and sincere" is how he described the writing he did after the long sickness. "It was never pessimistic. The way to life I had learned in my long sickness. I knew the illusions were right, and I exalted the illusions. Oh, I still turn out the same sort of work, stuff that is clean,

alive, optimistic, and that makes toward life. And I am always assured
by the critics of my superabundant and abounding vitality, and of
how thoroughly I am deluded by these very illusions I exploit" (*JB*,
276–77). After such knowledge, what forgiveness? London paid, and
paid dearly, for his illusions.

The chapters of *John Barleycorn* in which London touches on the
years of his Beauty Ranch are very different in mood and philosophy
from the false exuberance of Burning Daylight's rebirth. As he sur-
veys his rolling acres and looks over the legal pages that list the
names of former owners of the land, his mood is close to that of the
Preacher in Ecclesiastes. London's ranch was his last attempt to stamp
his imprint on the world before he passed beyond. If, through his
socialism, he had been unable to make the world better, at least he
could, through his ranch, make the soil better. If he himself had
withered for lack of soil in which to root, he would nevertheless
invest himself in the earth and so leave a part of him behind when he
was gone. "I have scrawled myself [on the earth] with a hundred
thousand eucalyptus trees" (*JB*, 325). But the earth once again
proved unreceptive to his seed. As he muses over the names of those
who farmed the land before him, and passed away, he thinks, "So I,
too, scratch the land with my brief endeavor and flash my name
across a page of legal script ere I pass and the page grows musty"
(*JB*, 326). Halleck, Hastings, Swett, Tait, Denman, Tracy, Grim-
wood, Carlton, Temple—the names of former owners "appear fast
and furiously, flashing from legal page to legal page and in a flash
vanishing. But ever the persistent soil remains for others to scrawl
themselves across" (*JB*, 325). The earth abides, and her persistence
mocks men's puny efforts to subdue her. "It is like a monster ever
unsubdued, this stubborn land that drowses in this Indian summer
weather and that survives them all, the men who scratched its surface
and passed" (*JB*, 324).

In *The Sea-Wolf* London put in Wolf Larsen's mouth a long passage
from Ecclesiastes, for the Preacher, says Larsen, "thought as I think:"
"'All is vanity and vexation of spirit,' 'There is no profit under the
sun,' 'There is one event unto all,' to the fool and the wise, the clean
and the unclean, the sinner and the saint, and that event is death"
(*SW*, 87, 88). The knowledge that death humbles even the mightiest
of men stuck in London's craw, for to him it reduced all human effort
to futility. "[Man] squirms on his dunghill, and like a child lost in

Jack London overlooking the Sonoma valley
(Reproduced by permission of The Huntington Library, San Marino, California)

the dark among goblins, calls to the gods that he is their younger
brother, a prisoner of the quick that is destined to be as free as
they—monuments of egotism reared by the epiphenomena; *dreams
and the dust of dreams, that vanish when the dreamer vanishes and are no
more when he is not"* (*JB*, 328–29; my emphasis). But all dreams do
not vanish with the dreamer. Some dreams are passed on to others
and are remembered and retold. Other dreams become the basis of a
new social order and live on long after the dreamers are dust. What is
culture but the dreams of dead men and women, embodied in stone
and song and social structure, to be chiseled and sung and shaped by
new generations of dreamers who add their own songs to the songs
of the past? If immortality means to have one's dreams live after the
body has returned to the earth, then Jack London has achieved the
immortality he so desired. He is known, remembered, and read
more than fifty years after his death. But he died without belief. He
died thinking that his dreams were dying with him. He was not
aware of having passed them on. "O, my daughter," he wrote to Joan
a year before he died, "I should like dearly to be able to talk to you
about men, and women, and race, and place."[5] As his daughters were
estranged from him, so was he estranged from his reading audience.
The act of communicating his dreams was confounded with pander-
ing illusions. London's dreams were sometimes his own, but they
were often enough those of a fictitious person so that he did not go
gently into that good night.

London called man's strivings "monuments of egotism." But is it
egotism that prompts the sower to put seed into the ground? Is he
not returning to the earth that which is of the earth? just as the
dreamer, in telling his dream, perhaps returns to his listener a forgotten memory? The sowing of a seed and the telling of a dream
need not be acts of detachment in which one bestows and the other
receives: they can be a mutual finding. But this mode of thinking and
being was not congenial to Jack London. Of his ranch he wrote, "I
am trying to master this soil and the crops and the animals that spring
from it, as I strove to master the sea, and men, and women, and the
books, and all the face of life that I could stamp with my 'will to
do.'"[6] In his battle with the earth, the earth won. In *John Barleycorn*
he recognizes the presumption of man's notion that he can own a
piece of the earth: "As if anything imperishable could belong to the

perishable" (*JB*, 313). London recognized the vanity of man's small efforts in the face of the rising sun and the abiding earth. But he could not consciously perceive himself as a part of the earth, a part of that imperishable body.

Under these circumstances, death meant a total annihilation of the consciousness that had paraded the earth in the shape of a man. Death was nihilation as well as annihilation: it negated what the man had stood for, his values, his dreams. It was as if they never were. Death, in this white light, was insupportable. The best London could do was blot from his consciousness the knowledge of death, for when he looked boldly on the Noseless One, so utterly useless did it make living appear that he was ready to quit it. To ward off the awareness of death, London employed anodynes. In *John Barleycorn* he tells an anecdote about a doctor who urged London to quit smoking.

> "That's what you ought to quit," he lectured. "It will get you in the end. Look at me."
>
> I looked. He was about my own age, broad-shouldered, deep-chested, eyes sparkling, and ruddy-cheeked with health. A finer specimen of manhood one would not ask.
>
> "I used to smoke" he went on. "Cigars. But I gave them up. And look at me."
>
> The man was arrogant, and rightly arrogant, with conscious well-being. And within a month he was dead. It was no accident. Half-a-dozen different bugs of long scientific names had attacked and destroyed him. The complications were astonishing and painful, and for days before he died the screams of agony of that splendid manhood could be heard for a block around. He died screaming. [*JB*, 280]

The structure and import of this story are familiar: the doctor is a splendid "specimen of manhood"; in supreme consciousness of his manhood, he was arrogant; but all this brought him was a slow and painful death. "He died screaming." Years ago London had witnessed a scene in the Erie County Penitentiary, when a young mulatto had asserted his manhood and was beaten to a bloody pulp. The message from both instances was that manhood was punished. To survive, one had to pretend to be less than a man. A posture of submission was preferable to the certainty of death. But the critical difference between the two situations is that, in the natural order, death is inevitable and will come to all, the meek and submissive as well as the arrogant. In the prison, punishment and death were perhaps just as inevitable, but they were part of a man-made social order and not part of the cosmic design. London failed to distinguish clearly between the cosmic order and the man-made social order that was subject to man-made change. Instead, he took flight from consciousness and drank to forget. John Barleycorn interpreted the story of the doctor in this way:

> "You see," said John Barleycorn. "He took care of himself. He even stopped smoking cigars. And that's what he got for it. Pretty rotten, eh? But the bugs will jump. There's no forefending them. Your magnificent doctor took every precaution, yet they got him. When the bug jumps you can't tell where it will land. It may be you. Look what he missed. Will you miss all I can give you, only to have a bug jump on you and drag you down? There is no equity in life. It's all a lottery. But I put the lying smile on the face of life and laugh at the facts. Smile with me and laugh. . . . It's a pretty dark world. I illuminate it for you. It's a rotten world, when things can happen such as happened to your doctor. There's only one thing to do; take another drink and forget it. [*JB*, 280–81]

London admits that he "took another drink for the inhibition that accompanied it" and that he took a drink "every time John Barleycorn reminded [him] of what had happened." In this way began the vicious circle that contributed to London's death at age forty: he drank to forget about death, but because drinking itself reminded him of death, it was necessary to take yet another drink to blot out the consciousness that the drink aroused.

In *Burning Daylight* Elam Harnish drank to forget his work when that work was finished for the day. In *John Barleycorn* London tells how this practice, which he employed after his daily writing was finished, led to a deadly complication. There came the time that the writing itself could not be done without the aid of a drink. "I would sit at my desk and dally with pad and pen, but words refused to flow. My brain could not think the proper thoughts because continually it was obsessed with the one thought that across the room in the liquor cabinet stood John Barleycorn. When, in despair, I took my drink, at once my brain loosened up and began to roll off the thousand words" (*JB*, 301). A further complication arose when the drink began to arouse the very truths against which it was designed to provide anesthesia. "The old long sickness, which had been purely an intellectual sickness, recrudesced. The old ghosts, long laid, lifted their heads again. But they were different and more deadly ghosts. The old ghosts, intellectual in their inception, had been laid by a sane and normal logic. But now they were raised by the White Logic of John Barleycorn, and John Barleycorn never lays the ghosts of his raising. For this sickness of pessimism, caused by drink, one must drink further in quest of the anodyne that John Barleycorn promises but never delivers" (*JB*, 303). Here, drinking is analogous to a neurotic ritual that imitates the very danger it is designed to ward off. The death that London so feared and defended himself against, through drink, was brought nearer by the drink itself. Flight from death is flight into death's arms.

Seduced by the White Logic, London once again opens the long-closed books, and "by paragraph and chapter [the White Logic] states the beauty and wonder I behold in terms of futility and dust" (*JB*, 315). London names some pessimistic philosophers in whom he reads, but his problem is not in these particular books but in the mode of perception that is implied by his invocation of the "books." The "books" have to do with a detached, analytical mode of perception, in which the perceiver is set apart from what he perceives, just as the young London, in reading the "Seaside Library" novels, read not about people in his own walk of life but about people of another social class. This mode of perception denies the reality of both the perceiver and the perceived. The White Logic says,

> "Appearances are ghosts; Life is ghost land, where appearances change, transfuse, permeate each the other and all the others, that are, that are not, that always flicker, fade, and pass, only to come again as new appearances, as other appearances. You are such an appearance, composed of countless appearances out of the past. All an appearance can know is mirage. You know mirages of desire." [*JB*, 316]

In mood, imagery, and mode of perception, this passage and sev-

eral others like it in *John Barleycorn* are remarkably similar to T. S.
Eliot's poetry of a hollow land in which a shadow falls "Between the
idea / And the reality . . . Between the emotion / And the response."[7]
To the list of London's spiritual kinsmen one should certainly add
Ernest Hemingway, who employed a similar set of anesthetics to
protect him from the painful truths of his lonely existence. Drinking,
fishing, writing, and praying are the defenses the Hemingway hero
employs to ward off consciousness. As for London, Hemingway's
flight from death was itself a dance of death, and he was whirled
faster and faster until he put a gun in his mouth and achieved cessa-
tion, if not rest. In Hemingway's writing, it is difficult to perceive the
nature of the truth the anesthetics kept at bay. He was more successful than London in holding the illusions in place, more artful in
shrouding the truth. Jack London's value as an artist and a seer
derives in part from his ability to catch intermittent glimpses of
truths that became less accessible and more mystifying to subsequent
generations of writers. What links London, Hemingway, and Eliot is
a similar mode of perception in which the knower is the known;
their bourgeois consciousness remains locked inside itself, never to
know release from the burden of self until release comes through
death. This consciousness speaks with the voice of the White Logic,
a logic that gave reason dominion over feeling, master dominion
over worker, men dominion over the creeping things of the earth.
Like London, Hemingway had intimations that the attempt to master
the earth was futile: of *The Sun Also Rises*, his own meditation on the
vanity of human effort, Hemingway remarked, the real hero of that
book was the earth. Unable to face the reality of their own situations long enough to recognize them in another, these spiritual kinsmen died without experiencing their kinship. Neither could they
recognize their kinship with the earth.

Only in dreams or in protofascist ideologies could Jack London
acknowledge his repressed desire for belonging, for oneness with the
natural order, for a collective awareness of what it means to be
human. How different death would have appeared to him if he had
felt himself planted in fertile soil. Then he might have taken his leave
in the manner suggested by Walt Whitman at the end of "Song of
Myself":

I depart as air, I shake my white locks at the runaway sun,
I effuse my flesh in eddies, and drift it in lacy jags,
I bequeath myself to the dirt to grow from the grass I love,
If you want me again look for me under your boot-soles.*

Unable to bequeath himself, except in secret ways hidden to himself,
London went to his grave a solitary singer, a solitary comrade.

*Reprinted by permission of New York University Press from *Leaves of Grass* by Walt Whitman, edited by Harold W. Blodgett and Sculley Bradley. © 1965 by New York University.

NOTES

INTRODUCTION

1. Stasz, "The Social Construction of Biography," pp. 51–71.
2. Stone, *Sailor on Horseback*, pp. 280, 329, 288.
3. O'Connor, *Jack London*, p. 158. Lynn, *The Dream of Success*, pp. 79, 110. Gossett, *Race*, pp. 216–17. Starr, *Americans and the California Dream, 1850–1915*, pp. 210–38. The quotation is from Starr, p. 213.
4. Sinclair, *Jack*, p. 173.
5. Lynn, *Dream of Success*, pp. 75–118. Starr, *Americans*, pp. 210–38.

CHAPTER ONE

1. Monkkonen, *The Dangerous Class*, p. 155.
2. Cloward, "Illegitimate Means, Anomie, and Deviant Behavior," pp. 156–78.
3. Hendricks and Shepard, *Letters from Jack London*, November 30, 1898, p. 6.
4. Atherton, "Jack London in Boyhood Adventures," London Papers, HL, pp. 1–41.
5. Ibid., pp. 111–12.
6. Ibid., pp. 1–8.
7. Ibid., pp. 57–60. Cf. Alger, *Ragged Dick*, pp. 149–52.
8. Quoted in Brace, *The Dangerous Classes of New York*, pp. 321–22.
9. Ibid., p. 38.
10. Lindsey and O'Higgins, *The Beast*, p. 150.
11. Jack London, *John Barleycorn*, p. 92; Barltrop, *Jack London*, p. 27.
12. Malcolm X, *Autobiography*, p. 52.
13. Atherton, "Jack London in Boyhood Adventures," London Papers, HL, pp. 41–43, 46.
14. See chap. 5 for a discussion of his disillusionment.
15. Charmian London, *The Book of Jack London*, 1:83.
16. Joan London, *Jack London and His Times*, pp. 47–48.
17. The story of Schmidt, from Taylor's *The Principles of Scientific*

Management, is quoted at length in Harry Braverman, *Labor and Monopoly Capital* (pp. 102–6), a lucid analysis of the effects of Taylorism on the labor process. London's awareness of Taylorism is further suggested by an article he clipped from a radical paper ("The Stop Watch System," *Freedom* 1 [April, 1911], pp. 1–14, London Papers, HL). London marked the following passage:

> Assuming that the stop watch system worked to a charm from a capitalist point of view, the human machines would turn out three times as much. As the workingman, underfed though he is, with an increased wage of 33 per cent, could hardly be expected to buy back as a consumer 300 per cent more of the product, there would be no demand for this labor. With two-thirds of the population idle, what would happen?
>
> The idle men would be forced to resort to destruction of property in order to maintain the price upon their labor, and having no property of their own, they would probably not hesitate to give Mr. Capitalist a dose of his own medicine. They might reason that inasmuch as they had produced the food, the shoes and the clothing, it was justly theirs anyhow. Having once grasped the idea that the land owners of America hold their land by right of conquest from the Indians, a desperate proletariat might proceed to acquire land by the same means. [p. 13]

London apparently intended this clipping for use in a story entitled "Sabotage."

18. Sinclair, *Jack*, p. 22. Jack London, "Tramp Diary," London Papers, HL.

19. London writes vividly of his prison experience in *The Road*, pp. 98–121, and in "How I Became a Socialist," in Foner, *Jack London*, pp. 364–65. See also Sinclair, *Jack*, pp. 23–26. For an extended analysis of American prison literature and the effects of prison experiences on writers' consciousnesses, see Franklin, *The Victim as Criminal and Artist*. Bruce Franklin and I were Fellows at Wesleyan University's Center for the Humanities when he was writing *The Victim*, and my thinking was at that time profoundly stimulated by his approach. Of particular importance, and relevant to this study of London, is Franklin's insight that in slave narratives and prison writing the experience of captivity fosters in the convicts a political awareness of their class position: they see in the prison a microcosm of the power relationships in the larger society.

CHAPTER TWO

1. Jack London, "How I Became a Socialist," in Foner, *Jack London*, p. 364.

2. Ibid., p. 395.

3. Douglas, *The Feminization of American Culture*.

4. See especially *ME*, p. 358; when women look at Martin in a suggestive way, he no longer cares. Lizzie Connolly says to him, " 'You ought to care

when women look at you that way, a man like you. It's not natural. It's all right enough for sissy-boys. But you ain't made that way.'"

5. See Ross, *G. Stanley Hall*, pp. 343, 317–18; E. S., "Celibate Education Today," pp. 425–27; Cattell, "The School and the Family," pp. 92–93.

6. Jack London to Mabel Applegarth, January 1899, London Papers, HL.

7. Hendricks and Shepard, *Letters from Jack London*, December 26, 1900, p. 118.

8. Ibid., July 31, 1900, p. 109.

9. Ibid., February 11, 1902, p. 130.

10. Ibid., December 26, 1900, p. 118.

11. Those who were tended to be labor aristocrats, such as craftsmen from the A.F. of L. See Austin Lewis's manuscript, "Jack London: 1898–1902," a summary of which is included in Franklin Walker's notes for an unfinished biography of London, in the Walker Papers, HL. Lewis was active in the Oakland Socialist Labor party and he provides useful comments on London's social and political orientation.

12. Lynn, *Dream of Success*, p. 84. Jack London, "What Life Means to Me," in Foner, *Jack London*, p. 396. Although I agree that London's consciousness was divided, I dissent from Richard O'Connor's opinion that London only posed as a socialist, that "he believed in it as an actor believes in the lines he is declaiming" (*Jack London*, p. 385). He was as sincere a socialist as he was any of his other identities.

13. Jack London, "What Life Means to Me," in Foner, *Jack London*, p. 396.

14. Ibid., p. 399.

15. Sinclair, *Jack*, pp. 29–30.

16. Hendricks and Shepard, *Letters from Jack London*, October 3, 1899, pp. 59–60.

17. Ibid., November 30, 1898, p. 7.

18. Charmian London, *Book of Jack London*, 2:78–79.

19. Hendricks and Shepard, *Letters from Jack London*, April 3, 1901, p. 124.

20. Charmian London, *Book of Jack London*, 2:81, 82. My emphasis.

21. Fromm, *Escape from Freedom*, p. 158.

22. Ibid., p. 151.

CHAPTER THREE

1. McClintock, *White Logic*, p. 97.

2. Jack London, *The Son of the Wolf*, pp. 6–7.

3. Ibid., p. 16.

4. For London's description of his great "Man-Comrade," see Charmian London, *Book of Jack London*, 2:82.

5. McClintock, *White Logic*, p. 77.

6. Jack London, *Great Short Works of Jack London*, pp. 308, 309.

7. See chap. 4 for more on London's materialist philosophy.

8. McClintock, *White Logic*, p. 114.

9. Jack London, *Great Short Works*, p. 299.

CHAPTER FOUR

1. Hendricks and Shepard, *Letters from Jack London*, November 30, 1898, p. 7.

2. Ibid., January 5, 1902, p. 127.

3. Ibid., January 6, 1902, p. 128.

4. Ibid., April 28, 1902, p. 135.

5. His advice to young writers includes the following: "Find out about this earth, this universe; this force and matter, and the spirit that glimmers up through force and matter from the maggot to Godhead. And by all this I mean WORK for a philosophy of life. It does not hurt how wrong your philosophy of life may be, so long as you have one and have it well" (Jack London, "First Aid to Rising Authors," London Papers, HL). See also his remarks "On the Writer's Philosophy of Life," in Walker, *No Mentor But Myself*, pp. 7–10.

6. Hendricks and Shepard, *Letters from Jack London*, July 12, 1902, p. 136.

7. Joan London, *Jack London*, p. 239.

8. The author's Ph.D. dissertation ("The True Americans: Henry Adams, Theodore Roosevelt, 'Prufrock,' and Others," Brown University, 1974) elaborates on this theme in the lives and works of Theodore Roosevelt and Harvard figures of the 1890s.

9. Lynn, *Dream of Success*, pp. 158–207.

10. Fitzgerald, *The Great Gatsby*, p. 111.

11. Jack London to Anna Strunsky, July 31, 1902, Walling Papers, HL.

12. Joan London, *Jack London*, p. 252.

13. London's need to reassure himself of his ties to "civilization" was taken by middle-class reviewers as evidence of London's "snobbishness": "he needs must assure the reader that in his own home he is accustomed to carefully prepared food and good clothes and daily tub—a fact that he might safely have left to be taken for granted" (as quoted in Joan London, *Jack London*, p. 247). "But," as Joan London replies to this, "Jack London had escaped too recently from the squalor and insecurity of the working class to take such a fact for granted, and, by the same token, had far less need to assure his readers of his comfortable status than himself" (ibid., pp. 247–48).

14. As quoted in Sinclair, *Jack*, p. 11.

15. Jack London to Anna Strunsky, August 16, 1902, and August 21, 1902, Walling Papers, HL.

16. Ibid., September 28–29, 1902, ibid.

17. Ibid., December 20, 1902, ibid. For similar stories in which working-class people wall off their consciousness from painful memories of their past, see Rubin, *Worlds of Pain*, pp. 23–48.

18. Joan London, *Jack London*, pp. 187, 248.

19. Ibid., p. 251.

20. In an undated manuscript note London wrote, "I must go to New York and write a companion book to the 'People of the Abyss.'" His jottings suggest that had he written it he would have viewed New York City from various points of view, e.g., that of a prostitute, a street gamin, an old man, and an old woman. London hated New York City, which may have been another reason he never wrote this book. His notes for "The American Abyss" include the somber reminder to himself, "Take Colt's automatic." MS note, "American People of the Abyss," London Papers, HL.

21. Sinclair, *Jack*, p. 85. Sinclair apparently believes that the book that London says is finished is not *The People of the Abyss* but *The Kempton–Wace Letters*, which Jack and Anna wrote together.

22. Jack London to Anna Strunsky, September 28–29, 1902, Walling Papers, HL.

23. Sinclair, *Jack*, p. 90.

24. Jack London to Anna Strunsky, December 20, 1902, Walling Papers, HL.

25. Ibid.

CHAPTER FIVE

1. Jack London, "What Life Means to Me," in Foner, *Jack London*, pp. 396–97.

2. See also *JB*, pp. 176–77.

3. The "logic" of this may be revealed by an analogy from another sector of the political economy: let us take the case of processed food. Food which has been highly processed has three characteristics: it is low in nutrients, deficient in natural fibers, and highly profitable. The first two characteristics have humanly undesirable effects for the consumers of this food—malnutrition and constipation. An obvious way of avoiding these undesirable effects is to eat unprocessed, whole grain foods. There is an elemental human economy gained by this simple solution, but the market, interested mainly in the third characteristic of processed food, applies a market solution: the manufacture and sale of billions of dollars worth of vitamins, food supplements, and laxatives. If these in turn have undesirable human effects, so much the better, for they will generate further market activity.

4. Hill, *Think and Grow Rich*, p. 186.

5. London, "What Life Means to Me," in Foner, *Jack London*, p. 395.

6. Ibid., p. 399.

7. Ibid.

8. Foner, *Jack London*, p. 63.

9. Jack London to Elwyn Hoffman, December 10, 1900, Hoffman Collection, HL.

10. Jack London to Anna Strunsky, October 15, 1902, Walling Collection, HL.

11. London, "What Life Means to Me," in Foner, *Jack London*, p. 397.

12. Braverman, *Labor and Monopoly Capital*, p. 179.

CHAPTER SIX

1. McClintock, *White Logic*, p. 123.

2. Hendricks and Shepard, *Letters from Jack London*, March 10, 1903, p. 149.

3. Dawley, *Class and Community*.

CHAPTER SEVEN

1. McClintock, *White Logic*, p. 123.

2. Franklin Walker notes (in the Afterword to *The Sea-Wolf and Selected Stories*, pp. 343–44) that Mugridge's nickname, "Cooky," was also the name of a cockney whom London met in the East End.

3. The burial service that Wolf Larsen provides is in part modeled on a sea burial that London witnessed when he was aboard the sealing ship *Sophie Sutherland* (Walker, Afterword to *The Sea-Wolf*, pp. 342–43).

4. When one of London's readers wrote to him to ask about Wolf Larsen's sexual preferences, London replied: "I have never dreamed of drawing a homosexual male character. Perhaps I am too prosaically normal myself, though I do know the whole literature and all the authorities of the 'curious ways'" (Hendricks and Shepard, *Letters from Jack London*, October 23, 1911, p. 354).

5. Charmian London, *Book of Jack London*, 2:30.

CHAPTER EIGHT

1. Charmian London's diaries, September 5, 1901, London Papers, HL.

2. Ibid., May 26, 1913.

3. Ibid., on back of March 20–25, 1905.

4. Ibid., on back of April 24–29, 1905.

5. Ibid., April 5, April 13, 1905; the quoted material is on the back of May 29–June 3, 1905.

6. Ibid., October 6, 1905.

7. Dickinson, "No Rack Can Torture Me," in *The Complete Poems of Emily Dickinson*, p. 183.

8. Charmian London's diaries, November 11, 1905, London Papers, HL.

9. Ibid., April 27, 1907.

10. Ibid., February 2, 1907.

11. Ibid., February 15, 1907.

12. Ibid., February 16, 1907.

13. Ibid., February 17, 1907.

14. Kevin Starr argues this persuasively in *Americans and the California Dream*, pp. 210–38.

15. Jack London to George Brett, October 7, 1914, London Papers, HL.

16. As quoted in Charmian London, *Book of Jack London*, 2:69.

17. She records several menstrual periods which came two weeks late; these may have been miscarriages.

18. Charmian London's diaries, April 27, 1906, London Papers, HL.

19. Ibid., March 16, 1907.

20. Ibid., March 14, 1908.

21. Ibid., December 24, 1908.

22. Ibid., February 6, 1908.

23. Charmian London, *Book of Jack London*, 2:34.

24. Ibid., 2:77.

25. Charmian London's diaries, December 26, 1907, London Papers, HL.

26. Charmian London, *Book of Jack London*, 2:36.

27. Ibid., 2:36–37.

28. Ibid., 2:36.

29. Charmian London's diaries, July 29, 1909, London Papers, HL.

30. Ibid., March 29 and April 5, 1912.

31. Ibid., January 8 and August 31, 1913.

32. Ibid., March 1, 1912.

33. Ibid., April 16, 1912.

34. Ibid., August 13, 1912.

35. Ibid., May 21, 1914.

36. Ibid., June 23, 1910.

37. Ibid., June 25, 1910.

38. Ibid., June 27, 1910.

39. Ibid., July 12, 1910.

40. Ibid., March 1, 1911.

41. Charmian London, *Book of Jack London*, 2:47.

42. Ibid., 2:43.

43. Charmian London's diaries, July 31, 1907, London Papers, HL.

44. Ibid., June 29, 1909.

45. Ibid., July 25, 1907.

46. Ibid., November 13, 1907.

47. Ibid., November 19, 1907.

48. Ibid., December 2, 1907.

CHAPTER NINE

1. George Brett to Jack London, August 27, 1903, London Papers, HL.

2. Hendricks and Shepard, *Letters from Jack London*, c. September 2, 1903, p. 152.

3. Jack London to Cloudesley Johns, September 5, 1903, London Papers, HL.

4. Hendricks and Shepard, *Letters from Jack London*, c. September 2, 1903, p. 153.

5. Ibid., July 11, 1903, p. 151; for the arrangement London suggested with Macmillan, see ibid., November 21, 1902, pp. 138-43. Brett extended the period of the contract from the one year suggested by London to two years, which gave him "a year to a novel instead of six months" (ibid., December 11, 1902, p. 144).

6. Jack London to Cloudesley Johns, September 5, 1903, London Papers, HL.

7. Hendricks and Shepard, *Letters from Jack London*, c. September 2, 1903, p. 153.

8. Enclosure in George Brett to Jack London, September 11, 1903, London Papers, HL.

9. Hendricks and Shepard, *Letters from Jack London*, September 2, 1903, p. 152.

10. Gordon Mills, "Jack London's Quest for Salvation," p. 12. Although I find Mills's description of this pattern accurate, I am at odds with his interpretation of it and his inclusion of *The Call of the Wild* in the category of these broken-backed novels. Mills argues that against Wolf Larsen's individualism London poses the idea of "universal brotherhood" and that this latter idea was associated with "the idea of romantic love, the two together representing gentleness and civilization, in opposition to the brutality of the materialistic world that [London] believed enveloped him" (p. 7). Mills finds this association of universal brotherhood and romantic love "both commonplace and perennially profound"; had he attempted to analyze this association he might have discovered the difference between profundity and mystification. He prefers to believe he is dealing with a mystery of the human heart. He notes that London's writing "sustained two desires: one, the desire for adventure, combat, power; the other, the desire for friendship, justice, and a serene intellectuality," which, he says, can be reduced to "the age-old problem of the unbridled will and the brotherhood of man. . . . It is true of London, as it is true that *the normal human being is in some degree a Dr. Jekyll and a Mr. Hyde*" (pp. 8-9; my emphasis). Mills makes no attempt to understand this pattern in its specific social and historical context; it is simply an "age-old problem."

11. Jack London, "Again the Literary Aspirant," p. 217.

12. Ibid., pp. 217, 218, 219.

13. Ibid., p. 219. Hendricks and Shepard, *Letters from Jack London*, November 21, 1899, p. 71.

14. Jack London, "Again the Literary Aspirant," p. 220.

15. Hendricks and Shepard, *Letters from Jack London*, March 7, 1907, p. 241.

16. Ibid., p. 242.

17. Jack London, "Again the Literary Aspirant," p. 220.

18. Melville, *Moby-Dick*, p. 220.

19. As quoted in Charmian London, *Book of Jack London*, 2:53–54.

20. Cf. Douglas's discussion of Melville in *The Feminization of American Culture*, pp. 289–329.

21. Labor, "Jack London's Symbolic Wilderness," pp. 149–61, and Labor, *Jack London*, pp. 124–46.

22. Hendricks and Shepard, *Letters from Jack London*, November 5, 1915, p. 463.

23. Maxwell Geismar draws attention to this statement by London's literary spokesman and suggests that the phrase "'consummate charlatanry' applied very well, not to art, but to the practice of the commercial art which he had misrepresented as the entire province of humane literature" (*Rebels and Ancestors*, p. 216).

24. Jack London, "Again the Literary Aspirant," p. 219.

25. Ibid.

26. At the beginning of his narrative Humphrey Van Weyden thinks "how comfortable it was, this division of labor which made it unnecessary for me to study fogs, winds, tides, and navigation in order to visit my friend who lived across an arm of the sea. It was good that men should be specialists, I mused. The peculiar knowledge of the pilot and captain sufficed for many thousands of people who knew no more of the sea and navigation than I knew. On the other hand, instead of having to devote my energy to the learning of a multitude of things, I concentrated it upon a few particular things, such as, for example, the analysis of Poe's place in American literature" (*SW*, 8).

27. Jack London, "Again the Literary Aspirant," p. 219.

28. MS note, "Forty Horses Abreast," London Papers, HL.

29. Envelope for "Again the Literary Aspirant," London Papers, HL.

30. *Dictionary of American Biography*, 13:335.

31. Hendricks and Shepard, *Letters from Jack London*, October 24, 1899, pp. 61–62.

32. Ibid., February 10, 1900, p. 91.

33. Ibid., February 3, 1900, p. 88.

34. Ibid., November 11, 1899, p. 68.

35. George Brett to Jack London, November 9, 1904, London Papers, HL.

36. Ibid., October 31, 1904.

37. Ibid., December 17, 1902.

38. Ibid.

39. Hendricks and Shepard, *Letters from Jack London*, February 16, 1903, p. 146.

40. George Brett to Jack London, July 1, 1915, November 3, 1915, London Papers, HL.

41. Hendricks and Shepard, *Letters from Jack London*, November 30, 1898, p. 8.

42. Gaby Deslys, "Why I Get All I Can and Keep All I Get," *American-Examiner*, 1911, London Papers, HL.

CHAPTER TEN

1. Foner, *Jack London*, p. 275. The four stories analyzed in this chapter may be found in Foner's collection, and subsequent page references to that text will be noted parenthetically.

2. Hendricks and Shepard, *Letters from Jack London*, November 30, 1898, p. 6.

3. Ibid., pp. 6, 7.

4. Ibid., p. 5.

5. McClintock, *White Logic*, pp. 127–28.

6. Ibid., p. 128.

7. Shortly after the time London wrote this story he apparently planned to write another, entitled "Sabotage," for which he clipped articles from the labor press describing the tactics of *"La Grève perlée,"* or the drop strike. In France, especially on the state-managed Western Railway, the workers were on the job, but they practiced "the delicate art of sending things astray." Goods intended for Paris ended up at Lille; trains with perishable goods were sidetracked; occasionally trains failed to slow up in time at the Gare du Nord, and the platform was destroyed. See clippings for "Sabotage," London Papers, HL.

8. Hendricks and Shepard, *Letters from Jack London*, December 26, 1900, pp. 118, 119.

9. As quoted in Sinclair, *Jack*, p. 115.

10. Hendricks and Shepard, *Letters from Jack London*, December 21, 1899, pp. 76–77.

11. Kaplan, *Mr. Clemens and Mark Twain*, pp. 114–15.

CHAPTER ELEVEN

1. As quoted in Joan London, *Jack London and His Times*, p. 315.

2. Foner, *Jack London*, pp. 87–97.

3. As quoted in Joan London, *Jack London*, pp. 313, 315.

4. Labor, *Jack London*, p. 103.

5. Norris, *The Complete Works of Frank Norris*, 3:177.

6. Labor, *Jack London*, p. 104.

7. Foner, *Jack London*, p. 89.

8. Lawrence, *Lady Chatterley's Lover*, pp. 362, 362–63.

9. Joan London, *Jack London*, p. 373. For a discussion of the influence of

Jung's *Psychology of the Unconscious* on London's late short stories, see
McClintock, *White Logic*, pp. 151–74.

10. Starr, *Americans and the California Dream*, pp. 235–36.

11. Faulkner, *Light in August*, pp. 161–62, 164.

CHAPTER TWELVE

1. Sam Baskett has written the most perceptive analyses of *Martin Eden*.
In his introduction to the Rinehart edition (New York, 1963), he articulates
the fundamental tension with which London struggles, yet he seems to
locate the contradiction in London's art, rather than in the society about
which he wrote and in which he lived. "London asks us first to believe in the
surpassing importance and dignity of Martin, and then he asks us to believe
in a malign and incomprehensible universe in which the individual has no
importance and dignity. Again, as a conscious artist, London has failed
to create a consistent work of art; but as a tormented human being he has
graphically represented his not untypical anguish as he confronts what
seemed to him some of the facts of twentieth-century life" (xii).

2. My thinking about *Martin Eden* has been stimulated by Carol Ohmann's
approach to the success parable in "*The Autobiography of Malcolm X*: A
Revolutionary Use of the Franklin Tradition," pp. 131–49. She notes that
both Malcolm's and Franklin's stories "are interested in external rather
than subjective events; they are both concerned with objectively measurable
achievements and how they may be obtained" (p. 133). Her discussion of
Malcolm's integration of his private self and his public self (pp. 146–49)
describes a voyage that neither London nor his autobiographical hero
was able to undertake.

3. See Lewis, *The American Adam*, an analysis of nineteenth-century
American literature, which Earle Labor invokes in his first chapter of
Jack London.

4. Hendricks and Shepard, *Letters from Jack London*, December 21, 1899,
p. 77.

5. Sam Baskett, "*Martin Eden*," pp. 23–26.

6. Review of *Martin Eden*, p. 93.

7. See his letter to Cloudesley Johns in chap. 4 and his characterization
of Wolf Larsen in chap. 7.

8. Jack London, "What Life Means to Me," in Foner, *Jack London*, p. 392.
George Munro's "Seaside Library" series put out cheap paper editions
of novels like *Jane Eyre*, *Adam Bede*, and *John Halifax, Gentleman*.

9. For an analysis of this syndrome at Harvard during the 1890s see my
"'Harvard Indifference,'" pp. 356–72.

10. Charmian London, *Book of Jack London*, 2:54–55.

11. See also *ME*, p. 158. London's manuscript notes for *Martin Eden*
(London Papers, HL) indicate that the Elizabeth Barrett–Robert Browning
relationship was in his mind early on as he conceived the novel.

CHAPTER THIRTEEN

1. Charmian London, *Book of Jack London*, 2:182.

2. Starr, *Americans and the California Dream*, pp. 210–38.

3. Starr calls attention to this passage and to London's preoccupation with physical health, ibid., pp. 211–12.

4. Charmian London, *Book of Jack London*, 2:33.

5. Hendricks and Shepard, *Letters from Jack London*, August 25, 1915, p. 459.

6. Ibid., February 7, 1913, p. 370.

7. Sam Baskett remarks on the affinities between Conrad, London, and Eliot in "Jack London's Heart of Darkness," pp. 66–77.

BIBLIOGRAPHY

MANUSCRIPT SOURCES

San Marino, California
   Henry E. Huntington Library
    Elwyn Hoffman Papers.
    Jack London Papers.

       The Henry E. Huntington Library has 16,000 pieces in the London
       Papers. Of particular use to this study were (1) London's unpublished
       letters, (2) his notes and clippings for unwritten stories, (3) the
       correspondence of George P. Brett of Macmillan Company, (4) Frank
       Irving Atherton's memoir, "Jack London in Boyhood Adventures,"
       and (5) Charmian London's diaries, 1900–1916. Although I con-
       sulted the originals of the letters in King Hendricks and Irving
       Shepard, *Letters from Jack London*, for the convenience of the reader
       I have cited the published record.

    Franklin Walker Papers.
    Anna Strunsky Walling Papers.

BOOKS AND ARTICLES BY JACK LONDON

There is no standard edition of Jack London's works. I have used the
editions most readily available, in the belief that these are as likely as any
to be available to the reader. For a full list of London's publications, see
Hensley C. Woodbridge et al., *Jack London: A Bibliography*.

London, Jack. "Again the Literary Aspirant." *Critic* 41 (1902): 217–20.
————. *Burning Daylight*. New York: Macmillan Company, 1910.
————. *The Call of the Wild*. New York: Grosset & Dunlap, 1915.
————. *A Daughter of the Snows*. Rahway, N.J.: J. B. Lippincott Company,
   1902.
————. *Great Short Works of Jack London*. Edited by Earle Labor. New York:
   Harper & Row, 1970.
————. *The Iron Heel*. New York: Macmillan Company, 1908.

———. *John Barleycorn*. New York: Century Company, 1913.

———. *Martin Eden*. 1909. Reprint. New York: Holt, Rinehart and Winston, 1963.

———. *The Mutiny on the Elsinore*. New York: Macmillan Company, 1914.

———. *The People of the Abyss*. 1903. Reprint. New York: Garrett Press, 1970.

———. *The Road*. New York: Greenberg, 1907.

———. *The Sea-Wolf and Selected Stories*. New York: New American Library, 1964. (*The Sea-Wolf* was originally published in 1904.)

———. *The Son of the Wolf*. Boston: Houghton Mifflin Company, 1930.

———. *The Star Rover*. New York: Macmillan Company, 1915.

———. *The Valley of the Moon*. New York: P. F. Collier and Son Company, 1913.

———. *White Fang*. New York: Grosset & Dunlap, 1906.

BOOKS

Alger, Horatio, Jr. *Ragged Dick and Mark, the Match Boy*. New York: Collier Macmillan Publishers, 1962.

Asbury, Herbert. *The Gangs of New York: An Informal History of the Underworld*. New York: Alfred A. Knopf, 1928.

Barltrop, Robert. *Jack London: The Man, the Writer, the Rebel*. London: Pluto Press, 1976.

Brace, Charles Loring. *The Dangerous Classes of New York, and Twenty Years' Work among Them*. New York: Wynkoop & Hallenbeck, 1872.

Braverman, Harry. *Labor and Monopoly Capital: The Degradation of Work in the Twentieth Century*. New York: Monthly Review Press, 1974.

Dawley, Allan. *Class and Community: The Industrial Revolution in Lynn*. Cambridge, Mass.: Harvard University Press, 1976.

Dickinson, Emily. *The Complete Poems of Emily Dickinson*. Edited by Thomas H. Johnson. Boston: Little, Brown and Company, 1960.

The Dictionary of American Biography. 22 vols. New York: Charles Scribner's Sons, 1934.

Douglas, Ann. *The Feminization of American Culture*. New York: Alfred A. Knopf, 1977.

Faulkner, William. *Light in August*. New York: Modern Library, 1932.

Fitzgerald, F. Scott. *The Great Gatsby*. New York: Charles Scribner's Sons, 1925.

Foner, Philip S. *Jack London: American Rebel*. New York: Citadel Press, 1947.

Franklin, H. Bruce. *The Victim as Criminal and Artist: Literature from the American Prison*. New York: Oxford University Press, 1978.

Fromm, Erich. *Escape from Freedom*. New York: Farrar & Rinehart, 1941.

Geismar, Maxwell. *Rebels and Ancestors: The American Novel, 1890–1915*. Boston: Houghton Mifflin Company, 1953.

Gilman, Charlotte Perkins. *Women and Economics: A Study of the Economic*

Relation between Men and Women as a Factor in Social Evolution. Boston: Small, Maynard and Company, 1898. Reprint. New York: Harper & Row, 1966.

Gossett, Thomas B. *Race: The History of an Idea in America*. New York: Schocken Books, 1965.

Hendricks, King, and Shepard, Irving. *Letters from Jack London*. New York: Odyssey Press, 1965.

Hill, Napoleon. *Think and Grow Rich*. 1937. Reprint. Greenwich, Conn.: Fawcett Publications, 1960.

Kaplan, Justin. *Mr. Clemens and Mark Twain: A Biography*. New York: Simon and Schuster, 1966.

Labor, Earle. *Jack London*. New York: Twayne Publishers, 1974.

Lawrence, D. H. *Lady Chatterley's Lover*. New York: Grove Press, 1962.

Lewis, R. W. B. *The American Adam: Innocence, Tragedy and Tradition in the Nineteenth Century*. Chicago: University of Chicago Press, 1955.

Lindsey, Ben B., and O'Higgins, Harvey J. *The Beast*. Garden City, N.Y.: Doubleday, Page & Company, 1911.

London, Charmian. *The Book of Jack London*. 2 vols. New York: Century Company, 1921.

London, Joan. *Jack London and His Times: An Unconventional Biography*. New York: Book League of America, 1939. Reprint. Seattle: University of Washington Press, 1968.

Lynn, Kenneth S. *The Dream of Success: A Study of the Modern American Imagination*. Boston: Little, Brown and Company, 1955.

McClintock, James I. *White Logic: Jack London's Short Stories*. Grand Rapids, Mich.: Wolf House Books, 1975.

Malcolm X; with the assistance of Alex Haley. *The Autobiography of Malcolm X*. New York: Grove Press, 1965.

Melville, Herman. *Moby-Dick*. Edited by Charles Feidelson, Jr. Indianapolis: Bobbs-Merrill Company, 1964.

Monkkonen, Eric H. *The Dangerous Class: Crime and Poverty in Columbus, Ohio, 1860–1885*. Cambridge, Mass.: Harvard University Press, 1975.

Norris, Frank. *The Complete Works of Frank Norris*. 10 vols. Garden City, N.Y.: Doubleday, Doran and Company, 1928.

O'Connor, Richard. *Jack London: A Biography*. Boston: Little, Brown and Company, 1964.

Ross, Dorothy. *G. Stanley Hall: The Psychologist as Prophet*. Chicago: University of Chicago Press, 1972.

Rubin, Lillian Breslow. *Worlds of Pain: Life in the Working-Class Family*. New York: Basic Books, 1976.

Sinclair, Andrew. *Jack: A Biography of Jack London*. New York: Harper & Row, 1977.

Starr, Kevin. *Americans and the California Dream, 1850–1915*. New York: Oxford University Press, 1973.

Stone, Irving. *Sailor on Horseback: The Biography of Jack London*. Boston: Houghton Mifflin Company, 1938.

Terkel, Studs. *Working*. New York: Avon Books, 1975.

Walker, Dale L. *No Mentor But Myself: A Collection of Articles, Essays, Reviews, and Letters on Writing and Writers*. Port Washington, N.Y.: Kennikat Press, 1979.

Walker, Franklin. *Jack London and the Klondike: The Genesis of an American Writer*. London: Bodley Head, 1966.

Woodbridge, Hensley C.; London, John; and Tweney, George H. *Jack London: A Bibliography*. Georgetown, Calif.: Talisman Press, 1966.

ARTICLES

Baskett, Sam. Introduction to *Martin Eden*. New York: Holt, Rinehart and Winston, 1963.

————. "Jack London's Heart of Darkness." *American Quarterly* 10 (1958): 66–77.

————. "*Martin Eden*: Jack London's Poem of the Mind." *Modern Fiction Studies* (1976): 23–36.

Cattell, J. McKeen. "The School and the Family." *Popular Science Monthly* 74 (1909): 84–95.

Cloward, Richard A. "Illegitimate Means, Anomie, and Deviant Behavior." In *Gang Delinquency and Delinquent Subcultures*, edited by James F. Short, Jr. New York: Harper & Row, 1968.

Hedrick, Joan D. "'Harvard Indifference.'" *New England Quarterly* 49 (1976): 356–72.

Labor, Earle. "Jack London's Symbolic Wilderness: Four Versions." *Nineteenth Century Fiction* 17 (1972): 149–61.

Mills, Gordon. "Jack London's Quest for Salvation." *American Quarterly* 7 (1955): 3–14.

Ohmann, Carol. "*The Autobiography of Malcolm X*: A Revolutionary Use of the Franklin Tradition." *American Quarterly* 20 (1970): 131–49.

Review of *Martin Eden*. *Athenaeum* (1910): 93.

Stasz, Clarice. "The Social Construction of Biography: The Case of Jack London." *Modern Fiction Studies* 22 (1976): 51–71.

S., E. "Celibate Education Today." *Popular Science Monthly* 73 (1908): 423–28.

Walker, Franklin. Afterword to *The Sea-Wolf and Selected Stories*. New York: New American Library, 1964.

PH.D. DISSERTATION

Hedrick, Joan Doran. "The True Americans: Henry Adams, Theodore Roosevelt, 'Prufrock,' and Others." Ph.D. dissertation, Brown University, 1974.

INDEX

Abysmal Brute, The, 135

Africa, 59

"Again the Literary Aspirant,"
154–56, 157, 160, 161

Alaska: fiction of, 48–55, 221–25;
image of, 93. *See also* Klondike

Alcohol. *See* Drinking

Alger, Horatio, 60; *Ragged Dick*,
6–9; *From Canal Boy to President*,
24

Alger (myth), 33; as model for London, 15–16; satirized, 25–26; in
ME, 200–212

America, 59

"American People of the Abyss," 69

American Press Association, 59

Anaesthetics, 21, 53; in *BD*,
225–27; and fear of death, 233,
234–35, 236; in Hemingway's
fiction, 236

Anglo-Saxonism. *See* Ideology: racial

Anodynes. *See* Anaesthetics

"Apostate, The," 169, 171–76, 178

Applegarth, Edward, 40

Applegarth, Mabel, 36, 40; letters
from London, 43, 56, 128, 167,
172

Art, 90, 145, 159 (n. 23); and inner
life, xv; and sentimental illusions,
40, 145; and loss of self, 46,
213–14; as self-realization, 47;
contradictions in, 154–58,
165–66; and unconscious, 158,

159; and editorial pressure,
163–65; and self-repression,
213–14. *See also* Audience; London, Jack: as artist

Asbury, Herbert, 4

Atherton, Frank, 7–9, 15

Atlantic Monthly, 82

Audience: and hobo-artist, 22–23;
bourgeois, 151, 154–61,
163–64, 165–67; London's scorn
for, 161, 163, 232

Austin, Mary, 158

Australia, 142

Autobiography of Malcolm X, The,
4–5, 13–14

Ban (horse), 137

Barrett, Elizabeth. *See* Browning,
Elizabeth Barrett

Baskett, Sam, 205

"Bâtard," 53

Bitch Goddess, 17, 75, 197

Black Cat, 155, 163

Blackwell's Island, 23

Blithedale Romance, The (Hawthorne), 54

Blond beast, 102, 104, 165, 173

Boer War, 59

Book of Jack London, The, 190

Books: and comradeship, 8; as
romantic escape, 20, 21; and false
consciousness, 21; as institution
of initiation, 21; and middle class,
32, 33, 34, 35, 46; and illusion,

33; London's mistake in opening, 58, 207; and London's notion of love, 74–75, 150; and White Logic, 91; in *SW*, 118, 128; in *ME*, 207, 208–10, 215–17, 220; and emotional detachment, 235

Brace, Charles Loring, 12

Brett, George P.: letters from London, 57, 94, 152; as London's editor, 151–52, 156, 163–64

British Journal of Psychiatry, 88

Browning, Elizabeth Barrett, 191, 209

Browning, Robert, 40, 209, 214

Burning Daylight, xv, xviii, 143, 188, 198; sentimental illusions in, 221, 226–30; illusion of immortality in, 221–22; attitude toward women in, 222–23, 225–27; preoccupation with health in, 224–25; drinking in, 225, 234; compared with *SW*, 227

Call of the Wild, The, xviii, 43, 47, 54, 94, 153 (n. 10), 157, 165, 171, 177; autobiographical elements in, 63, 96–99, 110; naturalism in, 95; restoration of hero in, 99, 102–11; collective consciousness in, 99–102, 107–8, 109–10; compared with *SW*, 112, 113, 114, 116; compared with *WF*, 137, 138; money from, 152; transformation of material in, 158; compared with "South of the Slot," 177, 180, 184; compared with *IH*, 188–89; compared with *ME*, 220

Capitalism and capitalist society, xviii, 51, 53, 79, 88, 90, 116, 132, 133, 153, 171, 187, 195; in *SW*, 112, 117, 177; in "The Apostate," 176; in "South of the Slot," 184; in *IH*, 188, 190, 191;

in *BD*, 222, 224. *See also* Dominant culture

"Cask of Amontillado, The" (Poe), 130

Century, 151, 152–53

Chaney, William, xvi, 5, 16

City, the: and naturalism, 60, 61; and Jack and Charmian's love, 143; in *BD*, 222, 226, 227

"City of Dreadful Night, The" (De Quincey), 93

Class, xvi, 15, 89, 90, 154, 184; and comradeship, 7–9; London's understanding of, 26–29; and language, 36, 40, 204–5; and power relationships, 37, 62; in "In a Far Country," 52; and sexuality, 74–75, 196–98; in *ME*, 75, 202, 204–6; in *SW*, 114, 116; in "South of the Slot," 177; and beast imagery, 203; and behavior, 209. *See also* Lower class; Middle class

"Class Struggle, The," 82

Clemens, Samuel. *See* Twain, Mark

Companionship. *See* Comradeship

Comradeship, 12, 14, 27, 45, 56, 57, 71, 81, 83–84; and drinking, 15–16, 17, 41–42, 86; with Nelson, 20; with Anna Strunsky, 37–38; need for, repressed, 40; and class, 41–44, 92; with Man-Comrade, 43, 45; in Alaskan fiction, 48–55; compared with courtship, 55, 154; and London's materialism, 58; in *PA*, 63–64; in *CW*, 110; in "South of the Slot," 183; in *BD*, 223–24

Conrad, Joseph, 135, 236 (n. 7)

Consciousness: false, 21, 98, 165; class, 66, 165, 202–3; bourgeois, 100, 154, 178, 236; sentimental, 130–33, 190–92; collective, 160, 161, 170, 176, 177, 184; machine, 174; human, 176

Contradictions: of society, xvii, 47, 110, 151; of class, xviii, 46, 92; within lower class, 16; of manhood, 35–37, 46, 195; in London's view of lower class, 68; of womanhood, 75, 195; in London's emotional life, 81; in art, 132, 154–58, 190, 195, 200 (n. 1)
Cooper, James Fenimore, 110
Coxey's Army, 27
Crèvecoeur, Michel-Guillaume Jean de, 14
Crime and criminality, 3–5, 10, 12, 22, 41; and manhood, 66, 118

Dangerous class. See Lower class
Daughter of the Snows, A, 54, 100–101
Dawley, Allan, 101
Death, 87, 116, 135, 165–66, 237; of consciousness, 45, 128–30; in Alaskan fiction, 48–54, 104–5, 225, 227; and orders of truth, 88–89; naturalistic, 115; in WF, 139–40; and sexuality, 198; and immortality, 229; London's defenses against, 233–35. See also Living death
De Quincey, Thomas, 93
Deslys, Gaby, 167
Dickens, Charles, 178
Dickinson, Emily, 138
Dirigo, 142, 147
Dominant culture, xvi, 23, 87–88, 92. See also Capitalism and capitalist society
Dowson, Ernest, 123
"Dream of Debs, The," 169, 176–77, 178, 181, 190, 200
Drinking: as manhood rite, 14–16, 18–20, 85; and John London's example, 15; and comradeship, 15–16, 17, 41, 42; London's childhood experience of, 17–18;

as anodyne, 21, 81, 234–35, 236; and false consciousness, 21–22; as escape from self, 46; and long sickness, 81, 84–86; to excess, 86, 142–43, 147; and "baby propositions," 146–47; in BD, 225–27; and writing, 234–35

Eames, Ninetta, 134
Eames, Roscoe, 134
Eliot, T. S., 236
Endings, happy, 6, 154, 163, 177, 216
"End of the Tether, The" (Conrad), 135
England, 94, 164. See also London, England
Erie County Penitentiary, 27–29, 31, 35, 39, 66, 96, 98, 101, 118, 233–34
Eternal life. See Immortality
Evolution. See Social Darwinism

Father figures in fiction, 106–7, 109, 111, 112, 120–21
Faulkner, William, 198
Fellowship. See Comradeship
Fish Patrol, 22
Fitzgerald, F. Scott, 61, 75–76, 143
Foner, Philip S., xvii, 176
Franklin, Benjamin, 26, 200–202
French Frank (oyster pirate), 13, 19, 35
Fromm, Erich, 45–46

"Game, The," 163
Gangs, 14, 15, 41, 110, 116, 143; London harassed by, 8–9; London joins, 10, 22; and industrialization, 10–11
Gangs of New York, The (Asbury), 4
Gilder, Richard Watson, 113, 151–52, 153
Gilman, Charlotte Perkins, 77–79, 134, 150

Glen Ellen, 134, 135, 136, 147
"God That Failed, The" (Johns), 163
Gossett, Thomas B., xv
Great Gatsby, The (Fitzgerald), 61, 75–76, 143

Hall, G. Stanley, 35
Hawthorne, Nathaniel, 53, 54–55, 157–58, 169, 206
Haydee (girlfriend), 34
Hegel, Friedrich, 138
Heinhold, Johnny, 15
Hemingway, Ernest, 195, 236
Henry Clay Debating Society, 33, 34
Hill, Napoleon, 76–77, 78
Hinkle, Beatrice, 196
Hoffman, Elwyn, 82–83
House of the Seven Gables, The (Hawthorne), 54, 158
"How I Became a Socialist," 82
Huckleberry Finn (Twain), 20, 22, 42, 144, 187
Huxley, Thomas, 82

Identity: and class, 179–80, 181–83; transformation of, in *IH*, 198–99. *See also* Consciousness
Ideology: racial, xv, 49, 98–99, 100–101, 165; of American dream, xvii; and women, 198; and search for belonging, 236. *See also* Alger (myth); Endings, happy; Illusion; Success: as ideology
Idylls of the King (Tennyson), 146
Illusion, xvii, xviii, 46, 58, 136–37, 146, 176, 229–30; and books, 33; and *SW*, 47, 94, 113, 115, 124, 132; of mastery, 49; of repeating the past, 61; as "cure" for long sickness, 72, 81–82, 84; contrasted with dream, 81; as "secondary truth," 135; unrelia-

bility of, 140; of eternal life, 140, 213; and search for belonging, 143; patriarchal, 144; and bourgeois audience, 151, 154; as escape from social reality, 153; in *BD*, 225; London's need for, 227–30; in art, 232; in Hemingway's fiction, 236. *See also* Books; Ideology; Sentimental love
Immortality: and middle class, 36, 213; in "The White Silence," 50; in *CW*, 105; and community, 110; and success, 128; and illusion, 143, 213, 227; and progeny, 144; and art, 144, 156, 160–61, 232; in *IH*, 192
"Impenitentia Ultima" (Dowson), 123
"In a Far Country," 49, 52–54
Industry. *See* Work
Intercollegiate Socialist Society, 82
Iron Heel, The, 82, 184, 185; critique of capitalism in, 188, 191; historical prophecy in, 189–90; sentimental consciousness in, 190–92; contradiction between form and content in, 191, 200; working class in, 192–93; repressed sexuality in, 193–95; compared with *SW*, 194; compared with *Lady Chatterley's Lover*, 194–95; association of class and sex in, 196–98; transformation of identity in, 198–99
Italy, 83, 84

Jack London (Labor), xvii
Jack London: American Rebel (Foner), xvii
Jack London and His Times (Joan London), xvii
Jack London and the Klondike (Walker), 48
Jacobs, Fred, 40
James, William, 75
"Jerry" (*Jerry of the Islands*), 164

John Barleycorn. *See* Drinking
John Barleycorn, 15, 18, 33, 40–42,
    83, 104, 142, 163, 233; long
    sickness and materialism in, 58,
    72–74, 81–82, 86–93, 234–36;
    illusion in, 229–30
Johns, Cloudesley, 41, 162–63;
    letters from London, 57, 58, 128,
    152, 155
Jung, Carl, 196

Kempton-Wace Letters, The, 38, 69
    (n. 21)
Kipling, Rudyard, 74, 159
Kittredge, Charmian. *See* London,
    Charmian Kittredge
Klondike, 48, 60, 95
Korea, 135

Labor, Earle, xvii, 158
Lady Chatterley's Lover (Lawrence),
    194–95
Langdon, Olivia, 187
Language, 88, 89, 106; and tradi-
    tion, 101; sentimental, 131; and
    disguise in art, 157, 170; and
    class, 178, 209, 213–14
Last Chance Saloon, 14, 15, 18, 19
Lawrence, D. H., 194–95
Lenin, V. I., 189
Light in August (Faulkner), 198
Lindsey, Judge Ben, 12
Little Lady of the Big House, The,
    xviii
Living death, 52, 130, 213, 227
Log of the Snark, The (Charmian
    London), 149
London, Bess (daughter), 144
London, Bess Maddern (first wife),
    37, 40, 41, 135, 136, 144, 185;
    marriage, 38, 180; separation,
    152
London, Charmian Kittredge (sec-
    ond wife): letters from London,
    43–44, 45, 133; marriage, 134,
    140, 185, 186–87; characterized,

134; as cure for long sickness,
    134, 136–37; relationship with
    London, 134–37, 144–47,
    148–50; courtship, 135–37;
    birth of daughter, 144; desire for
    children, 144, 146–48; miscar-
    riage, 144, 147; participation in
    London's writing, 146; reaction
    to daughter's death, 147–48;
    compared to character in *IH*,
    195; inscription to, in *ME*, 221
London, Flora Wellman (mother),
    xv, 15, 172; birth of London, 5;
    desertion of, by Chaney, 5; mar-
    riage to John London, 5; fear of
    Italians, 8, 17; spiritualism, 16,
    21; London's view of, 16–17;
    middle-class aspirations of, 18
London, Jack
    birth, xv–xvi, 5
    health, xvi; preoccupation with,
        87, 224 (n. 3); piles, 136, 139;
        tropical disease, 142, 145;
        teeth, 144–45; smoking, 150;
        in *BD*, 222, 224–25. *See also*
        Drinking; Long sickness
    search for belonging, xvi, 14, 20,
        128, 143–44, 230, 236
    authentic ("real") self, xvi, 14,
        43–45, 86, 133, 206
    as artist, xvi, 22–23, 32, 46, 47,
        48, 54–55, 131, 146, 154–61,
        163–64, 165–67, 178, 236;
        portrait of, in *ME*, 188, 190,
        205–7, 209–10, 213–14
    American heritage, xvi, 23,
        96–97, 101–2
    consciousness: divided, xvi,
        28–29, 47, 64, 65, 92, 98, 116,
        144, 186–87; false, 21; shaped
        by failure, 22–24; shaped by
        Alger myth, 25; humanistic,
        28, 104, 105, 119; masochistic,
        30–31, 45–46; sado-
        masochistic, 86–87; changed,
        38–39, 59, 63; desire to lose,

45–46, 83, 129; compared
with Martin Eden's, 48; in
Malemute Kid stories, 48–49;
fluid, 65–67; bourgeois, 88,
92–93; compared with Van
Weyden's (SW), 113; self-
contained, 128, 168
tramp life, 3, 22–24, 26–27, 44,
96
stepfather's influence, 5–6, 9–10,
15–17, 21
work experience, 6, 9–10, 12,
22, 24–26, 32, 43
money, 6, 10, 16, 25, 172; as
gateway to criminal subculture,
12–13; and comradeship, 16;
and manhood, 19–20; and
courtship, 33, 34; for Snark,
142, 200; and women,
149–50; for SW, 151, 152; for
CW, 152; from Macmillan,
152; worries, 152; as motivation, 162–63; in BD, 224, 225,
227
compared with: Ragged Dick
(Alger), 6–8; Tom Sawyer, 20;
Huck Finn, 20, 22, 42, 144;
Buck (CW), 96–99, 100; Van
Weyden (SW), 113–14,
130–31, 133; Wolf Larsen
(SW), 127–29, 130; Ishmael
(Moby-Dick), 144; prostitute,
166–67; Hawthorne, 169,
171; Lenin, 189; Rosa Luxemburg, 189; Hemingway, 195,
236; Ernest Everhard (IH),
198; T. S. Eliot, 236
childhood and adolescence,
6–22, 44, 46–47, 172–73, 200
friends, 7–9, 40–42, 70, 136
mother's influence, 8, 16–18
as oyster pirate, 10, 12–13,
14–22, 41–42, 65
emotional life, 14, 37–38, 77,
80–81, 135, 145, 148, 189;
repressed, 21–22, 33, 34–35,

40–45, 186–87; and fear,
28–29, 32, 63, 67–70;
conflicted, 29, 75, 185–87; and
need for idols, 39–40; and
masochistic strivings, 45–46;
betrayed by sentimental posture, 133; and art, 165–66, 190;
and limitations, 189, 190. See
also Comradeship; Long sickness; Power relationships
ambivalence toward women, 15,
16–17, 150; of middle class,
35–37, 79, 124, 131–32, 133,
227–29; and comradeship, 45,
223; and sexuality, 73–75, 80,
84–85, 146; and political vision, 79, 80; analyzed, 167–68,
195, 196–98
plasticity, 22, 67, 178
visions: of self in prison, 23; of
class structure, 26–29; of Social Pit, 32, 67, 70, 117; as
impulse to art, 32, 205; of
Man-Comrade, 45; of dependency and powerlessness, 46;
humanistic, 47, 89, 90, 116,
171, 184; of Truth, 58, 72,
73–74, 84, 112; of urban
jungle, 62, 63, 92, 94, 117; of
the "PEOPLE," 81–82, 84; of
dray horse, 88–89; and the unconscious, 93; in ME, 188,
205–6, 214, 216, 219; in IH,
188; in BD, 224–25
political vision, 24, 29, 77, 79; in
PA, 61–62; betrayal of, in WF,
138
prison experiences, 27–29, 44,
138; transformed into art,
29–31, 97–98, 138
socialism, 34, 37, 38–40, 39 (n.
12), 67, 82–84, 142–43, 230;
and the "PEOPLE," 39, 40,
187; in PA, 65–66; retreat
from, 69–71; in fiction,
169–85, 187. See also Oakland

Index

261

Socialist Labor party
marriage, with Bess, 37, 38, 72,
180, 185; with Charmian, 134,
140, 185, 186–87; separation
from Bess, 152. *See also* London, Charmian Kittredge
love affairs, with Anna Strunsky,
37–38, 69–71, 185; with
George Sterling, 185–86
social rise, 40–43
literary career, 43, 56; hobo apprenticeship for, 22; shaped by
lower-class experiences, 24;
established by Alaskan stories,
48; compared with Nathaniel
Hawthorne's, 54–55
solitude, 45, 81
suicidal fantasies, 46, 81, 83
in Alaska, 48
fatherhood, 65, 70, 144, 148
death, 84
diseased egotism, 86, 192
ranch, 137, 140, 143, 220, 230;
in *BD*, 221, 225, 227
philosophy. *See* Materialism
London, Joan (daughter), xvii, 70,
144, 232
London, John (stepfather), 18, 172;
marriage, 5; unstable work life,
5–6; ill and aging, 9; death, 9, 52,
172; as model for London,
15–16; and drinking, 21
London, Joy (daughter), 144
London, England, 58–71, 165, 179
Long sickness, xvi, 53, 58, 126,
145, 151, 159, 163, 179, 187; as
watershed in London's life and
art, xviii; "cure" of, 55, 72,
81–86, 132, 134, 136–37, 146;
begins, 71; London describes,
72–73; analysis of, 73–81; aftereffects of, 84–93; and London's
writing, 94; and *SW*, 113, 121;
and Charmian, 134, 135,
136–37, 229; London saved
from, 137, 140; return of, 235

"Love of Life," 53
Love of Life, 145
Lower class, 21, 22, 54, 59; as man's
world, xviii, 17–20, 31, 43, 46;
subcultures within, 3; hierarchies
within, 3–4, 5, 7; opportunities
within, 3–5, 12; values, 8, 9, 15;
ethnic differences within, 8–9;
description of, 10; contradiction
within, 16; and illusion, 16–17,
20–22; and political vision,
24–29; compared with middle
class, 32–37; and reality, 33, 46;
courtship in, 33–35; "savagery"
of, 43; and beast imagery, 61–62,
117, 175–76, 203; in *PA*, 61–66;
in *JB*, 91–92; as viewed by dominant culture, 92; in *CW*,
94–95, 110; in *SW*, 114, 115–17,
118–21, 125; in London's short
stories, 169, 171–72, 173–83,
187; in *IH*, 192–93; in *ME*,
192–93, 211–13, 217–19; and
sexuality, 213. *See also* Crime;
Gangs; London, Jack: prison experiences; London, Jack: tramp
life; London, Jack: work experience
Luxemburg, Rosa, 189
Lynn, Kenneth, xv, xvii, 39

McClintock, James, xvii, 48–49,
52, 176
McClure's Magazine, 156
Macmillan, 151, 163
McTeague (Norris), 61
Maddern, Bess. *See* London, Bess
Maddern
Malcolm X, 13–14
Mammy Jenny. *See* Prentiss, Virginia
Manchuria, 135
Man-Comrade, 43, 45, 51
Manhood, 9, 33, 62, 80, 133, 222;
and lower-class values, 15; London's initiation into, 24–29;

punished, 27–28, 66, 118–20,
132, 233–34; in London's writings, 31; contradictions of,
35–37, 46, 120, 195; London's
obsession with, 47. *See also*
Drinking: as manhood rite;
Lower class: as man's world
Marble Faun, The (Hawthorne), 54
Mariposa, 217, 220
Marriage: as institution of initiation,
6, 33; and power relationships,
37; compared with prostitution,
78; in *WF*, 138; and middle-class
identity, 180, 183; and immortality, 227
Martin Eden, xvi, xvii, 39, 44, 47,
48, 53, 58, 64, 185, 188, 197;
middle-class woman in, 36,
74–75; compared with *IH*, 192,
197, 199; contradiction between
form and content in, 200; autobiographical elements in, 200,
220; use of success formula in,
202; class relationships in,
202–5, 211–16, 217–19; portrait
of artist in, 205–7; 209–10,
213–14; literary models for behavior in, 207–11; compared
with *BD*, 221, 226, 227
Marx, Karl, 5, 29
Massillon, Ohio, xv, 18
Mastery: desire for, xvi, 47, 98–99;
in *ME*, 36–37, 215; and submission, 46; illusion of, 49; in *CW*,
103, 110; in *BD*, 221
Materialism, 57–58, 61, 85, 90, 92,
105; in short stories, 53; in *SW*,
112, 120, 123, 126, 168, 177; in
JB, 230–34. *See also* London,
Jack: visions, of Truth
Matthews, Brander, 161
Melville, Herman, xviii, 93, 111,
129, 144, 157–58
Middle class: as woman's world,
xviii, 31, 32–33, 35–36, 43, 46;
values, 3, 8, 15, 33, 69–71; Lon-

don's disillusionment with, 17,
39–40, 56–57, 72–75, 79–81;
compared with lower class,
32–37; and illusion, 33;
courtship in, 33, 34–35; London's initiation into, 33–35; and
socialism, 38–39; and sentimentality, 43; new, 60; and domesticity, 65; London embraces, 69–71;
and books, 92; in "South of the
Slot," 177–83; and repression,
178, 179, 180–81; in *ME*,
207–10, 213–16; and immortality, 213, 227
Millergraph, 148
Mills, Gordon, 153
Moby-Dick (Melville), xviii, 144,
157
Monkkonen, Eric, 3
Moran of the Lady Letty (Norris), 60,
191
Mortality. *See* Death
Munro, George, 207 (n. 8)
Munsey, Frank A., 161–62
Munsey's Magazine, 161–63
Mutiny on the Elsinore, The, 146,
159

Native Son (Wright), 171
Naturalism, 60–61, 164–65, 191;
in *CW*, 95; in *SW*, 115; and blond
beast, 165; in *IH*, 198
"Negore the Coward," 145
Nelson, "Young Scratch," 18–20,
22, 27, 35, 40–41, 42
Nevada, 22
Newsboys' Lodging House, 9
New York (city), 69 (n. 20), 142;
slum people of, 61; and drinking,
147
New York *Independent*, 82
Niagara Falls, 96
Nicholson (doctor), 139
Nietzsche, Friedrich, 113, 159,
221–22, 224
Norris, Frank, 60–61, 191

Oakland, 32, 44, 136, 140, 142–43;
    London's childhood and ado-
    lescence in, 3, 5–10, 12–13, 14–
    22, 59–60, 200
Oakland Free Library, 202, 203,
    215
Oakland Socialist Labor party, 33,
    38, 39, 82
O'Connor, Richard, xv
Ouida, 6
Outing, 140
Overland Monthly, 77

Panella, Mike (gang leader), 8, 9
Paradox. *See* Contradictions
Paris, 83
People of the Abyss, The, 47, 59–60,
    178, 211; origin of idea for, 59,
    200; political vision in, 61–62;
    double consciousness in, 63–67;
    writing of, 67; change in Lon-
    don's consciousness after, 67–71,
    94; compared with *SW*, 113–14,
    117; editorial suggestions for,
    163–64; revisions in, 164
Phillips, David Graham, 60, 156
Poe, Edgar Allan, 112, 130,
    157–58
Power relationships: in prison, 27
    (n. 19); in marriage and family,
    37; in lower class, 46; in *SW*,
    116–20; in prostitution, 166–67;
    in "The Apostate," 176; in *ME*,
    215. *See also* Mastery
Positivism. *See* Materialism
Prentiss, Virginia, 12
"Prince of the Oyster Pirates," 21
Prison, 12, 36, 37, 59; as institution
    of initiation, 24, 27–29, 33; liter-
    ature of, 27 (n. 19); in *SR*, 29–31;
    old friends in, 41; of conscious-
    ness, 83; in *WF*, 138–39. *See also*
    Blackwell's Island; Erie County
    Penitentiary; London, Jack:
    prison experiences; San Quentin
Proletariat. *See* Lower class

Psychology of the Unconscious (Jung),
    196

"Queen, the" (mistress), 13, 21, 35

Race. *See* Ideology: racial
Ragged Dick (Alger), 6–7, 8–9
Razzle Dazzle, 10, 13
"Red Kelly" (gang leader), 8
Reno, 148
Road, The, 6, 31, 156, 185, 196
Romantic love. *See* Sentimental love
Roosevelt, Theodore, 35
Ruskin Club, 39, 65
Russo-Japanene War, 135

"Sabotage," 26 (n. 17), 176 (n. 7)
Sailor on Horseback (Stone), xv
Saloon: as institution of initiation,
    14–15, 17, 21, 31, 33; as roman-
    tic escape, 15, 20; and com-
    radeship, 83–84
Salvarsan 606, xvi
San Francisco, 41, 134, 136, 142; in
    fiction, 176, 177, 184
San Quentin, 31, 38, 138
Saturday Evening Post, 152, 184
"Scab, The," 82
Scarlet Letter, The (Hawthorne), 53,
    54, 158
"Schmidt" (pig-iron handler),
    25–26
Schopenhauer, Arthur, 113
Scientific management, 25, 26, 30,
    87–88
Scotty (sailor), 87
Seaside Library, 39, 207, 235
Sea-Wolf, The, xvi, 47, 54, 146, 154,
    160, 163, 165, 167, 176, 177,
    194, 227; materialism in, 53,
    112, 120, 123, 126, 230; and
    naturalism, 60; illusions in, 94,
    122, 123, 124, 130–33;
    capitalism in, 112, 116–17, 133;
    repression in, 112–13, 123–24,
    126, 132, 133; as dialogue with

White Logic, 113; and long sickness, 113, 121, 126, 132; compared with *PA*, 113–14; power relationships in, 116–21; brutality in, 120, 121, 151–52, 153; negotiations with Gilder over, 151–53; as attack on Nietzsche, 159; compared with "South of the Slot," 179; compared with *IH*, 191–92

Sentimental love, 43, 55, 131, 133, 153 (n. 10), 186–87, 195; in *BD*, 221, 225–27. *See also* London, Charmian Kittredge

Sexuality: and class, 34–35, 73–75, 213; repressed, 35, 80; homoerotic, 67, 122–23; and success, 76–77, 78; and economics, 77–79, 150; and positivistic vision, 84–85; repressed, in *SW*, 123–24, 126, 132, 133, 152; embodied in Wolf Larsen (*SW*), 168; repressed, in *IH*, 193–95; politics of, 196; associated with class oppression, 196–97; and mortality, 198; repressed, in *ME*, 211–13

Shattuck, Louis, 33, 34, 212

Shepard, Eliza London (half-sister), 173

Shingle Sanitorium, 136

Shorty (sailor), 13

Shorty ("homeboy"), 13

Signa (Ouida), 6

Sinclair, Andrew, xvi, 69

Snark, 137, 142, 145, 149, 150; *ME* written aboard, 200

Social Darwinism, 43, 62, 116–17, 180–81

Socialist Labor party. *See* Oakland Socialist Labor party

Social Pit, 5, 22, 32, 43, 59, 67, 68, 70

Solidarity. *See* Comradeship

"Song of Myself" (Whitman), 236

Sonoma valley, 140; novels of, xviii

Sophie Sutherland, 22, 115 (n. 3)

"South of the Slot," 47, 169, 176–85, 188; and *CW*, 177, 180, 184; autobiographical elements in, 178, 179, 180

Spencer, Herbert, 126

Starr, Kevin, xv, xvii, 196, 221

Star Rover, The, 29–31

Stasz, Clarice, xv

Sterling, Carrie, 136

Sterling, George, 136; letters from London, 143, 186; London's love for, 185–86

Stone, Irving, xv, xvi, xvii

"Strength of the Strong, The," 159, 169–71

Strunsky, Anna, 73; socialism, 37, 69; relationship with London, 37–38, 69–71, 185; letters from London, 44, 56–57, 61, 67–68, 69, 70, 83–84, 162, 202

Success: and self-destruction, xvii; legitimate and illegitimate roads to, 3; lower-class standards of, 5; as Bitch Goddess, 17; as ideology, 24–25, 60–61; in London's consciousness, 72–73; in *The Great Gatsby*, 75–76; in Napoleon Hill, 76; and idealized middle-class woman, 79; as search for immortality, 128; in *ME*, 200–202, 216

"Success." See *Martin Eden*

Sun Also Rises, The (Hemingway), 236

Swinburne, Algernon, 36, 40, 208–9, 217

Taylor, Frederick Winslow, 25–26, 222

Taylorism. *See* Scientific management

Tennyson, Alfred Lord, 43, 91, 116, 146, 210

Terkel, Studs, 166
Think and Grow Rich (Hill), 76–77, 78
"To Build a Fire," 49, 51, 53–54
Trotsky, Leon, 188, 189–90
Truth, 58, 79, 153, 168; repressed, 24, 155–56; orders of, 88–89, 90–91, 157–58; dialogue concerning, 155; hidden by drink, 235; in Hemingway's fiction, 236; in London's art, 236
Twain, Mark, 20, 60, 144, 187

University of California, 38, 40, 48, 202

Valley of the Moon, The, xviii, 18, 99, 143; Charmian's notes for, 146; miscarriage in, 147
Villard, Oswald Garrison, 161–62
Violence: and naturalism, 165, 191; in *IH*, 193

Wake Robin Lodge, 190
Walker, Franklin, 48
"What Life Means to Me," 39, 80–81, 82, 207

White Fang, 137–40
White Logic, 229, 235, 236; dialogues with, 87, 91; and dominant culture, 90–92; described by London, 93; and *SW*, 113
White Logic (McClintock), xvii, 48–49, 52, 176
"White Silence, The," 49–52, 53, 54; compared with *CW*, 105
Whitman, Walt, 67, 236
Womanhood, 62, 166–67, 195
Women and Economics (Gilman), 77–79, 134
Work: as institution of initiation, 6, 24–26, 33; changes in, 12; in *SR*, 30; in *CW*, 102–5; in *SW*, 112; described by prostitute, 166; in "The Apostate," 171, 173–76. *See also* London, Jack: work experiences; Scientific management
Work ethic, 3, 5, 12, 15, 16; London satirizes, 24–26
Working (Terkel), 166
Working class. *See* Lower class
World War I, 164
Wright, Richard, 171